"I heartily recommend and endorse *Justice on the Cross*. The book is a most valuable exposition of Palestinian liberation theology—its origins, content, and the issues it attempts to address. Like all liberation theologies, Palestinian liberation theology arises directly out of the daily lives and situation of Palestinian Christian and attempts to read Scripture and to understand the Christian faith as supportive of their liberation struggle and as an adequate answer to real existential questions."

—**JONATHAN KUTTAB**, executive director, FOSNA

"*Justice on the Cross* is an indispensable introduction to Palestinian liberation theology. Christison surveys the history of Palestinian oppression and shows how liberation theology is at the core of Christian efforts to end that oppression through a process of liberation grounded in the gospel. Her introduction to liberation theology—its origins and multiple adaptations by oppressed groups—is alone worth the price of this fine book."

—**JUAN M. C. OLIVER**, custodian of the Book of
Common Prayer of the Episcopal Church

Justice on the Cross

Justice on the Cross

Palestinian Liberation Theology, the Struggle
against Israeli Oppression, and the Church

Kathleen Christison

WIPF & STOCK · Eugene, Oregon

JUSTICE ON THE CROSS
Palestinian Liberation Theology, the Struggle against Israeli Oppression, and the
Church

Wipf & Stock
An Imprint of Wipf and Stock Publishers
199 W. 8th Ave., Suite 3
Eugene, OR 97401

www.wipfandstock.com

PAPERBACK ISBN: 978-1-6667-5288-5
HARDCOVER ISBN: 978-1-6667-5289-2
EBOOK ISBN: 978-1-6667-5290-8

03/06/23

To the Palestinian people,
whose struggle for freedom has inspired me for so long

To Bill Christison,
without whose love and inspiration I would never have continued

What does the Lord require of you but to do justice, and to
love kindness, and to walk humbly with your God?

—MICAH 6:8 (NRSV)

We will stand for justice. We can do no other. Justice alone guarantees a peace
that will lead to reconciliation and a life of security and prosperity for all
the peoples of our land. By standing on the side of justice, we open ourselves
to the work of peace; and working for peace makes us children of God.

—SABEEL ECUMENICAL LIBERATION THEOLOGY
CENTER, Jerusalem, *The Jerusalem Sabeel Document:*
Principles for a Just Peace in Palestine-Israel

Freedom is not a state; it is an act. It is not some enchanted garden
perched high on a distant plateau where we can finally sit down and rest.
Freedom is the continuous action we all must take, and each generation
must do its part to create an even more fair, more just society.

—JOHN LEWIS, *Across That Bridge: A Vision*
for Change and the Future of America

Contents

Preface

The reason I speak to them in parables is that "seeing they do not perceive, and hearing they do not listen, nor do they understand." With them indeed is fulfilled the prophecy of Isaiah that says: "You will indeed listen, but never understand, and you will indeed look, but never perceive. For this people's heart has grown dull, and their ears are hard of hearing, and they have shut their eyes."

—MATT 13:13–15 (NRSV)

IN THE EARLY MONTHS of 2020, before the global COVID-19 pandemic and widespread social and economic turmoil descended, and as I was turning over in my mind thoughts of writing this book on Palestinian Liberation Theology, I had a dismaying encounter with an Episcopal seminarian. Although popular awareness of the Palestinian plight under Israeli domination was then and is still growing slowly in the United States, my conversation with the seminarian brought home to me just how prevalent it remains that, where Palestine and Palestinians are concerned, as Jesus lamented, "the people's heart has grown dull, and their ears are hard of hearing." I have long been aware of the widespread American ignorance of Palestinians, but I was still taken aback when this seminarian, just returned from a church-led tour to the Holy Land, dismissed my inquiries about what he had seen and learned of Palestine with an impatient, "But this was a tour of the Holy Land; it wasn't a political tour."

When I asked if his group, which spent several days in the Palestinian city of Bethlehem on the West Bank, had visited one of Bethlehem's

Palestinian refugee camps, he seemed puzzled, as if wondering why any tour group would do such a thing. I imagine he didn't know there are three refugee camps in Bethlehem—each one, like the many such camps elsewhere in the West Bank and in neighboring Arab countries, home to several thousand Palestinians, with their descendants, who in 1948 were expelled from their homes and land in what became the state of Israel. He was even more puzzled when I asked a question indicating that there is a difference between the state of Israel and the Palestinian territories occupied by Israel. Why would I ask, I could almost hear him wondering: wasn't it all the same—Israel, the West Bank, Jerusalem?

When I inquired if his guide had been Israeli or Palestinian, he was dismissive and clearly did not know or care whether his group had heard the Israeli or the Palestinian perspective on the Holy Land from this guide, or indeed whether there is a Palestinian perspective. He did volunteer that the guide was an American now living in Israel, which gave me the answer to my question, although my friend remained uninterested that this clearly indicated the guide was a Jewish Israeli. It was after recounting the guide's assertion that the Trump Administration's May 2018 action in moving the US embassy from Tel Aviv to Jerusalem had "not been a big issue," not arousing much attention or protest—to which I responded that, on the contrary, sixty Palestinians who protested nonviolently that day in Gaza had been shot to death by Israeli sharpshooters—that he cut off our conversation because it was becoming too political.

I should have known better, or expected less. But this was a well-educated, politically moderate professional man on the young side of middle age newly becoming immersed in the compassion and the social justice message of Jesus Christ who I had assumed, precisely because of who he was and where he had just traveled, might know something about the Palestinian people as living, breathing souls inhabiting—*still* inhabiting millennia later—the land where Jesus journeyed, literally and spiritually. But clearly my assumption that he would have learned anything about Palestine, Palestinians, and especially Palestinian Christians from traveling on a tour led by a Western Christian church was naïve. My own longstanding immersion in things Palestinian and my particular interest in Palestinian liberation theology had led me in a giant leap of imagination to the assumption that any seminarian in a mainstream Protestant church would surely know liberation theology and have at least a bare knowledge of Palestinians. But sadly, those who should know best about Jesus' ministry to the oppressed, as he carried it out himself and as his successors should be doing today, too often "see but do not perceive, hear but do not listen, and fail to understand." It is not an exaggeration, in fact, to say that Western Christianity—meaning all denominations in the West, from Roman Catholic, to mainstream Protestant, to evangelical Protestant, and especially to fundamentalist Christian Zionist—knows next to nothing, and usually cares less, about the indigenous people who live, and have always lived, in the very land where Christianity was born, where Jesus Christ was born, lived, and died.

My seminarian friend's sterile experience in that land is not unusual. Nor can he really be criticized himself for his ignorance of Palestinians as real people who inhabit this supposedly holy land. For, because of centuries of rote church practice, as well as the state of modern international geopolitics, "Palestine" in much of the public imagination is not a real place with real people—and certainly not descendants of original Christians—but a kind of plastic Disney-esque land: a place now called Israel where, we are told, Jews have been wonderfully redeemed by their establishment of a state, but where Christian redemption is recognized only at memorial sites where Jesus walked two millennia ago. We cannot picture any actual Christians in this imagined land, except perhaps some Western missionaries and the caretakers of ancient Christian holy sites. For reasons unfathomable to too many Westerners, Muslims also live in this fantasy land, but they cast a vaguely dangerous pall; they are the ultimate "other," clearly interlopers.

I can see why my seminarian friend fails to understand that there are real people, real children of God, besides those who are Jewish, living in this land that so many call holy. But what I cannot fathom is why the Christian church that he is preparing to serve in ordained ministry can be so ignorant of, and in particular so uncaring about, the native inhabitants of this land where Christianity began and where indigenous Christians still live. As I have delved more deeply into liberation theology, in Palestine and elsewhere, it has become more and more puzzling to me how institutional Western Christianity could have strayed so far from its roots: so far from any knowledge of the people who have always lived in Jesus Christ's own land, so far from the love of humanity that Jesus showed and preached, so far from the totally obvious moral and ethical lessons of liberation that Jesus taught through the gospels.

How has it been possible to ignore the very scriptural message that underlies and provides the basics of the faith? What Jesus taught was clearly *love and liberation*; the gospels clearly comprise a *book of liberation.* How can it not be evident to everyone—from the poorest, least educated child of God who simply hears the words of the gospel without being able to read them, to the most elevated, most beautifully vested and mitred, best theologically educated official in any church hierarchy in the West—that Jesus' primary mission and most heartfelt concern on earth was to minister to the needy and oppressed, and to pass this mission on to his disciples and to their disciples in turn: to feed the hungry, clothe the naked, comfort the imprisoned, heal the sick, dine with the shunned, wash the feet of sinners, bless the downhearted and the poor in spirit, grieve with the bereaved, bless those who suffer under political and social injustice, embrace *all of humanity as equals*?

When in Matthew's Gospel Jesus blesses those who help "the least of these" because they are helping him,[1] he is enunciating the ultimate liberation theology. And when he then reverses this teaching and con-demns those who do *not* help—"I was hungry and you gave me no food, I was thirsty and you gave me nothing to drink, I was a stranger and you did not welcome me, naked and you did not give me clothing, sick and in prison and you did not visit me" (Matt 25:41-46, NRSV)—it seems clear that he is pronouncing a judgment for the ages on everyone, including church and state leaders, who does not do these things for the hungry, the naked, the imprisoned. Moreover, in every chapter and verse of the gospel, Jesus focuses on the poor, lifting up the oppressed and offering words and parables of blessing and compassion. This is not just a nice story to be read and forgotten. These words have been there for millen-nia; similar stories of aiding the poor and oppressed have been in the Hebrew Scriptures for even longer—all the while providing the outline for what has come to be called God's "preferential option for the poor."

But we haven't seemed—ever in history—to absorb Jesus' words and their meaning very well; in fact, we Western Christians have seldom been taught the deep meaning of those words. On a personal level, I cannot remember ever being told by the Catholic nuns and priests who were my educators from elementary school through university that God *loved* me or anyone else, and certainly not the marginalized in my society. I learned about faith, hope, and charity, but not about faith, hope, and *love.*

---

1. Matt 25:35-36, 40 (NRSV): "[F]or I was hungry and you gave me something to drink, I was a stranger and you welcomed me, I was naked and you gave me clothing, I was sick and you took care of me, I was in prison and you visited me (. . .). Truly I tell you, just as you did it to one of the least of these who are members of my family, you did it to me."

Whatever message of compassion my schoolmates and I received was mostly drowned out by the more emphatic messages about avoiding sin.

On a much broader level, I believe that, at least until fairly recently, the church has generally failed to emphasize the message of real love, and particularly love for the poor and oppressed, that is Jesus' clear mission and message. It is only in the last approximately half century, in fact, that the Catholic Church, through Vatican II, has focused on God's "preferential option" for the disadvantaged in a truly serious way, and even then not as fully as needed. With too few exceptions, church hierarchies do not respond well to the myriad cries for help from their faithful—and, it must be said, do not heed Jesus' very clear gospel injunctions to open their hearts to those most in need. This is precisely why liberation theology has grown up in so many places where its wisdom and love are so sorely needed.

As for Palestine, it is little wonder that so many of the world's faithful, never guided to see the obvious in what Jesus was saying, view the actual Holy Land in Palestine-Israel as a kind of Disneyland without real people. The critical struggle for Palestinian Christians as they shape and work through a theology of liberation for their particular needs is, starkly, to resist their erasure and that of their Muslim compatriots, not only physically from the land, which Israel continues to expropriate, but also psychologically from the minds of world publics and politicians and of their own church hierarchies that seem often to have forgotten them.

As I sat down to write this book about Palestine and Palestinians and a theology of liberation for Palestine a few months after my encounter with the seminarian, in the summer of 2020 and beyond, the world seemed to come tumbling down, and the curtain of ignorance about Palestine became even more opaque. A global pandemic was bringing sickness, death, and economic disaster to a world already nearing catastrophe from planetary destruction. The massive suffering that has afflicted the poor and marginalized everywhere during this pandemic has deeply affected Palestinians, who all live either directly under Israel's domination or in exile because of it, and whose fate was already being largely ignored by the world. Some of the worst Israeli atrocities have become more evident in recent years through gaps in that curtain of ignorance, but much of the world, particularly the Western world, remains oblivious to the horrors of Israel's regime of control. This was even true with regard to Israel's initial refusal during the early months of the pandemic to make vaccines available to the five million non-citizen Palestinians living under its control in the occupied territories, even though the 700,000 Jewish settlers who live among Palestinians in those territories were vaccinated.

During a random week in that summer of 2020, as Palestinians were being denied life-saving vaccines while a distracted world failed even to notice, I began to keep a catalog of what was happening to Palestinians on the ground in Palestine—the kind of ordinary cruelty that Israel visits on Palestinians every day, day after day, year after year. I finally decided, however, that I could not catalog this cruelty. Any week's catalog would simply be too lengthy, the atrocities too wide-ranging, affecting every large and small aspect of Palestinian living and dying, the list too rapidly expanding. So, in the interests of getting on with my primary task of describing the fullness of Palestinian liberation theology and its importance to oppressed Palestinians, I will say simply that, through both its military forces and the hundreds of thousands of illegal settlers whose vandalism in the occupied territories the military supports, Israel regularly, and increasingly, commits a full catalog of unthinkable atrocities against the Palestinian population under its control.

In a heartening indication that the international human rights community, if not political leaders or the media, are finally noticing, several leading Israeli and international human rights monitors issued major reports in 2021 and 2022 declaring Israel to be an "apartheid regime." These reports have confirmed and added intricate detail to a surfeit of other, more informal reporting that has been circulating outside the mainstream of politics and the media, by United Nations, Palestinian, Israeli, and many other observers. This "alternative" reporting provides evidence enough, as we will see later, to affirm the depth of Palestinian suffering.

The oppression Palestinians face is unquestionably growing worse. The Israeli government and military no longer even try to conceal or make excuses for their daily harassment and torment of Palestinians: the unprovoked killings, the imprisonment for no reason, the Gaza bombings, the property destruction, the land expropriation, the harassment and closure of Palestinian human rights and civil society organizations—precisely the organizations that expose Israeli human rights abuses.[2] At the political level in the United States, among those in the administration and in Congress who make policy, the degree of attention paid to Israel's anti-Palestinian policies and actions is virtually nil. In fact, at this policymaking level, support for Israel grows stronger with each administration, whether Democratic or Republican, more or less coincident with the increasingly rightward swing of each Israeli government. President Joe Biden has continued to follow or has failed to undo, almost all the several policy initiatives instituted by the Donald Trump administration—which was far more enthusiastically supportive of Israel and restrictive toward the Palestinians than any previous administration. Israel gathers support with each US election cycle.

The editor of an alternative Israeli media site, Edo Konrad of +972 *Magazine*—one of many Israelis, it is important to note, who is able to see through US policy—commented in September 2021, when the United States gave Israel $1 billion for additional military equipment, on top of the annual grant of $3.8 billion in military aid, that the continued US failure to demand any progress from Israel toward resolving the conflict in return for massive amounts of aid "is a testament to just how recklessly little US leaders care about Israeli intentions or Palestinian lives. Perhaps more than anything," he continued, these latest US policy moves send "a clear signal that, whether it's Trump or Biden (. . .) there is hardly anyone with any modicum of power who will stand up and say enough to Israel's accelerating, endless military rule. For now, Washington remains committed to ensuring that time is on the side of apartheid."[3]

This failure to address the actual situation in Palestine is not for want of available information. The abundance and steady growth of reporting in progressive media organs make it more and more difficult for political leadership levels to ignore what is going on in Palestine; the abysmal understanding exhibited by these political elites is increasingly becoming untenable. Although the mainstream media do not report the Palestine situation in any depth and have always shown a marked bias

2. In October 2021, the Israeli government issued closure orders against six Palestinian human rights groups for supposed terrorist connections, but has never produced evidence of such connections. In August 2022, Israeli police raided the offices of these six organizations, as well as of a seventh, and welded the doors shut. In the course of this activity, the Israeli forces also broke into the compound of St. Andrew's Episcopal Church in Ramallah, where one of the human rights groups rents office space, tearing the church door from its hinges and breaking glass.

3. Konrad, "Washington's Three Gifts to Naftali Bennett."

toward Israel, alternative media—including multiple blogs, websites, and various other online publications in the United States, in Palestine and Israel, and elsewhere—have been reporting voluminously and with increased frequency in recent years. Although currently being ignored by the powers-that-be virtually everywhere, this very abundance of reporting, including the plethora of human rights reports detailing Israel's apartheid governing system, gives poignant meaning to the statement of enduring "hope in the absence of all hope" that stands as the centerpiece of the *Kairos Palestine* document issued in 2009 by Palestinian Christians, which we will examine later.

In his longstanding embrace of Israel—most recently exhibited during a trip to Israel in July 2022 and, several weeks later in August, following a three-day Israeli bombing assault on Gaza—President Biden exhibits a remarkable blindness to reality and gross unconcern for Palestinians. Not only did Biden, as always, excuse Israel's three-day attack on Gaza in August 2022 as being within its "right to defend itself," even though Israel itself described the bombing as a preemptive attack intended to head off an allegedly impending action by Palestinian militias. But after Israel had killed forty-nine Palestinians, Biden hailed the Israelis for "saving lives." He meant, of course, Israeli lives. While a few of the Palestinian dead had been targeted as leaders of the Islamic Jihad movement, the fact that the vast majority of those killed were innocent civilians and that nineteen, more than one-third of the total, were children was of no evident concern to Biden.

This Biden trip was a license—granted to Israel, to the media, to the US political class and the public—to forget the Palestinians. With this trip, capped by Biden's inane repetition of the mantra that the United States desires "equal measures of freedom, prosperity, and democracy" for Israelis and Palestinians, it has become unmistakably clear that the state of official ignorance about Israel's oppression of Palestinians has reached the point of absurdity. Israel's atrocities have become so obvious that ignoring them requires a concentrated effort of will. Biden managed to call up that will during his trip, acceding completely to Israel's policy agenda and explicitly pushing the Palestinians and Palestinian interests to the background. He ignored the near-universal verdict of the international human rights community that Israel is an apartheid state; he excused the killing by Israeli soldiers only two months earlier of a popular Palestinian-American journalist, *al-Jazeera* correspondent Shireen Abu

Akleh; and he totally ignored Israel's closure of the major Palestinian organizations that monitor Israeli abuses.

I actually wonder how it is possible that Biden and his officials know
so very little, or can so easily pretend ignorance, about the unbearable
human effects on the Palestinians of Israel's perpetual dominance. An
Israeli human rights leader recently wrote a stinging commentary about
the exceptional hypocrisy shown by Biden during his Israeli visit, pointing out that the United States officially does not want to know. Hagai
El-Ad, director of Israel's leading human rights organization B'Tselem,
and a person of remarkable compassion, noted that in advance of the
Biden trip the While House urged Israeli officials to avoid actions that
might cause embarrassment—as had occurred years earlier when, during
a Biden visit in 2010 as US vice-president, Israel symbolically slapped
him in the face by announcing plans to build a massive number of new
housing units in an illegal settlement. The 2022 request smoothed the
way for Biden to make adulatory remarks during his visit about Israel
and the "core values" it shares with the United States, without being con-
tradicted by a public display of oppressive Israeli actions. Pointing to the
myopia evident in this US request, El-Ad condemned "the bloody legacy
of 'shared values.'" Apparently, he wrote, "Palestinian blood spilled *after*
the president's visit is more easily scrubbed than that more viscous type
of blood—the kind that tends to leave unsightly stains if spilled in the
days before."[4] Atrocities are acceptable, in other words, if Biden does not
have to know about them.

El-Ad's impassioned criticism demonstrates a clear recognition of
the way in which all US officials are so easily able to avert their eyes and
deny reality when Israel carries out oppressive actions. "Grotesque as it
may be," he wrote,

> this act of American micro-diplomacy is telling. For it genuinely
> illustrates the foreign policy of successive U.S. administrations
> over the decades: endless Palestinian subjugation framed as
> "stability"; the generous underwriting of Israeli apartheid while
> paying the occasional lip service to the "two-state solution,"
> which places equal responsibility on the occupier and the oc-
> cupied; and shielding Israel from any real consequences. Mean-
> while, the U.S. continues to kick the can down the road (. . .).
> The road, stained with the blood of innocents, is decades old,
> and the can being kicked down its dusty lanes is, in fact, a people

4. El-Ad, "Bloody Legacy of 'Shared Values.'" Emphasis in original.

oppressed by a regional superpower that is armed, financed, and backed by the United States.[5]

The massive and massively powerful apparatus that makes up the oppressive Israeli government and military machine, along with the US political, propaganda, and military apparatus that supports Israel, is clearly not easily overcome. When an emperor has no clothes, it takes more than a child in a fairy tale blurting out the truth to force the emperor and his admirers to recognize that he is naked and looking more and more foolish. But there are some small and not-so small signs that the romantic tale of Israel's "goodness," of its so-called moral superiority and democratic values, has begun to wear thin. There is increasing global recognition that this is a fairy tale; more and more people now recognize the emperor's nakedness.

This may be a major reason for hope in the perpetual paradox of hope and despair that surrounds this tragic struggle. The very absurdity of the attempt to ignore Israel's behavior when it is so blatantly oppressive could be the seed from which major change will grow. Global public awareness is slowly rising. In the words of one activist, there is "wall-to-wall consensus" among human rights experts and organizations throughout the world that Israel's governing system and laws in the entire area under its control, from the Mediterranean Sea to the Jordan River, meet the definition of "apartheid." More and more people and institutions recognize that Israel has been intent from its beginnings on separating from and, wherever and whenever possible, actually eliminating the non-Jewish Palestinian people in the land.

Although this reality is roundly denied by the political powers in Israel and the West, it is undeniable; even the best political propagandists cannot long deny that this emperor has no clothes. Change is perceptible at the grassroots level and is spreading among social justice activists, on social media, among non-mainstream media commentators, even among a few congresspeople. Some mainstream Christian churches are awakening. Even in Israel, the numbers and activities of human rights activists are growing. In a great many ways, although under ever-tightening siege, the Palestinians themselves are stronger and more determined.

The Palestinian cause is justice, purely and simply: justice for a century in which Palestinians have endured colonial and settler-colonial

---

5. El-Ad, "Bloody Legacy of 'Shared Values.'"

*in*justice, in which they have faced what in any other context would be dealt with as crimes and gross human rights violations, faced wars and war crimes against them, lived under apartheid, and experienced near-total societal destruction, including theft of land, homes, and means of livelihood. And, most unbearable, most inconceivable, a century in which they have been tagged as the guilty party in the eyes of much of the world—the accused, their mere existence and efforts to survive in their own homeland portrayed as a threat by those who took that homeland.

Liberation theology will not resolve the Palestinians' struggle. It will not end Israel's oppressive policies or anytime soon turn Israel's apartheid settler-colonial system toward real democracy or away from Jewish exclusivity and supremacy. But liberation theology is nonviolent resistance: it gives strength to maintain steadfastness, which is itself resistance. And resistance is survival. For the small Palestinian Christian community, the spiritual strength comes from knowing through liberation theology that they are descended from the first Christians of Jesus' time, that they have a right and an obligation to remain in Palestine because simply, as one Palestinian has put it, this is "where Jesus was and where Jesus wants me." This conviction of rightness and of God's presence with them in the struggle for justice is of surpassing political as well as spiritual importance. It is a rampart against despair and forgetting. Because it speaks to the political oppression that all Palestinians face, its call for resistance can nurture and build hope for both Christian and Muslim Palestinians. Without resistance, there is only surrender and suffocation; without breath, there is only death.

Acknowledgments

I AM HONORED THAT several theologians helped me along the way as I gathered whatever theological wisdom and political knowledge have gone into the writing of this book. First and foremost, I thank the Rev. Dr. Naim Ateek, who conceived Palestinian liberation theology thirty-plus years ago, helped inspire and lead a theological and political awakening in the Palestinian Christian community, and remains one of the preeminent Palestinian voices of nonviolent resistance to Israeli oppression for Muslim as well as for Christian Palestinians. I am more indebted to him than I can adequately convey for his theological guidance and mentorship, and for his reading of much of this manuscript.

Two theologians read my entire manuscript and offered invaluable comments and insights. Dr. Marc H. Ellis, a Jewish theologian who has written extensively, and sensitively, about liberation theology for both Jews and Palestinians, has a unique perspective on the Palestinian theology because he worked closely with Naim Ateek in the early days of the Palestinian theology's conception and the founding of the Sabeel Ecumenical Liberation Theology Center in Jerusalem. The Rev. Dr. Juan M. C. Oliver, Custodian of the Book of Common Prayer of the Episcopal Church in the United States, is an expert, in both the spiritual and the academic sense, on the theology and meaning of liturgy and worship. He is immersed in the theology of the cross and of Jesus' suffering in order to bring justice to the oppressed.

Others read portions of the manuscript and gave me helpful remarks: The Rev. Edwin Arrison, South African Anglican priest who was a protégé of Archbishop Desmond Tutu, heads the Desmond and Leah Tutu Legacy Foundation, and helped Palestinian Christians draft *Kairos*

Palestine in 2009; Mark Braverman, theologian and clinical psychologist whose Jewish perspective on Palestinian theological and political matters has been extremely valuable; Dr. Eric C. Smith, Assistant Professor of Early Christianity and Contemporary Christian Practices at the Iliff School of Theology, who assisted me through a thesis on Palestinian liberation theology that became the initial seed of this book and whose views on Palestinian-Israeli issues helped me maintain my objectivity; and the Rev. Dr. Donald E. Wagner, a leading expert on Christian evangelicalism and particularly Christian Zionism, whose compassion has for decades led him into intense involvement with the Palestinian struggle theologically, academically, and directly on the ground.

In addition to their comments on this book, the published work of all these individuals provided me further insights. I am grateful and immensely honored that these experts gave me their time and shared their thinking on this critically important topic. It goes without saying that any errors and stumbles are totally my own.

Introduction

*The great pastoral, and therefore theological, question is: How is it possible
to tell the poor, who are forced to live in conditions that embody a denial of
love, that God loves them? (. . .). Liberation theology had its origin in the
contrast between the urgent task of proclaiming the life of the risen Jesus and
the conditions of death in which the poor of Latin America were living (. . .).
The liberation of our continent means more than overcoming economic,
social, and political dependence. It means, in a deeper sense, to see the
becoming of humankind as a process of human emancipation in history. It is
to see humanity in search of a qualitatively different society in which it will
be free from all servitude, in which it will be the artisan of its own destiny.*

—GUSTAVO GUTIÉRREZ[1]

*Movements are always about the people. Yes, we march for freedom.
Yes, we march for justice. But we do it because we know and love
people who are bound; people who suffer from injustice.*

—WILLIAM J BARBER II[2]

IN NOVEMBER 2018, THE London *Economist* published an article more
or less pronouncing the death of Liberation Theology in Latin America
and, by implication, everywhere else as well. Observing with far too

1. Gutiérrez, *Theology,* xxxiv, 56.
2. Barber, "Moral Movements."

1

much certitude that the radical critique of capitalism's inequality and poverty that characterized Latin American liberation theology and clerical activism in the 1960s and 1970s had by now "passed into the standard thinking of the Vatican," and noting further that the assassinated El Salvadoran Archbishop Óscar Romero had been canonized for his liberation work, the article suggested that liberation theology might now take its success and pass peacefully from the political scene, like other transitory social movements.[3]

The *Economist*'s pronouncements, premature even for Latin America and quite out of touch with the fundamental nature of liberation theology—to say nothing of the pervasiveness of the very oppression from which liberation is sought—are an indication of how poorly this theology is understood. Not only has liberation theology not passed from the scene in Latin America or any place where there remain oppressed and marginalized populations crying out for its guidance and for God's succor, but this theology of the oppressed has sadly not become the "standard thinking" of either the Vatican or any other part of institutional Christianity. And therein lies much of the long story of the difficult theological struggle to liberate humanity from the injustices that supremacist colonial and ecclesiastical centers of power have for centuries imposed on indigenous populations, people of color, and the downtrodden around the world.

Although the *Economist*'s assessment was marginally correct in that the precise term "liberation theology" is used less often in the world of today's justice struggles, it is critically important to note that in fact the impetus, and indeed the theology, behind social justice movements, civic protest, freedom struggles, and the like have vastly strengthened since liberation theology first emerged in Latin America half a century ago. Many social justice movements today, although not specifically identified as part of a liberation theology movement, can nonetheless be described as faith-based or spiritually guided struggles for liberation from oppression. As only one example, the Rev. William Barber, cited above, heads two movements: Repairers of the Breach and the Poor People's Campaign: A National Call for Moral Revival. Neither calls itself a liberation theology movement, but the mission of both is liberation theology, and both are interfaith, religiously oriented social justice organizations. Barber co-chairs the Poor People's Campaign with another Protestant leader, Presbyterian minister the Rev. Liz Theoharis.

3. B.C., "What Happened to Liberation Theology?"

More directly to our interest here, the Palestinian liberation theology that we will discuss in this book continues to call itself explicitly a contextual liberation theology movement, and to function as such.

How is liberation theology involved in this story of colonization and power, and what exactly is it? Simply put, liberation theology, as it was first articulated in Latin America and wherever it is practiced today under whatever name, is a grassroots, bottom-up rather than a top-down theology; it comes not from the church and its scholars passing down doctrine and preaching the gospel *to* the poor and marginalized, but from the oppressed themselves speaking out about their own concerns through the gospel, precisely through the *mission of justice* that Jesus Christ practiced and taught, *against* the collective power of secular governments and coopted churches. This is a theology of praxis and resistance: the marginalized and dispossessed preach the gospel of justice to church hierarchies, not the reverse, in a kind of resistance that challenges the Eurocentric, colonialist structures that have dominated church and state in the West, and wherever the West wields power, for so many centuries.

Liberation theology is a people's theology, a real-world appeal to God as a God of love, invoked by and on behalf of all humanity and especially humanity's marginalized. It is the theology of those weighed down by political, social, and/or economic oppression who call upon God to be present with them in their suffering. In its pursuit of "liberation"—liberation precisely from the physical and spiritual misery that results from oppressive rule—and its appeal to God for spiritual help and solidarity, it is the theological expression of what has come to be widely known in the twenty-first century as intersectionality: the intertwined political and social struggles of the oppressed against the injustices of racism, colonialism, settler colonialism, ethnic privilege, elite privilege, patriarchy, heteronormativity, capitalism and economic dislocation—of all "othering."[4] The multiple liberation theologies, each in its own context, speak truth to and challenge the impunity of power structures. By their very nature,

4. Law professor and critical race scholar Kimberlé Crenshaw coined the term "intersectionality" in the 1980s to describe the way various power structures interact in the lives of minorities. Crenshaw initially used the term and conceived the theory to address the reality that Black women and others of color often faced racial and gender discrimination simultaneously, although anti-discrimination law at the time looked at race and gender separately, leaving them doubly afflicted but without adequate defense. Decades of civil rights and social justice work have brought changes in law and brought the term to broader usage for all marginalized and oppressed populations. See Adewunmi, "Kimberlé Crenshaw on Intersectionality."

these are theologies of struggle against the status quo imposed by Power and by those, including in church establishments, who collude with, or by their silence reinforce, secular Power. These theologies are by definition inseparably political and theological; any movement that speaks out against dominating systems is inevitably political. Jesus was political. In their political justice orientation, these liberation theologies often naturally draw opposition from religious no less than from secular authority, as Jesus also clearly did.

The term "liberation theology" actually describes a set of diverse contextual theologies formulated by and in response to particular populations suffering under injustice and speaking out in their particular vernaculars. Each of these is unique: to the Latin American poor and disenfranchised; to marginalized Latino communities throughout the Americas; to Black people in the United States facing the centuries-long injustices of slavery and the continuing oppression of White supremacy; to the South Africans who struggled successfully against the particular evils of racial apartheid and still struggle to resist the legacy of White domination; to the LGBTQ+ community struggling for legal and cultural acceptance as equal to all other human beings; to women, Black and White, suffering the separate oppressions of patriarchy and racism in their various forms; to Native Americans who honor a supreme Great Spirit; and—our particular interest here—to Palestinians, both Christian and Muslim, living under decades of brutal, intensifying Israeli abuse and human rights violations.

Despite their contextual differences, these theologies are united in their common recognition of the oppressed as all children of God, however the Divine is named, and as all equally deserving of freedom, justice, and human dignity. The particular nonviolent message of these theologies is directed at all centers of exploitative power: colonial, postcolonial, secular, economic, religious. There is a profound beauty in the spiritual succor and the hope that these theologies give the marginalized, whether their suffering is political, social, economic or, most likely, some combination of these. The reassurance that God cares is profoundly comforting.

A Palestinian Christian theologian, for instance, explains that when Israel was created in 1948 and Palestinians were driven from homes and land, traditional theology and the institutional Christian church failed them. The church helped the displaced in material ways, but Christian theology, by relying on Hebrew scriptural promises and conveying the common impression that Israel's creation was a miracle from God, seemed to justify Palestinian suffering and "provide divine approval for our predicament." Only when Palestinian liberation theology was formulated decades later did Palestinian Christians begin to fathom that Jesus' life and gospel teachings provided the true model for their lives: Jesus too had "lived under an oppressive Roman occupation and showed us the way of non-violent resistance." Jesus had resisted, spoken truth to power, and thus gave Palestinians a path to follow for their own resistance, and their survival.[5]

Liberation theology in all its variations, although based in Christianity, speaks in the voice of the voiceless of any faith, and of none—the voice of all who suffer injustice, at the soul level of all who cry out for consolation. This theology is shaped by each community's view of how God relates to them as people with distinct needs but universally deserving of justice, equality, and dignity in their separate circumstances. God's relationship with humanity and especially with oppressed humanity is the point at which liberation theology's universality enters in: this point is God's love for all humankind equally and God's desire that all of humankind live in justice. This point of universality is what Scripture shows us is God's "preferential option" for the poor and disadvantaged, and God's desire that all people be raised to an equal level of justice and love, where all have agency and are the subjects, not merely the objects, of their own destiny. This theology is the *cri de cœur* of the downtrodden calling out in God's own voice for God's solidarity as they struggle against the powers that imposed injustice in the first place, and it is God's promise, in response, to be with all those who suffer.

The political context of Palestinian liberation theology, as we will see, is the oppressive situation in which all Palestinians live, and have lived for the better part of a century, under Israeli domination or in exile because of Israeli injustice. The theological context is the Bible, the ministry of Jesus Christ, the Word of God. The Bible is fundamental for all liberation theologies, but for Palestinians, who actually live in the land of the Bible and where Jesus lived and died, this theological context is more immediate and concrete, in some ways more deeply spiritual because it is so immanent and so real. The father and formulator of Palestinian liberation theology, Palestinian Episcopal priest the Rev. Dr. Naim Ateek, notes that the Palestinian theology "calls attention to the heart of the biblical message," emphasizing the "liberating aspect of the Word of God." This

5. Duaybis, "Theologies of Palestine."

liberating message has been there in the Bible all along, he points out, but it has been neglected and, in the specific case of the land of Palestine, misused and abused. In this particular context, liberation theology "brings the Word of God to [Palestinians] in our daily lives, attuning our ears to what God is saying to us today and to what God wants to do through us (. . .). God has something very relevant and very important to say to both the oppressed and the oppressors" in Palestine. God's message comes through Jesus Christ, Ateek says: "the *Word* of God incarnate in Jesus the Christ interprets for us the *word* of God in the Bible."[6]

As with any theology, any communication with God, there is an ineffable quality to liberation theology that defies easy verbal description and indeed easy human understanding. Spiritual communion with God by its nature is a profound experience, strongly sensed but not easily spoken about. The thought of feeling God's love in suffering describes a nearly mystical experience. Liberation theology is not mysticism; it is not necessarily contemplative; it is not always only personal. But it is deeply spiritual and emotional. It does attempt to bring the oppressed faithful to a deep contemplative sense that God is present with them, individually and, because they suffer as a community, collectively. Black theologian Barbara Holmes, who knows the history and foundations of Black spirituality and mysticism in America, is a spiritual leader well able to write clearly about the ineffable:

> When we are fully alert in spirit, mind, and body, we are more than we imagine and can accomplish more than we suppose. Moments of awareness occur as a dawning of meaning, when the familiar suddenly becomes infused with new insights or unfamiliar ideas merge with the wellspring of experiences and beliefs that pervade human consciousness. Such occasions feel like personal discoveries (. . .) an inner unveiling [that] has finally allowed me to see (. . .). An awakening is necessary to reconnect us to our origins and one another.[7]

Holmes speaks elsewhere of this awakening, this unveiling, in the Black church as part of a contemplative practice that often occurs in community and that, by being witnessed in community, becomes richer than

---

6. Ateek, *Justice and Only Justice*, 6, 80. Emphasis in original.

7. Holmes, *Race and the Cosmos*.

private personal experience. This practice, she says, depends on "an intense mutuality" and a "shared religious imagination." In radiant words, Holmes describes the "joy unspeakable" that the enslaved and the downtrodden find when God "tiptoes into the hush arbor" and shares with them God's own suffering.[8] Although the African experience of bondage of which Homes writes is different from the kinds of oppression that liberation theologies address today, at the same time it is painfully similar. For all oppressed peoples, not least for the Palestinians with whom we are primarily concerned here, liberation theology is the vehicle through which God tiptoes into the soul, testifies to the universality of suffering, and brings hope and a kind of unspeakable joy at being together.

It is no surprise that liberation theology is widely misunderstood in a world where secular politics is so often seen, and desired, to be divorced from anything religious or spiritual—and no surprise that Palestinian liberation theology is misunderstood in all worlds. An Israeli friend, a compassionate but non-religious activist for justice and peace who works closely with Palestinians, has complained to me that he thinks Palestinian liberation theology, at least as expressed in much writing about it, is "too ecumenical"—by which I believe he means too prayerful and faith-oriented, especially not political, and perhaps not leftist, enough. He is an activist working to oppose Israel's oppressive domination of Palestinians and Palestinian land. To him, being "political" means activism and above all zeroing in on promoting explicitly political steps to resolve this long-running struggle. Although he no longer considers himself a Zionist and he genuinely cares about relieving the oppression Palestinians endure, his activism tends, simply because he lives in Israel, to focus less on the Palestinian perspective and on resistance that is specifically Palestinian than on finding an avenue for Israeli resistance, a way for Jewish Israelis to end Israel's violation of Palestinian rights. Spiritual-cum-political, or spiritual-cum-resistance concepts simply do not resonate for him, and so he is not absorbed in this theology's principal objective, which is to *build Palestinian spiritual strength and build nonviolent political resistance,* individually and collectively, by bringing hope for justice where there otherwise seems little or no reason for hope.

---

8. Holmes, *Joy Unspeakable*, xvi–xvii.

Although there is an ineffable quality to this theology, as a grassroots theology, it is anything but abstruse and other-worldly; it *is* resistance. Naim Ateek, the Palestinian Episcopal priest who founded Palestinian liberation theology, often says that "we don't do theology in a vacuum; we do theology in relation to what's going on around us"—and "what is going on" is always political. Another young Palestinian theologian and minister, the Rev. Munther Isaac—who directs the regular "Christ at the Checkpoint" conference at the Bethlehem Bible College and pastors the Christmas Lutheran Church in Bethlehem—gives a similar concrete and decidedly political edge to the spirituality of liberation theology, noting like Ateek that Palestinians "do not write theology in libraries; we write it at the checkpoint." Palestinian theology "from behind the [Israeli separation] wall," Isaac notes, is concerned as much with the day-to-day issues that Palestinians face living under Israeli domination, as it is with intangible issues such as justice, nonviolence, and spiritual strength.[9] Similarly, the late South African Archbishop Desmond Tutu has said, "I don't preach a social gospel; I preach the gospel, period. The gospel is concerned with the whole person. When people are hungry, Jesus didn't say, 'Now is that political or social?' He said, 'I feed you.' Because the good news to a hungry person is bread."

Philosopher and intellectual Cornel West refers to what these Palestinian clergymen and Tutu are speaking about—doing theology and living it, preaching and practicing the gospel, caring about humanity— simply as having "soul." A frequent outspoken defender of Palestinian rights, this Black Christian civic and religious activist and theologian says he is committed not to any particular "brand" like nationalism or capitalism, but to a cause that epitomizes liberation: the "cause of poor working people all around the world, with deep, deep stress on struggles against white supremacy and male supremacy, homophobia, transphobia, or *any ideology that loses sight of the humanity of people.*" Eschewing theological absolutism and any notion of himself as a purely academic professor of philosophy teaching esoterica from a textbook, West recently told an interviewer that he grew up in a Baptist tradition that has "a sense of the whole, (. . .) a sense of our vocation and mission and purpose." He draws, he says, from Malcolm X and James Baldwin and bell hooks as much as from Socrates and Erasmus, as much from Gandhi and Howard Thurman as from the ancients. Speaking in 2022 during Russia's invasion

---

9. Isaac, *Other Side*, 19.

of Ukraine—a rare instance of a public personality recognizing ongoing Palestinian suffering—West expressed as much concern for the Palestinian plight as for what Ukrainians were suffering. He said he wants "whatever wisdom I have, whatever sense of joy, quest for truth and beauty I have, to be filtered directly into the empowerment of people so they can see more clearly, feel more deeply, and act more courageously."[10]

Despite these theologians' broad, interconnecting theology and the ineffable nature of their spirituality, I nonetheless found my Israeli friend's difficulty with the Palestinian theology difficult to navigate. How to describe the critical theo-political aspects of this Palestinian theology to a political activist who, not unlike many others in solidarity with Palestinians, seems to dismiss theology and religion simply because they do not seem relevant to him? I could make it clear that neither this nor any theology need be pious, and that theology is universal and never solely Christian—either or both of which might be areas where his skepticism was focused—but I could not avoid dealing with the theological and spiritual foundations of this particular Palestinian thinking. Theology is, after all—well, theological. And ultimately, when a theology deals with humanity's relationship to God, it becomes deeply spiritual and enters the realm of the ineffable—the "unspeakable," as Barbara Holmes would have it. There was little likelihood that I could lead my friend to feel this ineffable spirituality. But, while I think he does not see this theology as a critically important form of resistance and of survival in resistance, his view is prevalent in secular society, and so we continued our discussion. I hoped to persuade him to maintain his cooperation with all aspects of the Palestinian struggle, even if they were not his particular cup of tea.

It is first important to understand what this specific Palestinian theology is about. In its own context, Palestinian liberation theology is equal parts political and theological—and, indeed, more political than most people understand. Not primarily a struggle against social and economic oppression like its Latin American counterpart, this Palestinian theology is a quest for *God's justice and mercy* against the highly political injustices imposed by Israel's oppressive system of domination and fundamentally

10. Hedges, "Dr. Cornel West." Emphasis added. In his introduction to the interview, Chris Hedges described West as "the premier standard bearer for the Black prophetic tradition, the most important intellectual and spiritual movement in our history (. . .). Rooted in the experience of American racism, capitalist exploitation, and imperialism, this tradition has provided an ongoing critique of our economic, social, and political institutions and beliefs, as well as calling out the country's spiritual bankruptcy."

by the Israeli settler-colonial regime under which Palestinians have lived since Israel's establishment and their own resultant dispossession in 1948. In addition, again unlike Latin American liberation theology, the Palestinian theology is a protest not against oppression imposed on a Christian population by national governments that are also Christian, but is a protest against the oppression of a Muslim and Christian population imposed by a Jewish state and governing ideology. But the point of this theology is oppression, not professed religions: if, as noted, liberation theology is a vehicle for surviving oppression, a way of beseeching God to "tiptoe into the soul" and whisper hope, it matters not at all to the oppressed, or to God, what faith the oppressor professes; nor does it matter what faith the oppressed practices. Where the theology comes in is in the ineffable, in the transcendent: in the spiritual way of prayer and of seeking relief from pain through that appeal to God for justice and mercy.

For liberation theology, nothing about ethnicity, religious practice, faith confession, biblical covenants, geographic location is relevant, for God is transcendent. Biblical scholar Brad East, describing the common phenomenon in works of art of depicting Jesus, or Jesus with his mother, with ethnic features and in cultural settings that link these artworks to particular identities and geographies, notes that each of these human depictions locates Jesus and his mother as members of a particular people—because Jesus is transcendent. Although Jesus was a Jew, "by an unfathomable mystery, he is incarnate" as a member of one or another ethnic group. East points out that such visual depictions of Jesus, when serving as commemoration of the victims of injustice, are christological: "Jesus, in drawing near to the oppressed, assumed their condition as his own; and vice versa, (. . .). Those who endure abuse or suffer unjustly represent or embody the power of Christ in the world." Thus, the life and passion of Jesus Christ "can be 'written' (. . .) in terms of those he especially loves, whom the world would render powerless victims; and they in turn can be 'written' in terms of his triumph in and through death."[11]

Speaking particularly about Black liberation theologian James Cone's conception of Jesus as Black and of what this "mystery of divine identification" means for Black—and, one might also say, for all other— victims of injustice, East captures the transcendent nature of Cone's liberating theology: Jesus lived and died in a particular time and place, was born in a land under a foreign, pagan occupation that victimized his

11. East, "Jewish Jesus, Black Christ."

people, and suffered for this. Because Jesus was both human and divine, his identity is "not only past, but present; not only historical, but spiritual. It (. . .) extend[s] beyond his own context into the lives and bodies of others, even into the here and now." Jesus is immanent. The mystery of Jesus' identity as divine and human, at once universal and particular, renders Cone's affirmation that "He *is* black because he *was* a Jew" true and reasonable. The reality of Jesus' true humanity "displays God's solidarity with us (. . .). That he was truly divine (. . .) means that this solidarity was not a onetime affair, not limited to the particularities of his person."[12]

If it is liberating for the Black faithful to be told so surely that, because of "the mystery of divine identification," Jesus is Black, how equally liberating, how absolutely redemptive, must this mystery be for Palestinians, who can know with equal surety that *Jesus is a Palestinian Arab because he is also a Palestinian Jew—he is and was and will always be Palestinian!*

No matter who the oppressor or the oppressed, the struggle represented by liberation theology remains a spiritual form of resistance by an oppressed population to political, state-imposed oppression. Directly addressing the colonialist/imperialist nature of this injustice and oppression, one theologian has noted that Jesus died a victim of state-sanctioned—that is, political—violence, and the political instrument of his death is now seen as a religious symbol. The Rev. Suzanne Watts Henderson, a Christian Church (Disciples of Christ) minister and colleague of Palestinian Lutheran pastor the Rev. Mitri Raheb, has pointed out that the "cross" had a political purpose, as a means of execution, long before it became a religious symbol. Furthermore, she notes, the "pages of history are full of people on the cross," including both the oppressed—"victims of imperial violence justified as necessary tools for keeping the peace"—and those who stand with the oppressed. They are all expressing political resistance.[13]

As my friend and I delved more deeply into his criticism, I pointed out that the essence of Latin American liberation theology, which he admired as a leftist and perhaps a bit of a 1960s revolutionary himself, seems to me very similar to the essence of the Palestinian theology. Both Gustavo Gutiérrez, the Peruvian Catholic priest who first widely articulated the Latin American theology, and the Palestinian Episcopal

12. East, "Jewish Jesus, Black Christ." Emphasis in original.
13. Raheb and Henderson, *Cross in Contexts*, 22.

priest Naim Ateek are clerics who have shaped their objectives in similar terms—terms that are both religious and ultimately very political. The question Gutiérrez asks in the epigraph at the top of this Introduction both poses a profound question of theodicy and describes the essential challenge of liberation theology: in one way, it asks how God can permit anyone to live in godforsaken circumstances, while in a larger sense, the question says simply, without judging or questioning God's will, that liberation theology's difficult mission is to bring the poor to the deep sense that, however abject their circumstances, God remains present with them. In either sense and however profoundly theological, Gutiérrez's question is inextricably linked to the equally profound political and social realities of the poor and marginalized in Latin America. Although the Palestinian context arises from different circumstances altogether, Naim Ateek asks the same theological question, ultimately employing similar thinking, similar terminology, similar prayers to probe how theology can assure Palestinians—who live without freedom or virtually any human or political rights under Israeli domination—that God loves them, opposes the injustice they face, and cares for their survival despite their extreme circumstances.

My friend was not convinced. "But Latin America had Marxism" was his still-skeptical response. True enough in some measure, but this misses the point and the true vision of liberation theology. Indeed, Marxism's revolutionary socialism and theories of struggle against the social and economic contradictions that lead to poverty and marginalization have been an inspiration for many liberation struggles, nowhere more so than in Latin America in the 1960s and 1970s. But the fundamental aspect, the overriding goal, of Latin America's liberation theology has been *liberation* from oppression, rather than the political theories engaged to facilitate that liberation. Marxism has sometimes been an instrument, but never the goal. In the 1970s, a prominent Latin American liberation theologian, the late Brazilian Archbishop Dom Hélder Câmara, a self-described socialist but not a Marxist or communist, famously spoke to the link, and the inevitable tension, between his liberationist pastoral praxis and the political lens through which that praxis was often viewed, when he said, "When I give food to the poor, they call me a saint. When I ask why they are poor, they call me a communist."[14]

14. *Wikipedia*, "Hélder Câmara."

The goal of Palestinian liberation theology is also liberation, of course, but the political theories and strategies are, and must be, different. Both Latin American and Palestinian liberation theology, in their own ways, invoke moral law to lift up and end the suffering of the downtrodden in their societies, but where the Latin American theology has relied on political and social/economic theory underpinned by the gospel, the Palestinian theology must rely on principles of universal moral and ethical law, including specific tenets of international law, as well as on anti-colonial and anti-racist theory—all also underpinned by the gospel. Marxist theories are of little use to Palestinians. Any liberation theology is *sui generis*, arising from its own context, with its own theories, its own relationship to God, focusing on its own needs—and, in the end, because each is a contextual resistance struggle, following its own path to finding justice. Primarily, any liberation theology is formulated for the comfort and succor of those who suffer, not for the politics of those who would support them.

In Palestine, the instruments for liberation are a combination of several things. There are the anti-colonial and anti-racist theories that have animated Palestinian opposition to Zionism's settler colonialism from the beginning; these are theories that are also in one way or another currently raising public consciousness and increasingly inspiring public protest around the world against all types of oppression. There are also, importantly, the moral and ethical principles underpinning the body of international law meant to set a global standard for inter- and intra-state human conduct—a critical moral standard to which few if any national governments adhere. In addition, and particularly critical in Palestine, although not in any other location where liberation theology is put forth, Palestinian liberation theology is based on scriptural exegesis that stands in direct opposition to Israel's professed biblical rationale for its existence as an exclusively Jewish state.

This last, in fact, is the very place where the Palestinian theology differs most obviously from other liberation theologies, for the Palestinian context is not only the common struggle for justice against political and social oppression, but involves a larger struggle for the very existence of the Palestinian people against a Zionist oppressor that employs Scripture to justify dispossessing and altogether removing them from the land. Nothing is more political and also religion-based than Zionism's use of Scripture to justify Jewish exclusivity in Palestine. Similarly, nothing is more political and at once religious than the use—and serious misuse—of Scripture by the growing Christian Zionist movement in the United States and Europe, which supports Israel's takeover of Palestinian land for its Jewish state. The scriptural citations that Naim Ateek and other Palestinian liberation theologians put forth against Zionism's biblical justifications constitute a serious political as well as theological challenge to the Israeli Zionist political system, going well beyond the "ecumenical" and beyond prayerful spiritual injunctions. They are fighting on a theo-political battlefield and with the very theo-political weapons employed against them by their Zionist oppressors.

I don't believe my friend, or very many other people, have thought deeply about how inextricably political and religious any liberation theology is, and must be. I also doubt that the large segments of public and media opinion that ignore or disparage religion—and indeed even most churches whose business is religion—recognize the true humanity of the suffering for whom this theology is put forth. Despite the widespread dismissal of religion's importance, it should not be lost on any modern political and social justice activists that spirituality, faith, and Scripture together play a prominent role in virtually all justice advocacy. Ultimately, it is also important to affirm that just as any liberation theology is *sui generis*, so also is any resistance *sui generis*. No one and no group outside a resistance movement can gainsay the utility and purpose of any kind of nonviolent resistance, whether it involves active protest on the ground, or preservation of culture and identity, or only producing literature or scriptural exegesis.

It is no mere coincidence in fact that so many of the most prominent and influential leaders in civil rights and freedom struggles in the modern era have been religious figures speaking for a political cause in a language redolent with religious overtones. Although we will deal with this more deeply at a later point, it is also no coincidence that all of these people have led civil rights, social justice, and justice and peace struggles in their individual capacities outside of institutional religious boundaries. These spiritual-political leaders have included, over the last century: Mahatma Gandhi; Dietrich Bonhoeffer; Martin Luther King Jr.; Desmond Tutu and other leading South African clerics; the Dalai Lama; the late congressman and ordained minister John Lewis; the late C. T. Vivian, Joseph Lowery, and countless other Black civil rights leaders in ordained ministry; Cornel West, William Barber, and numbers of other still-active American Black civic and spiritual leaders, some ordained, some not; Liz Theoharis, the White Presbyterian minister who co-chairs the Poor People's Campaign with Barber; Sikh activist Valarie Kaur; the collective of religious leaders, Black and White, who gathered at Ferguson, Missouri, in 2014 in a protest that sparked today's anti-racism campaign; many of the new generation of young Black Lives Matter leaders who emerged from Ferguson and other similar protests[15]; the Native American Water Protectors at Standing Rock Reservation in North Dakota; the multiple Latin American religious martyrs, including Óscar Romero, assassinated and later canonized for preaching and leading a liberation struggle.

These men and women are only the most prominent of the innumerable religio-political social justice activists who have struggled over the last century against imposed oppression. To my Israeli friend, I can only say: the liberation struggle is always political; liberation theology is always resistance to injustice, even when it is not precisely called liberation theology; and liberation theologians always speak in spiritual terms—in their own language—and cite scriptural passages in the struggle for justice, a struggle that is never only spiritual or apolitical. Jesus was political; he was, in fact, the first liberation theologian of the Christian era.

In a real sense, liberation theology arose from a modern, post-World War II awareness of the horrors long inflicted on humanity by political systems, as well as an awakened ethical sense that victims of injustice must be rescued, must be protected and, importantly, must speak out themselves in their own voices, asserting their own human rights and no longer accommodating or silently surrendering to their oppressors. A world weary of war after two global conflicts in less than half a century and deeply horrified after a genocidal assault on the Jewish people, initially held out hope that the essential rights of humankind to liberty from colonial domination and freedom from oppression of all kinds could, and somehow would, be guaranteed. The United Nations was established to forge global peace, international laws were written to prevent war crimes and human rights violations, the Universal Declaration of Human Rights (UDHR) promised respect for human dignity.

The United Nations, itself created on the promise to prevent future wars and preserve the rights of humanity, describes the UDHR as "a roadmap to guarantee the rights of *every individual everywhere*." The

15. See, for instance, Burnley, "Movement for Black Lives."

principal leaders of the group that conceived and drafted the declaration were Eleanor Roosevelt, the driving force behind the drafting committee, and René Cassin, a French jurist who composed the first draft and was later honored with a Nobel Peace Prize for his work on the declaration. The Chilean representative on the drafting committee captured the immense moral purpose behind the declaration—and, it must be noted, its theo-political character—when he described it as an expression of a critical consensus on "the *supreme value of the human person*, a value that did not originate in the decision of a worldly power but rather in *the fact of existing*—which gave rise to the inalienable right to live free from want and oppression and to fully develop one's personality."[16]

The declaration, formally adopted by the UN General Assembly in December 1948, lays out in thirty articles an equal number of individual rights owed to every human being on earth. These are rights whose promulgation, the declaration proclaims, is "the foundation of freedom, justice and peace in the world" and is as well "the highest aspiration of the common people." In a clear reference to the horrors of World War II and especially of the Holocaust, the declaration notes that "disregard and contempt" for human rights had previously resulted in "barbarous acts which have outraged the conscience of mankind."[17] Even if, as is in fact likely, the UDHR's drafters had in mind only, or primarily, the Jewish people who had so recently been the victims of barbarous acts, the declaration's very universality rendered it an instrument intended to affirm the *right to survival* of all peoples on earth, individually and collectively.

There is a tragic irony for Palestinians in these high-flown pledges, however. In the heady, hopeful atmosphere of the early postwar years, there can be no gainsaying the sincerity of the UDHR's drafters or their genuine hope of charting a new course for humanity and human interaction. Nor is it surprising or at all hypocritical that the horrors so recently perpetrated against Jews during the Holocaust were at the forefront of the drafters' minds, particularly the mind of René Cassin, who was himself Jewish. But, like many similar statements of high purpose for humanity, this document was flawed in concept from the beginning, based as it was on the well-meaning but elitist paternalism of the White-, Western-, colonial-privileged position from which its drafters operated, and *it is obvious beyond the shadow of a doubt that the fate of the forgotten population*

16. United Nations, "Universal Declaration of Human Rights: History." Emphasis added.

17. United Nations, "Universal Declaration of Human Rights."

of Palestine, even then being swept away by another new colonial venture, never clouded the vision or even entered the thoughts of the drafters.

The initial atmosphere of hope built upon the UDHR, not surprisingly, soon proved ephemeral. The fragile legal and ethical structure built around the declaration rested not only, for its vision, on the selective ethics of an elite core of drafters who were blind to the oppression in their own nations but also, for its implementation, on governing systems around the world that had no intention of respecting the justice and human rights needs of their populations. This denial of the oppression of populations everywhere in the world living in deep injustice and poverty was as true of Eleanor Roosevelt, who apparently had little thought for the United States' own legacy of slavery and Jim Crow discrimination against Black people, to say nothing of its oppression of Native Americans, as it was of the Soviet Union and China, both UDHR signatories clearly known at the time to be totalitarian states.

The particular tragedy for the Palestinians lay in the exact coincidence of the UDHR's widely hailed issuance with the massive human rights and existential catastrophe that befell them when Israel was established as a Jewish state on Palestinian land. The declaration was ratified by the UN General Assembly in December 1948, just months after the establishment of Israel in May of that year and in the midst of Israel's ethnic cleansing of the Palestinians, which continued throughout 1948 and beyond. The irony here goes beyond the simple coincidence of timing in one people's achievement of justice after immense suffering and another people's hugely unjust near-destruction, but rests in the fact that the Jewish people's salvation occurred, directly and deliberately, at the price of the Palestinians' tragedy.

The major impetus for the UDHR in the first place was clearly the redemption of the Jewish people in the wake of the horrors they suffered during the Holocaust. Hailing the prominent role played by Jews in working to establish a new, more just postwar world order, one scholar quotes René Cassin himself as saying that "support for the human rights of all people is an obligation incumbent upon all Jews, as we believe that universal human rights are intrinsic to Jewish values."[18] Perhaps only God can judge whether, when Cassin spoke of human rights as "intrinsic to Jewish values," he was being hypocritical or only blind to what the new Jewish army was doing on the ground to Palestinians as he was drafting

18. Halper, "Prophetic Judaism of Human Rights."

the UDHR. But it seems clear that, just as Jewish statehood was achieved at the cost of Palestinian expulsion, so also did the beautiful concept of Jewish redemption from suffering occur at the cost of totally obscuring the Palestinians' consequent suffering.

The UDHR was not the first betrayal of the Palestinians, nor certainly the last; it marked, in fact, the start of seventy-plus years of repeated, ongoing betrayals by governments—notably including, of course, those of Israel and the United States but also including Arab governments—as well as by international organizations, global public discourse and, it must be said, churches. The founder of Palestinian liberation theology, Naim Ateek, personally believes that the drafters of the UDHR and its vision of a supposed new, more moral world order, were well aware of the human rights violations being perpetrated against Palestinians, but that they did nothing to improve the declaration or assure its enforcement.[19]

It is not the purpose of this book to chronicle the nearly seventy-five years of Israel's existence in the land between the Mediterranean Sea and the Jordan River. But it is critical to understand how deeply Israel's presence and expansion—from its creation in 1947 by United Nations proclamation as a Jewish state on more than half this land, through its expansion in 1948 to 78 percent of the land, to its control since 1967 over the entirety of the land—have affected the indigenous Palestinian Arab population of this area. This is an indigenous population that includes not only the minority of Palestinian Christians with whom this book is concerned, but the majority population of Palestinian Muslims. It is a population roughly equal in numbers to the Jewish population, each totaling approximately seven million, but which lives completely under Israel's undemocratic control, with rights that are restricted in some way or, for the vast majority, with no freedom or political rights at all. Three major reports by human rights organizations published in 2021 and 2022, all declaring Israel to be an "apartheid regime" throughout the entire territory under its control, make it dramatically clear, without requiring that we here lay out years of detail on Israel's policies, that Israel's Zionist governing system has always been racist, discriminatory, and oppressive to Palestinians. The three organizations are Israel's major human rights

---

19. Personal email communication from Naim Ateek (March 11, 2019).

group B'Tselem, the international human rights monitor Human Rights Watch (HRW), and the largest global monitor, Amnesty International.[20]

These well-known and, in two cases, international human rights bodies are by no means the first organizations to tag Israel with the apartheid label; several small Israeli and Palestinian groups have long recognized this reality, and every one of the last several UN Special Rapporteurs for the Occupied Territories serving during recent decades has applied this label. In a more recent development, three mainstream Christian denominations in the United States—alone among mainstream churches—have adopted a church-wide stance recognizing and condemning Israeli apartheid. We will discuss these declarations in more detail in a later chapter.

Of the three major human rights reports, the one by B'Tselem was issued first, in January 2021. The Hebrew word *b'tselem*, literally meaning "in the image of"—and, significantly, used in Hebrew synonymously with "human rights and dignity"—is taken from Genesis 1:27: "And God created humankind in his image, in the image of God he created them." Founded over thirty years ago, B'Tselem seeks to end Israel's occupation of Palestinian territories as "the only way to achieve a future that ensures human rights, democracy, liberty and equality to all people, Palestinian and Israeli alike."[21] It is a highly credible organization, well-known and internationally respected for honest reporting by both Palestinian and Israeli sources; its director, Israeli activist Hagai El-Ad, writes and lectures, including in 2020 before the United Nations, with great human compassion.

In a shift from its previous focus only on Israel's control over Palestinians in the occupied territories—the West Bank, Gaza, and East Jerusalem, which Israel captured in 1967—B'Tselem's 2021 report examined Israeli control throughout the entire area between the Mediterranean Sea and the Jordan River. Entitled "A Regime of Jewish Supremacy from the Jordan River to the Mediterranean Sea: This is Apartheid," the report pronounced Israel to be unquestionably an apartheid regime throughout the entire area over which it rules. Contrary to the common perception that this territory exists under two different governing systems—the supposedly democratic state of Israel, existing alongside the occupied Palestinian territories—the report asserted that in fact this entire geographic area must be regarded as governed by a single regime with differing sets

20. The three reports are: B'Tselem, "Regime of Jewish Supremacy"; Human Rights Watch, "Threshold Crossed"; and Amnesty International, *Israel's Apartheid*.

21. See B'Tselem website.

of rights for Jews and Palestinians. The entire area between the river and the sea is organized "under a single principle: advancing and cementing the supremacy of one group—Jews—over another—Palestinians." Israel "engineers" space within this geographic area differently according to whether Jews or Palestinians live there.[22]

Thus, although there is demographic parity between the two peoples in the entire area—as noted, seven million Jews and seven million Palestinians—there is no parity of laws or rights. For instance, approximately 700,000 Jewish settlers live among about three million Palestinians in the West Bank and East Jerusalem and enjoy full rights in the Israeli state because they are Jews; they live "as though the entire area were a single space." Palestinians, on the other hand, live in a "fragmented mosaic" with differing rights, differing systems of injustice, differing restrictions on movement, according to which fragment they live in. Palestinians in the West Bank and in Gaza, where two million live under a fifteen-year Israeli blockade, are denied all political rights and all but minimal human rights. Palestinians in East Jerusalem, an occupied territory illegally annexed by Israel, have a "residency status" that allows them freedom of movement (they have yellow license plates like Israeli citizens) and limited rights to local, but not national voting. The 1.9 million Palestinians who are citizens of Israel enjoy some of the usual benefits of citizenship, but their rights are not equal to those of Jews, and they are disadvantaged by multiple institutionally discriminatory laws. Israel regards itself officially as a state of the Jews rather than a state of its citizens, and in July 2018 the state formally enshrined Jewish supremacy in law by adopting a "Nation State Law"—a so-called Basic Law, which has the force of a constitutional provision—granting self-determination only to Jews.[23]

The 2021 HRW report on Israeli apartheid, entitled "A Threshold Crossed," is a frank, no-punches-pulled, 213-page compendium of what it refers to as Israel's "crimes against humanity," including *apartheid* and *persecution*, as defined under international law. Issued in April, three months after the B'Tselem report, this lengthy study began with a summary assertion of the situation for Palestinians that essentially affirmed the groundbreaking B'Tselem report. Across the entire territory between the Mediterranean Sea and the Jordan River, HRW asserted,

22. B'Tselem, "Regime of Jewish Supremacy."
23. B'Tselem, Regime of Jewish Supremacy." For the text of the law, see "Basic Law."

and in most aspects of life, Israeli authorities methodically privilege Jewish Israelis and discriminate against Palestinians. Laws, policies, and statements by leading Israeli officials make plain that the objective of maintaining Jewish Israeli control over demographics, political power, and land has long guided government policy. In pursuit of this goal, authorities have dispossessed, confined, forcibly separated, and subjugated Palestinians by virtue of their identity to varying degrees of intensity. In certain areas, as described in this report, these deprivations are so severe that they amount to the crimes against humanity of apartheid and persecution. Several widely held assumptions, including that the occupation is temporary, that the "peace process" will soon bring an end to the Israeli abuses, that Palestinians have meaningful control over their lives in the West Bank and Gaza, and that Israel is an egalitarian democracy inside its borders, have obscured the reality of Israel's entrenched discriminatory rule over Palestinians (. . .). A number of Israeli officials have stated clearly their intent to maintain this control in perpetuity and backed it up through their actions, including continued settlement expansion over the course of the decades-long "peace process."[24]

In the remainder of the report, HRW clearly defined and graphically described what constitute Israel's crimes against humanity—crimes labeled by HRW as "among the most odious crimes in international law"—and how these affect Palestinians. Under international law,[25] the crime of apartheid is defined as consisting of three elements: an *intent to maintain domination* by one racial group over another, *systematic oppression* by one racial group of another, and *commission of "inhumane acts"* against a racial group specifically because of its identity. These inhumane acts include forcible transfer or expulsion, expropriation of land, creation of separate reserves and ghettos, denial of free movement, and denial of "the right to a nationality." The crime of persecution consists primarily of "intentional and severe deprivation of fundamental rights" committed because of a group's racial, national, or ethnic identity.[26]

24. Human Rights Watch, "Threshold Crossed."

25. The particular international laws cited are the 1973 International Convention on the Suppression and Punishment of the Crime of Apartheid, which defines apartheid, and the 1998 Rome Statute of the International Criminal Court, which defines the crime of persecution. Human Rights Watch, "Threshold Crossed," 3.

26. Human Rights Watch, "Threshold Crossed," 5–9.

While the B'Tselem report did not focus on the grim situation in Gaza beyond including it as one of the "mosaic pieces" where Palestinians enjoy no rights, the HRW report devoted considerable space to detailing the factual realities of the horror that is life in this territory. Even the barest outlines of the Gaza situation indicate a suffocating, nearly unimaginable reality. Gaza is a small strip of land, one hundred forty square miles, an area not even one-fifth the size of Rhode Island, the smallest US state, but with a population of two million and rising. It is one of the most densely populated places on earth, and its population is virtually imprisoned there, having endured a tight Israeli blockade since 2007. Israel severely limits imports and exports, as well as population entry and exit. Unemployment is in the 40- to 50-percent range; this figure, along with the rate of grinding, rock-bottom poverty, is rising inexorably. Water sanitization plants and sewage treatment plants have been repeatedly bombed and have not been adequately repaired because of the Israeli blockade. Gaza's water is polluted and unsafe for human consumption; raw sewage pours into the Mediterranean. The United Nations predicted several years ago that Gaza would be "unlivable" by 2020.[27] The eruption of the COVID-19 pandemic in the same year of 2020 added another disaster atop continuing disaster.

Since the blockade began, Israel has launched four major military, largely aerial bombing, assaults on the territory—in 2008, 2012, 2014, and 2021—plus multiple smaller assaults, that have killed thousands of Palestinian civilians, including children, and destroyed tens of thousands of homes and other structures. Although Hamas, which has governed Gaza since Palestinian elections in 2006, and other militants frequently fire locally made rockets into Israel, and did so in the thousands during the crisis in 2021, Israel's massive response against a confined population with nowhere to run is often likened to "shooting fish in a barrel." In 2018, Palestinians began a regular nonviolent protest, the Great March of Return, at the Israeli-constructed barrier closing Gaza in, that continued every week for about eighteen months. One of the organizers of the March called it "a scream for life."[28] With the exception of some rock-throwing and occasional Molotov cocktails, protesters who approached

27. See United Nations Country Team, *Gaza in 2020*. The report concluded that, without the intensification of "on-going herculean efforts by Palestinians and partners in such sectors as energy, education, health, water and sanitation," Gaza would not be "a liveable [sic] place" by 2020. See 16.

28. See Seddon, "'Scream for Life' Gaza."

the barrier on the Gaza side were unarmed, but were met with sniper fire and some heavy arms fire from the Israeli side. More than three hundred Palestinians, including almost fifty children, were shot to death, and 36,000 were injured, of whom about one-quarter were children. Israeli snipers also shot and killed several clearly identifiable medical personnel and journalists. Approximately two hundred of the injured, shot in the leg, required limb amputation.[29] These are only the bare realities of life in Gaza, but virtually no one outside Gaza heard or responded to its "scream for life." Gaza could have invented the term *dystopia*.

Amnesty International's report, issued in February 2022, is the most detailed and is as hard-hitting as the HRW report. Running to almost three hundred pages and the result of more than four years of research, including interviews on the ground with both Palestinians and Israelis, along with analysis of Israeli laws, government regulations and directives, military orders, and public statements by political and military officials, the Amnesty report concluded, in the simplest terms, that "Israel has perpetrated the international wrong of apartheid (. . .) wherever it imposes [its] system," in violation of both the Apartheid Convention and the Rome Statute.[30] After over two hundred pages of detail, Amnesty expanded on the apartheid charge, concluding with more specific and sweeping charges that Israel's system of "institutionalized segregation and discrimination against Palestinians, as a racial group, in all areas under its control amounts to a system of apartheid, and a serious violation of Israel's human rights obligations. Almost all of Israel's civilian administration and military authorities, as well as governmental and quasi-governmental institutions, are involved in the enforcement of a system of apartheid against Palestinians across Israel and the OPT [occupied Palestinian territories] and against Palestinian refugees and their descendants outside the territory."[31]

Importantly, the report copied HRW in affirming that this apartheid system, which it called "a systematic as well as widespread attack" against the Palestinian people, has been in effect as long as Israel has existed. As noted above, Amnesty considers that even Palestinian refugees expelled in 1948 and their descendants, whom Israel has refused the right to return to their homes and land, are victims of apartheid. The

29. United Nations, "Two Years On."
30. Amnesty International, *Israel's Apartheid*, 12.
31. Amnesty International, *Israel's Apartheid*, 267.

report asserted in addition that, since its establishment in 1948, Israel "has pursued an explicit policy of establishing and maintaining a Jewish demographic hegemony and maximizing its control over land to benefit Jewish Israelis while minimizing the number of Palestinians and restricting their rights." Racial discrimination against Palestinians and Israel's system of segregation are "the result of deliberate government policy." The violations of Palestinians' rights "are not accidental repetitions of offences [sic], but part of an institutionalized regime of systematic oppression and domination."[32]

In a striking catalog of crimes and rights violations, the Amnesty report listed "the continuing forced displacement of a majority of Palestinians from their land and property in 1947–49 and subsequently in 1967; the forced deportations, forcible transfers and arbitrary restrictions on their freedom of movement; the denial of nationality and the right of return; the racialized and discriminatory dispossession of their lands and property; and the subsequent discriminatory allocation of and access to national resources (including land, housing and water)." In an additional listing, the report named "administrative detention and torture, unlawful killings and serious injuries," all clearly committed as a means of maintaining the system.[33]

These violations combine "to hinder Palestinians' current enjoyment of their rights, including access to livelihood, employment, healthcare, food security, water and sanitation, and education opportunities." They further guarantee a permanent lower status for Palestinians than Jewish Israelis enjoy throughout the land; this intended permanence was crystallized in 2018 with passage of Israel's Nation State Law, cited also in the HRW report. Amnesty asserted that the law—which in fact merely formalized a situation existing for decades—"constitutionally enshrined racial discrimination against non-Jewish people" by declaring that self-determination is a right only for Jews.[34]

Israel has always regarded Palestinians as a threat to the establishment and maintenance of a Jewish majority, Amnesty asserted, and as a result Palestinians "were to be expelled, fragmented, segregated, controlled, dispossessed of their land and property and deprived of their economic and social rights." Beyond its efforts to reduce the numbers of

---

32. Amnesty International, *Israel's Apartheid*, 13.

33. Amnesty International, *Israel's Apartheid*, 30, 267.

34. Amnesty International, *Israel's Apartheid*, 30, 267.

Palestinians and restrict the rights of those remaining in Palestine, the report charged that Israel has obstructed even the Palestinians' ability to challenge the oppressive campaign against them.[35]

B'Tselem concluded its groundbreaking apartheid report, the first of these several major reports, with the hope that the dramatic statement would arouse a critical firestorm of debate that might ultimately lead to overturning apartheid.[36] But, in yet another indication of how thoroughly the Palestinians and their plight have sunk below the world's radar screen, the firestorm never arose: the mainstream US media, led by the *New York Times* and the *Washington Post*, both often eager to shield Israel from criticism, ignored the B'Tselem report altogether for three months, until HRW issued its more detailed report. The then-new US administration of President Joe Biden, along with Israel's government and society, have also largely ignored the entire apartheid issue, except to deny its relevance. Something like a small "firestorm" of strident criticism of the apartheid reporting arose in the United States a year later in reaction to Amnesty International's report—including harsh criticism in tones of wounded outrage from the major Jewish organizations, some parts of the media, and virtually all politicians of both political parties, including the Biden administration itself. But there was no true debate of the sort B'Tselem had hoped for in circles where debate might have made a difference, and no direct criticism or rejection of any of Amnesty's or the other organizations' evidence. Again, the media primarily strove to ignore the report; the *New York Times* took almost two months—fifty-two days, by the count of the anti-Zionist blog *Mondoweiss*—even to mention the

35. Amnesty International, *Israel's Apartheid*, 13–14.

36. In an impassioned article published in the UK, coinciding with release of the B'Tselem report, Director Hagai El-Ad opened with the lament that the oppressive knowledge always hanging over Israel-Palestine—that "this place is constantly being engineered to privilege one people and one people only: the Jewish people," while an equal number of Palestinians live there as lesser beings—is a reality that "fills the air, bleeds, and is everywhere on this land." In speaking of this reality aloud for the first time, El-Ad insisted that the ugly reality must change: he said he wants to stay in the land where he was born (in Haifa in 1969), but he "demand[s] to live in a very different future. The past is one of traumas and injustices. In the present, yet more injustices are constantly reproduced. The future must be radically different—a rejection of supremacy, built on a commitment to justice and our shared humanity." See El-Ad, "We are Israel's Largest Human Rights Group."

report, and then did so only in a brief article on a related subject and only online rather than in its print edition.[37] This news has not been what the *Times* considers "fit to print."

The essence of the Palestinians' century-long struggle for justice has been to resist the denial and attempted erasure of their very existence. The struggle has been against Zionist settler-colonial efforts literally to erase their presence in Palestine: to erase the identity of the land of Palestine itself, as well as their identity as a distinct people; also to erase the world's memory of Palestinian distinctness, even to try to erase the Palestinians' own self-perception as people with a common identity, ethnicity, culture, language. Although Palestinian political leadership has always been wanting, the Palestinian people have maintained a strong sense of community arising from having been unjustly victimized. The common plight of exile and oppression that all Palestinians faced after their dispossession and ethnic cleansing by Israel in 1948, which came to be called the *Nakba*, or catastrophe, has had the effect of forging greater unity and sense of resistance. Even at their lowest period in the immediate aftermath of the Nakba, when there was little thought, and no possibility, of collective organized resistance against Israel, Palestinians in refugee camps and various other places of exile consciously preserved their identity, their culture and dialect, and their spiritual bond with homes and homeland. Often, separate neighborhoods inside refugee camps in Lebanon, Jordan, and Syria (which each housed refugees numbering in the tens of thousands from various areas of Palestine) were organized according to villages of origin before 1948. Neighborhoods took the names of villages, and streets were named after village streets or village heroes. Children have grown up in refugee camps knowing they came from such-and-such a village in Palestine and only gradually learning that they were refugees. Their Palestinian identity was fostered from the beginning.

This profound need to preserve identity as a powerful means of resistance to oppression is, of course, common to most peoples suffering such oppression. This is preeminently the case with Jews, whose Zionist leaders fail to honor or even recognize in Palestinians the same impulse that motivated them in establishing a Jewish state. As we will see, other peoples, including Black Americans, are no different. The late civil rights

---

37. North, "'NY Times' Gives In."

icon Rosa Parks, for instance, was powerfully motivated by notions of resistance and liberation. She had her own experience, similar to that of Palestinian refugee children, of being raised from childhood to "know that we were not free" but to have pride in being Black. At age eight, she read a book that introduced her to the notion that Black people were regarded by Whites as inferior; this thought—that her own people were "not considered to be complete human beings"—angered her even as a child and planted in her the seeds of resistance. She came to the realization early in life that Black survival and Black accomplishments were the ultimate weapons for resistance to White supremacy. Reclaiming the history of Black resistance and being educated "for liberation" became Parks' driving passion.[38]

Parks was also moved and empowered by the notion of a God who seeks justice on earth and the equality of all people—a kind of liberation theology that had not yet made its way up to traditional theologians but that had long been known by the oppressed. She spoke for many Black Americans when she talked of the "Lord's power within me to do what I have done." She achieved an inner peace because of her faith, once observing that she "prayed hard not to give in and not to fall by the wayside."[39] This "power of the Lord" in us and the steadfast determination not to fall by the wayside define the essence of all liberation theologies, as we will see.

Questions such as where God is, where God has been throughout history's catastrophes, are at the heart of all theologies, perhaps especially of all liberation theologies. For the Palestinians, the central question is how God could permit the gross violation of Palestinian rights that has been the direct and ongoing result of Israel's establishment as a Jewish state more than seven decades ago. Looking back to the time of the world's welcome to that Jewish state, Palestinians wonder how God could have permitted the hypocrisy that allowed every nation to turn away from Palestinian human rights while endorsing a "universal" declaration supposedly supporting precisely those rights. How could the church have ignored Palestinian humanity and the Palestinians' human and spiritual needs so egregiously for so long? These deep questions apply as well, of

38. Theoharis, *Rebellious Life*, 4–5.

39. Theoharis, *Rebellious Life*, 6, 102, 124.

course, to other peoples living in unrelieved oppression whose humanity has long been ignored.

We will attempt to tackle critical questions such as these, and especially the role of the church in exercising—or not exercising—God's "preferential option" for the poor and marginalized, as we survey the growth of liberation theologies throughout the world and examine in much greater depth the rise of Palestinian liberation theology, how this theology fits in to the general context of other such theologies, as well as how it relates to the situation of Palestinians on the ground and of their Israeli oppressor.

1

Liberation

The Theology

*For the hanged and beaten. For the shot, drowned, and
burned. For the tortured, tormented, and terrorized. For the
abandoned by the rule of law. We will remember.*

*With hope because hopelessness is the enemy of justice. With courage
because peace requires bravery. With persistence because justice
is a constant struggle. With faith because we shall overcome.*

—INSCRIPTION, *National Memorial for Peace and Justice*
(The Lynching Memorial), Montgomery, Alabama

IT IS REASONABLE TO assume that a major impetus for the rise of liberation theology in the decades after World War II lay in the world's failure—at perhaps the most opportune time in history, when peoples and
governments seemed eager for renewal—to create a global moral order
that truly lifted up and ended the suffering of the downtrodden in societies everywhere. The Universal Declaration of Human Rights might have
been the instrument for creating such a new order, but it has never fulfilled the vision its framers imagined. Deep, profoundly existential questions and issues of theodicy, such as have driven theologians like Gustavo
Gutiérrez and Naim Ateek, began to be posed throughout the world in
the wake of a half century of global warfare that was hugely destructive to

humanity. When, however, despite high-flown verbal aspirations, secular political systems and even institutional churches failed to be able to ease humanity's grief and suffering in any substantial way and showed themselves unprepared even to attempt to address the fundamental questions of why God permits such suffering, liberation theology arose from the grassroots as a nonviolent, loving, compassionate resistance effort to support and guide the suffering through their pain to a realization that God is always present to sustain and suffer with them.

German theologian Jürgen Moltmann was one of the first intellectuals in the postwar era, and perhaps the first in Europe, to articulate a theology for and by the oppressed. Although he is not usually thought of specifically as a liberation theologian, his theology is deeply concerned with the condition of those who live in any kind of oppression, and he has provided support and inspiration to theologians throughout the world, notably including Latin Americans dealing with liberation theology. Gustavo Gutiérrez has called Moltmann's body of work "undoubtedly one of the most important in contemporary theology."[1] Noted Croatian-American theologian Miroslav Volf, who came to know Moltmann as a doctoral student under him, has hailed the "energy and power" of the German's theology and its ability to capture hearts and minds in Asia and North and South America, no less than in Europe. In Volf's view, there is "no theologian from the second half of the twentieth century who has had as powerful a global resonance as Moltmann has."[2]

Moltmann knew suffering himself, and his own experience led him to the radical understanding both that, through the cross, God knows and stands with suffering humanity and that, through the risen Christ, God gives hope to humankind. Coming from an unchurched family, Moltmann was conscripted into the German army as a teenager in the last year of World War II and then spent three years in British prisoner-of-war camps, where he experienced profound guilt and near-despair over Germany's conduct during the war. He speaks of God finding him, rather than the reverse, during his years of searching and reading Scripture in prison. In this way, he came to know God in a personal way as one who suffers in solidarity with the afflicted of humanity. Moltmann was

1. Gutiérrez, *Theology*, 125.
2. Volf, "Foreword," vii.

particularly touched by Jesus' words on the cross—"My God, my God, why have you forsaken me?" (Matt 27:46, Mark 15:34, Ps 22, NRSV)—and felt this cry of abandonment as Jesus' participation in Moltmann's own personal suffering.[3]

In later years, he grieved the trauma of friends living under military dictatorships in the postwar world, especially East European compatriots living under Soviet domination. He wrote that the oppressed in any society that was "blind to the sufferings of others" could find hope and God's solidarity in the cross, "if they remember that at the centre of the Christian faith stands an unsuccessful, tormented Christ, dying in forsakenness."[4] In this way, Moltmann laid the basis of a theology rooted in the notion of a personal, grieving God who relates deeply to the oppressed and what they endure, and he thus reinforced the foundations of other developing liberation theologies.

Moltmann's belief that God enters into human suffering out of "a passionate love" for humankind positioned him in direct opposition to traditional theologians committed to the belief that God is impassible and impervious to humanity's distress. He has been harshly critical of the church's rigidity and its failure, essentially, to relate to humanity: the church has been blind to the real world; Christian dogmatism does not understand the feelings and the trauma of those in pain and therefore cannot offer liberating hope. Moltmann's own view, on the contrary, is of God not as distant and impenetrable, but as suffering Godself. In the face of this suffering of humanity, Moltmann challenges the church to create a "truly Christian theology"—which he specifically says *"means a liberating theology."* Unless the church can put aside its perpetual, unreasoned optimism and begin to see and feel the pain of the negative, Christian hope is neither liberating nor even realistic. A church that cannot change "in order to exist for the humanity of man [sic] in changed circumstances becomes ossified and dies."[5]

Painting a realistic, and warmly human, picture of Jesus as rebel—a picture that models and mirrors oppressed humanity, ignored and abandoned by society and by the church—Moltmann characterizes Jesus as

---

3. Volf, "Foreword," ix.

4. Moltmann, *Crucified God*, xi–xii.

5. Volf, "Foreword," ix, and Moltmann, *Crucified God*, front matter, especially xi–xiii, xxv, 9. Emphasis added.

folly to the wise, a scandal to the devout and a disturber of the peace in the eyes of the mighty. That is why he was crucified. If anyone identifies with him, [that person] becomes alienated from the wisdom, religion and power politics of his society. The crucified Christ became the brother of the despised, abandoned and oppressed. And this is why brotherhood with the "least of his brethren" is a necessary part of brotherhood with Christ and identification with him (. . .). Christian identification with the crucified Christ means solidarity with the sufferings of the poor and the misery both of the oppressed and the oppressors.[6]

Liberation theology is nothing if not a personal theology of God's deep relationship with and love for all of humanity, and as Moltmann's theologies of hope and of "the crucified God" evolved, he came to describe a kind of spiritual sanctuary for the oppressed that evokes the suffering, consoling presence of God, a place where God shares human alienation. He never expressed and, we can most likely assume, never felt a particular awareness of Palestinians, or indeed of Latin Americans or other specific populations of the oppressed. But, through his own deep sense of being with God, and his understanding of Jesus as not a mere symbol but a real presence who scandalized and "disturbed the peace" of the mighty, he has conveyed his own and God's true love and solidarity with all peoples who suffer. "In the vicious circle of meaninglessness and god-forsakenness" in this life on earth, he tells us, God "comes forward in the figure of the crucified Christ, who communicates *the courage to be*."[7]

Although Moltmann was not the inspiration for the proliferation of liberation theologies that occurred more or less simultaneously among suffering peoples in different geographic locations throughout the world, his theology was well-known in this new school. These theologies arose spontaneously during the first decades after World War II, with no interdenominational coordination and in differing political and geographic contexts, and all coincidentally adopted the same name without knowing about the others.[8] Black theologians in the United States began to preach liberation particularly for Black people. At the height of the civil rights era, for instance, noted Black theologian James H. Cone published two books

6. Moltmann, *Crucified God*, 29.

7. Moltmann, *Crucified God*, 493–94. Emphasis added.

8. Rieger, "Protestantism," 36.

about a theology he explicitly called liberation theology, even though he was unaware that Gustavo Gutiérrez's classic on the Latin American theology was being published almost simultaneously.[9] Cone discovered Jürgen Moltmann before he had ever heard of the Latin American theologians, and he cited Moltmann's revolutionary theology in his books.[10] Before long, the connection between Cone and the Latin Americans was made—Brazilian educator and liberation philosopher Paulo Freire wrote the foreword to a later edition of one of Cone's books—and the circle of liberation theologians expanded.[11] The German's early works also became a fruitful resource for several Latin Americans. In fact, Moltmann's book, *The Crucified God*, figured poignantly in a catastrophic event in El Salvador: in November 1989, six Jesuit priests, along with their housekeeper and her daughter, were brutally murdered in their home by Salvadoran soldiers, and when the murderers tipped over a bookcase near one of the victims, Moltmann's book fell out and was later found blood-stained on the floor. Moltmann considers this a symbol that these martyrs were "the seed of the resurrection of a new world."[12]

Connections such as this indicate a kind of deep spiritual bond among liberation theologians. Naim Ateek himself may have felt a similar kind of inner bond. He says he knew little about the wider school of liberation theology when he first approached a publisher in 1988 with the manuscript of his first book, *Justice and Only Justice*. But without realizing it, he was speaking from the same kind of pain that his fellow liberationists experienced. He had not at that point read Gutiérrez or other liberation theologians and says his editor was the "first to recognize that what I was writing was a *Palestinian* liberation theology." Ateek was, he

9. Cone's books were published in 1969 and 1970. See Cone, *Black Theology and Black Power*, and Cone, *Black Theology of Liberation*.

10. Cone quotes from a 1968 essay by Moltmann, written before *Crucified God* was published, as follows: "If we believe the crucified Christ to be the representative of God on earth, we see the glory of God no longer in the crowns of the mighty but in the face of the man who was executed on the gallows (. . .). It follows that the freedom of God comes to earth not through crowns—that is to say, through the struggle for power—but through love and solidarity with the powerless." See Cone, *A Black Theology*, 107.

11. Freire, "Foreword," xi.

12. Moltmann, *Crucified God*, xv–xvi. In telling this story, Moltmann notes a particular emotional connection between himself and Spanish-Salvadoran Jesuit Jon Sobrino, who lived in the house with the other Jesuits but was out of the country when the murder occurred. It was a bookcase in Sobrino's room from which Moltmann's book fell out.

says, "addressing my own context of injustice and oppression. I was, as a follower of Jesus Christ, applying my faith in God and my knowledge of the Bible to respond to the unbelievable atrocities committed by the Israeli government in its occupation of my country. Looking back, it was all providential. Thanks be to God."[13]

Providential indeed. The existential questions that liberation theologies seek to answer are the thoughtful and at least implicitly theological questions that any people must ask when faced with collective suffering and near-extinction—questions that in a great many ways link humanity in a kind of spiritual bond, of which they may not always even be aware. In his landmark *A Theology of Liberation*, which remains a classic enunciation of a revolutionary school of theology, Gustavo Gutiérrez touched on the miserable, voiceless, powerless condition that, in 1970 when he wrote it, characterized and still characterizes so much of humanity's social and political underclass.[14]

This underclass constitutes a great mass of populations everywhere who are too often simply dismissed as "the poor." For Gutiérrez and his liberation theology colleagues in Latin America, these poor are not a faceless mass; they are the people who populate the gospels and to whom Jesus ministered. They encompass a broad spectrum of humanity, and they matter critically; they mattered to Jesus, and they should matter to us today. Yet, as Gutiérrez says, poverty is the very negation of humanity. In poverty, human beings do not matter; they are unimportant and have no elementary rights. Poverty "destroys peoples, families, and individuals," he writes; it "means death." Poverty, by his all-encompassing definition, is "lack of food and housing, the inability to attend properly to health and education needs, the exploitation of workers, permanent unemployment, the lack of respect for one's human dignity, and unjust

---

13. Email from Ateek. Emphasis in original.

14. Gutiérrez is the most prominent of the Latin American liberation theologians, but he is by no means the only one. Among the most well-known are Leonardo Boff of Brazil and his brother Clodovis Boff; Ignacio Ellacuria of Spain and El Salvador, who was one of the six Jesuit priests murdered by Salvadoran soldiers in 1989; Jon Sobrino, also a Spanish-Salvadoran Jesuit who lived with the six murdered priests but was out of the country at the time of the massacre; and the late Juan Luis Segundo of Uruguay, also a Jesuit priest. Leonardo Boff was censured by the Vatican and has left ordained ministry. His brother Clodovis is a lay theologian. Sobrino has also been criticized but not silenced by the Vatican for his position on Christology.

limitations placed on personal freedom in the areas of self-expression, politics, and religion."[15]

Gutiérrez saw that theology has a critical function, going well beyond that of economic and social development programs—and well beyond the secular visions of the Marxist struggle—in being present to humanity's progress. Critical to theology's presence in this human progress, he wrote in an early description of liberation theology's purpose and role, is the struggle in underdeveloped and oppressed countries "to construct a just and fraternal society, where persons can live with dignity and be the agents of their own destiny."[16] A huge and indeed superhuman, supernatural task, involving the building up of *"a new humanity"*—a phrase Gutiérrez himself set in italics. Liberation, he reemphasized farther on in *A Theology of Liberation*, means not only overcoming economic, social, and political dependence, but "in a deeper sense, [seeing] the becoming of humankind as a process of human emancipation in history. It is to see humanity in search of a qualitatively different society in which it will be free from all servitude, in which it will be the artisan of its own destiny."[17]

Creating this "qualitatively different" society means being actively involved in the struggle for justice. Gutiérrez's insistence that the oppressed must be the agents of their own lives and futures—in his words the "artisans" who fashion and lead the struggle—speaks to an essential aspect of liberation theology that distinguishes it from traditional theologies. The notion of agency is critical to his work, signifying the basis of this theology as originating in the grassroots: the idea that the oppressed populations occupying the bottom rungs of societies are the ones who must speak out for themselves, becoming the subjects of their own lives rather than the objects and the victims of others. Although not a theologian, Brazilian educator Paulo Freire developed much of the foundation of liberation theology with his classic 1968 study, *Pedagogy of the Oppressed*. This book promoted the notion that education is a tool of social justice and should be designed to awaken critical consciousness in the oppressed, thereby showing the way to freedom from oppression. Having grown up in poverty and realizing the limiting effect poverty has on the mind's ability to learn, Freire coined the term *conscientização*

15. Gutiérrez, *Theology*, xxi, 249n49.

16. Gutiérrez, *Theology*, xiv.

17. Gutiérrez, *Theology*, 56. Emphasis in original. More of this passage is cited in the epigraph of this chapter.

or "conscientization" to describe the process of educating the poor to achieve liberation through praxis.[18]

Even before Freire fully developed his educational philosophy and published *Pedagogy*, Gutiérrez had discussed the value of critical pedagogy as a process through which the poor overcome their own "naïve awareness," broadening their consciousness, becoming more acutely aware of the brutal realities of their situation, not surrendering but "find[ing] their own language" in which to work against those realities. Through this continuing process of critical awareness, or conscientization, the poor become better able to examine issues and ideas frankly and without inhibition, "replac[ing] magical explanations with real causes," and engaging in dialogue and debate.[19]

Much of this process of conscientization occurred via the establishment throughout Latin America of Christian Base Communities, small local groups organized by lay people in towns and villages for the purpose of educating peasants in reading and other basic skills, along with some religious teaching, and thus empowering them socially and creating precisely the personal and community agency that Gutiérrez and Freire were trying to inspire. Through these base communities, the poor themselves led small-scale social justice movements and were able to bring significant change by highlighting their own struggle for liberation. Although liberation theology as it began in the 1970s has evolved considerably, under the pressures both of Vatican opposition and of economic movements such as neoliberalism, the fundamental impetus of the theology did nonetheless have a lasting impact, largely through the base communities, in terms of awakening the poor to their own power to bring change and in turn pressing the church to recognize the scriptural basis of social justice and begin to involve the poor in religious discourse. Liberation theology ultimately, in the view of one scholar, moved the church's focus "away from solely eternal salvation to the more pressing necessity of earthly liberation of the poor from oppression and suffering."[20]

Conscientization by its nature generates connections, and Freire has had a particular influence on the development of social justice movements outside Latin America. His teachings had an impact on Black resistance well before the Black Lives Matter movement emerged in 2013. As we

18. See Freire, *Pedagogy of the Oppressed*.
19. Gutiérrez, *Theology*, 57.
20. Singer, "Liberation Theology in Latin America."

have seen, theologian James Cone connected with Freire in the 1980s. At about the same time, the American Black writer and social activist bell hooks made a significant connection with Freire. hooks wrote that, in studying Freire, she gained an "identity in resistance." His teaching that the oppressed "cannot enter the struggle as objects in order later to become subjects" was transformative for her because it furnished a language for her own growing awareness of being in struggle against the colonizing process under which Black people live in the United States. hooks's own transformation was in recognizing that she and the Black community, who are the *objects* of colonization, need always to see themselves, and to act, as *subjects* in maintaining the struggle for a *de*colonizing process.[21] Most liberation theologians have gone through their own transformative processes and, as we will see, this has been true for Palestinians as well: although they are the objects of Israel's colonizing process and indeed of its attempt to erase them as a people, in developing a resistance struggle and a specific theology of resistance and liberation, they have come to see themselves rather as the subjects of their own struggle.

The supreme spiritual challenge of liberation theology—achieving the spiritual and psychological liberation of humanity, and the question of theodicy that it raises—is the one posed by Gutiérrez in the epigraph of this chapter: "How is it possible to tell the poor, who are forced to live in conditions that embody a denial of love, that God loves them?"[22] How to convince the downtrodden that God is present in suffering and in misery—that God sustains everyone in the struggle to live freely, liberating all from what Freire called the "fear of freedom" and the fear of personal transformation that would come with it?[23] How to give everyone, as Jürgen Moltmann would have it, the "courage to be?" Gutiérrez captured the essence of liberation theology when he wrote that,

> the freedom to which we are called presupposes the going out of oneself, the breaking down of our selfishness and of all the structures that support our selfishness; the foundation of this freedom is openness to others. The fullness of liberation—a free gift from Christ—is communion with God and with other human beings (. . .). The gradual conquest of true freedom leads to the creation of a new humankind and a qualitatively different

21. hooks, *Teaching to Transgress*, 46–48.
22. Gutiérrez, *Theology*, 24.
23. Freire, *Pedagogy of the Oppressed*, 35.

society. This vision provides, therefore, a better understanding of what in fact is at stake in our times.[24]

Another prime challenge of liberation theology, part of the mission of this theology, is to stand as a challenge to the church. Taking note of the widespread and growing postwar awareness of the oppressive, alienating situation in which so much of humanity lived—and characterizing this situation as a sin, "offensive to humankind and therefore to God"—Gutiérrez expressed regret that this global consciousness was only barely seeping into the institutional church. Although the church tried to maintain a façade of spiritual other-worldliness, placing itself above profane, temporal affairs, Gutiérrez pointed out that, for all its supposed spirituality, the church hierarchy virtually everywhere in the Western Christian world maintained close ties to the exploiting classes that wielded political and economic power. The established church in fact lent legitimacy to oppressive and dictatorial governments—betraying the poor and the oppressed in the process—through its failure to criticize the status quo, its efforts to rein in clerics who did criticize and, in Gutiérrez's words, its continued meaningless preaching of "a lyrical spiritual unity of all Christians."[25]

The Second Vatican Council in the early 1960s, as well as a key 1968 conclave of the Latin American Bishops' Conference at Medellín, Colombia, committed the Catholic Church more fully to eliminating social and economic injustice. But this period of raised consciousness dissipated before long, and conservative elements in the hierarchies, fearful of radical influences, soon moved to suppress liberationist sentiment and action.[26] Attention to the poor and disadvantaged has not been totally lost; young Latin American priests who learned a liberating mission from the early liberation theologians, and have passed this down to their still younger successors, continue to preach and minister to poor populations throughout the continent. The Christian base communities continue to

24. Gutiérrez, Theology, 24–25.

25. Gutiérrez, Theology, 40–41.

26. See Ruether, "Catholicism," 17–19, for a brief description of the period in the 1960s and 1970s that saw a greater opening to the poor in the Roman Catholic Church, soon followed by a more conservative turn back to marginalization of liberating forces.

educate. Liberation theologies elsewhere still believe in and practice a ministry whose preferential option is for the poor. But Gutiérrez's lament fifty years ago—the lament around which he framed his theology and his book—remains a critical comment on the institutional church today: on what Gutiérrez characterized as traditional theology's longstanding failure to reflect on "the conflictual character of human history, the confrontations among individuals, social classes, and countries." Theology has failed here because, as he has noted, conflict and movement—"the passage from the old to the new person, from sin to grace, from slavery to freedom"—are human progression, the heart of human existence.[27]

Humanity changes, was Gutiérrez's message, but theology has not kept pace. It is critically true that the church in the West has failed at virtually every step along this human progression. It is by now widely acknowledged, perhaps especially by church people, that Christianity accommodated itself to empire almost two millennia ago when the first Roman emperor, Constantine, embraced the Christian faith in the fourth century as a tool of his imperial rule. Constantine and his imperial successors have long since passed away, but imperialism and colonialism remain in various forms of state government, and the church remains in alliance with those political systems. The Rev. Richard Rohr—a Franciscan friar, founder of the Center for Action and Contemplation, and noted spiritual leader who focuses on linking spiritual contemplation to action—has written bluntly that liberation theology is "mostly ignored by Western Christianity," largely because an "empowered clergy class" linked to empire and the politically powerful has forced its own perspective on the faithful, rather than speak on behalf of or care for the marginalized and the downtrodden. On another occasion, Rohr wrote that, when "the Christian tradition chose an imperial Christ, living inside the world of static and mythic proclamations, it framed belief and understanding in a very small box (. . .) [a Jesus] with little heart (. . .) and almost no flesh or soul (. . .). This is what happens when power and empire take over the message."[28]

Some theologians refer to the church having always been "in bed with" imperialism. John Philip Newell, an expert on Celtic spirituality, observes that when Christianity became the religion of empire, the church began to move toward a doctrinal orthodoxy favored by the state.

27. Gutiérrez, *Theology*, 23.
28. Rohr, "Knowing from the Bottom," and Rohr, "Practical Christianity."

From having an abundant collection of writings about Jesus, including first- and second-century Christian writings and hidden gospels that have only recently come to light, the church pared and narrowed the canon early on and moved toward adherence to "a tightly defined canon of scripture."[29]

Jewish theologian Marc Ellis, who has worked closely with Naim Ateek and written prolifically on liberation theology as it applies to Palestinians and Jews, uses the term "Constantinianism" to signify the church's enduring cooptation by empire. He asserts grimly that "the *ethical center of Christianity was gutted* as it assumed its Constantinian character." Indeed, Ellis maintains that Constantinianism is a part of all religions, including Islam and Judaism, and declares unequivocally that the most critical aspect of this "joining of religion and state" is that it "challenges the ethics of any and all traditions."[30] It is telling, although perhaps not surprising, that some of the clearest insights into Christian church policy and practice come from non-Christians, who often seem better able to see institutional Christianity's insensitivity to humanity. Mahatma Gandhi also chastised the church for not doing as Jesus preached: to love our enemies. Gandhi, a Hindu, called Jesus the great "Asian prophet" and had as the only adornment in his ashram room a picture of Jesus with the inscription, "He is our Peace." But he lamented that "Christianity became disfigured" when it moved from its birthplace in the East and went West, where it "became the religion of kings." Had the church followed Jesus' pleas to love the enemy, Gandhi believed, the world would long ago have been transformed.[31]

Political caution in the church has most often dictated listening to kings and presidents and rejecting or simply ignoring moral pleas from the people. Moreover, what is too often forgotten or wrongly dismissed as not relevant is the debt that colonialism and postcolonialism, with their harsh and lingering consequences for indigenous peoples around the globe, owe to the church's alliance with empire. Religious missionaries accompanied conquering colonial armies and explorers in the Americas and in Africa. Invading armies carried crosses aloft and marched under the banners of "holy" imperial rulers. The church justified slavery and native submission to foreign rule as God's will, trading in slavery and

29. Newell, *Christ of the Celts*, ix–x.

30. Ellis, "Judaism," 87. Emphasis added.

31. Quoted in Newell, *Rebirthing of God*, 79–80.

treating slaves and the indigenous as subhuman. The fifteenth-century Doctrine of Discovery officially justified and gave papal approval to European states' freedom to take possession at will of non-Christian lands without regard to the sentiments or the lives of native populations. John Philip Newell recounts his experience delivering a talk in Canada on the prologue of John's Gospel (John 1:9, NRSV), in which John speaks of "the true light that enlightens everyone coming into the world." Newell invited his listeners to search for that light within themselves, as well as in every other person and in other traditions. At the end of the talk, a Mohawk elder rose to speak, in tears, saying he had been thinking about that light during Newell's talk and wondering where "I would be today. I have been wondering where my people would be today. And I have been wondering where we would be as a Western world today if the mission that came to us from Europe centuries ago had come expecting to find Light in us."[32]

Fear of undermining the church's longstanding alliance with the state, and of endangering the security that alliance provides, is undeniably an underlying reason for the church's limited interest in the fate of the oppressed. It is not only Latin America's liberation theology that has faced obstacles in gaining the concentrated interest and attention, far less the support, of the church establishment. Protestant theologian Joerg Rieger, writing of general church impassivity to the plight of the poor and oppressed, has observed that liberation theology is "an invitation to the church to search for new encounters with God in places where theologians and church people hardly bother to look."[33] Liberation theology is that upstart theology that speaks to the church forthrightly, through "invitations" and bolder challenges, in an effort to persuade church people to search in those unlikely places amongst the most miserable of God's children for precisely that thrilling new kind of encounter with God that often only the downtrodden and the suffering experience. Sadly, success in awakening church hierarchies to this realization and inducing them to venture onto new paths outside the security of alliance with state power has been elusive.

As the testimonies of theologians like Moltmann and Gutiérrez indicate, the church has been notably hesitant about responding to those invitations to search for "new encounters with God." Although pressures

---

32. Newell, *Christ of the Celts*, 14–15.

33. Rieger, "Protestantism," 49.

in recent decades from the public square and from a new popular awakening to social justice have encouraged greater institutional church participation in "liberation" activism, involving the church and church people deeply in movements for justice has always been and remains a hard pull. Hierarchies tend to be leery of addressing prophetic calls for resistance and change, ever reluctant to venture away from safe, welltrodden doctrinal paths and from the political security of alliance with state power to go in search of any of those new encounters.

Virtually every liberation theology challenges the established church to some degree, whether because the church fails to respond to cries for help from oppressed populations or, more critically, in those contexts in which the church itself is a major source or cause of oppression through its cooperation with the state. For the Palestinians, as we will examine more deeply in later chapters, the Western church has been actively complicit with Israel in almost totally erasing public awareness of Israel's oppression of the Palestinians—and indeed awareness of the existence of Palestine and the Palestinians. Christianity's profound guilt over centuries of virulently antisemitic church practice and policy, which was arguably a major factor leading to the Holocaust, has led the Western church, in its post-Holocaust effort to make amends to the Jewish people, to turn its back almost completely on its substantial numbers of Palestinian Christian members—as if blaming innocent Palestinians for the church's own persecution of Jews. The numbers of church leaders who know next to nothing about Palestine and who care less are legion.

The story of El Salvadoran Archbishop Óscar Romero stands out as a striking anomaly in the church's record of failing the poor and disadvantaged; he is perhaps the exception that proves the rule. Romero was assassinated in 1980 by the rightwing Salvadoran government because of his outspoken criticism of its violence and human rights violations. Ironically, although Romero took this stance in defiance of church cautions, he was canonized by the church years later, in 2018, for having courageously championed the poor and marginalized—for, in other words, doing precisely what the church hierarchy had cautioned him against doing. As archbishop of San Salvador, Romero was effectively "the church" in his country, but he boldly stepped out of his own and the church's usual cautious mold and indeed defied church injunctions against speaking out, becoming a vocal critic of government oppression. Although he had always been a conservative himself and in fact had been hailed by other conservatives as a "safe" choice as archbishop, the political murder of a close priest friend just weeks after his consecration as archbishop in 1977 opened Romero's eyes to the horrific injustice endemic to El Salvador at the time, and changed his heart. Many of his fellow bishops opposed his newly outspoken stance, and Pope John Paul II, in the supposed interest of church unity, refused Romero's request that the Vatican condemn El Salvador's oppressive governance and use of death squads.[34]

Although Romero is said to have been uninterested in liberation theology, in fact in both his preaching and his practice, he was the very exemplar of a liberation theologian. In his three years as archbishop, he wrote newspaper columns, gave radio broadcasts, preached in the cathedral and in village churches, gave sanctuary to the distressed—his public word always concerned with liberating the oppressed from suffering, directly opposing government violence and oppressive policies, and bringing God to the poor as one who loved and suffered with them. He preached love as the instrument of justice and salvation; after the murder of his priest friend, he said that "the cause of love cannot be separated from justice. There can be no true peace or love that is based on injustice or violence or intrigue."[35] Achieving salvation through preaching and practicing the word of the gospel was not intended only for the soul at death but meant justice and liberation for "the person living in history."[36] And, he believed, it was the church's obligation to work for that liberation: "A church that does not provoke any crisis, preach a gospel that does not unsettle, proclaim a word of God that does not get under anyone's skin or a word of God that does not touch the real sin of the society in which it is being proclaimed: what kind of gospel is that?"[37]

This prophetic statement was both a description of Romero's own outspoken ministry to the oppressed and a challenge to the established church that failed to stand with him. As another Salvadoran liberation theologian, the Jesuit priest Jon Sobrino, who ministered to the oppressed alongside Romero, noted shortly after the assassination, Romero "became someone new" after his consecration, "demonstrat[ing] the true

---

34. Kurtz, "Introduction," 1–15, and *Wikipedia*, "Óscar Romero."
35. Kurtz, "Introduction," 8.
36. Romero, *The Violence of Love*, 4.
37. Romero, "Quotes."

humility of those who believe in God." Unlike so many of those who rise
to the top in the church hierarchy and then tend toward "immobility,"
this archbishop, Sobrino saw, began to encounter God "from the perspective of the poor": in the faces of the poor whom he served, he came to see
"the disfigured countenance of God."[38] He gave inspiration to the poor
and, like the liberationist he was, took inspiration from them.

For Black citizens in the United States, the White institutional church has
undeniably been one of many oppressors, and a major one. It is impossible to do justice here to the depth and breadth of Black suffering under
centuries of oppression by White institutions and citizens in the United
States, or to the continuing Black struggle for liberation. But it is important to recognize that for the last half century and more, Black liberation
theology has stood at the forefront of the Black freedom struggle, as a
strong affirmation of Black identity and human dignity. This Black theology has been enunciated by civil rights leaders; it has been highlighted in
numerous books, as mentioned earlier, by the late scholar and theologian
James H. Cone; and it is in many ways the basis of the anti-racism movement that is flourishing today. Critically, a Black spirituality that goes
beyond rigid definitions and doctrines has for centuries been a spiritual
liberating force unique to the Black community.

Howard Thurman, although not known specifically as a liberation
theologian, was an early precursor of the theology, opening the subject
of liberation as early as 1949.[39] Widely regarded as the father and inspiration of the civil rights movement, and still revered as such today, because
of his social justice writing and preaching, Thurman wrote about the
meaning of Jesus' religion for "people who stand with their backs against
the wall" and criticized the inadequacy of church ministry, in ways that
liberation theologians everywhere have emulated. Martin Luther King Jr.
was also not formally a liberation theologian, but fifty-plus years after his
assassination he remains the United States' best-known advocate of Black
liberation. Although he is by no means alone among memorable civil
rights leaders and liberation preachers, King's eloquence has preserved
a special place for him in the pantheon of Black leaders. His 1963 "Letter from Birmingham Jail" still stands as a major protest against White

38. Sobrino, "Theologian's View," 26–27.
39. See in particular Thurman, *Jesus and the Disinherited.*

church reluctance to allow social justice protests to disrupt the so-called "normalcy" of the status quo. King addressed his letter, written from his jail cell in Birmingham, to a group of White churchmen who had more or less officially, as a body representing Christian churches in the city, opposed his preaching and civil rights activism and cautioned him against stirring up trouble in Birmingham. The clergymen's admonitions were a classic example not only of White church racism, but of a pervasive church caution, complaining as they did that "outsiders" were coming to the city and that King's protests were "unwise and untimely." King's pointed response, as one of those so-called outsiders, was that prophets and preachers, including Jesus' disciples, had always traveled afar to preach justice and that he was "in Birmingham because injustice is here." Moreover, as he famously noted, America's communities are all closely interrelated and, as a result, "injustice anywhere is a threat to justice everywhere. We are caught in an inescapable network of mutuality, tied in a single garment of destiny. Whatever affects one directly, affects all indirectly."[40] These continue to be words that all churches, all theologies, indeed Christianity in general, should live by but too often fail to heed.

James Cone, writing and teaching from the conviction that any theology is "a prophetic word about the righteousness of God that must be spoken in clear, strong, and uncompromising language," formulated a theology for Black people that was indeed radical and uncompromising, provocative, bluntly angry in its motivation and its expression. Cone brought three essential convictions to his enunciation of Black liberation theology: a belief that true Christianity is fundamentally a religion of liberation, formulated by Jesus Christ to free the downtrodden and oppressed; a belief that the proper function of theology is to demonstrate to humankind what liberation means so that they can clearly see that the justice struggle is consistent with Jesus' gospel; and what he frankly called his "rage" at the reality that White racist, White supremacist theologians were defining the nature of the gospel and of Christianity itself, for Black Christians as well as for Whites, but essentially *against* anyone who was Black.[41] He saw White Christianity as a betrayal of the gospel and a "heresy." In his posthumously published 2018 memoir, *Said I Wasn't Gonna Tell Nobody: The Making of a Black Theologian*, he wrote that when "it became clear to me that Jesus was not biologically white and that white

40. King, "Letter from Birmingham Jail."

41. Cone, *Black Theology*, ix, xviii. Cone's other notable books include *Black Theology and Black Power* and *The Cross and the Lynching Tree*.

scholars actually lied by not telling people who he really was, I stopped trusting anything they said."[42]

Cone wrote two books in two years at the height of the civil rights movement: *Black Theology and Black Power* in 1969 and *A Black Theology of Liberation* in 1970. He saw these books as a way, by exposing White theology for the racism on which it was based, to reframe faith and religion for Black people and to "speak a different word" theologically. He called these books "a manifesto against whiteness and for blackness," intended to "liberate Christians from white supremacy." Believing that theology is not only discourse about ultimate reality but prophetic discourse about current reality, in this case the reality of Black suffering and resistance, he sought to interpret the gospel so that it spoke to African Americans about their situation and empowered their resistance, rather than as he had always heard the gospel interpreted—for Whites. He was inspired by Malcolm X—more so, he felt, than by King, because he said Malcolm expressed what he himself felt "deep within my being." Cone quoted Malcolm as expressing adherence to "a religion that believes in freedom" and as rejecting "a religion that won't let me fight a battle for my people."[43] A theological declaration of liberation.

Although he concentrated initially only on Black suffering and liberation, Cone later acknowledged the limitations of his focus, in the Preface of a second, 1986 edition of *A Black Theology*. As he had explained in the book's 1970 edition, he felt an urgency about his mission to formulate a Black liberation theology "so they can know" that their struggle for justice "is consistent with the gospel of Jesus Christ." Despite his initial focus only on the Black community, by the time of the book's second edition, Cone had become aware of the wider scope of suffering throughout the world, outside himself and his community. He had come to know, he said, "the multidimensional character of oppression"—and that there is "an interconnectedness of all humanity that makes the freedom of one people dependent upon the liberation of all."[44]

At the end of his life, he embraced all oppressed peoples in the United States and throughout the world. According to a posthumous tribute by journalist (and ordained Presbyterian minister) Chris Hedges, Cone's extensive body of writing stands as a critical exposition of the "moral

---

42. Quoted in Hedges, "Heresy of White Christianity."

43. Cone, *Black Theology*, xvi–xviii, and Hedges, "Heresy of White Christianity."

44. Cone, *Black Theology*, ix–x, xxi–xxii.

failure" of the United States and in particular of "the white liberal church and white liberal power structure." Speaking out on behalf of all oppressed peoples living in suffering, including Palestinians, Cone pleaded eloquently in his memoir for Christians and especially theologians to recognize that suffering:

> I write on behalf of all those whom the Salvadoran theologian and martyr Ignacio Ellacuria called "the crucified peoples of history." I write for the forgotten and the abused, the marginalized and the despised. I write for those who are penniless, jobless, landless, all those who have no political or social power. I write for gays, lesbians, bisexuals, and those who are transgender. I write for immigrants stranded on the U.S. border and for undocumented farmworkers toiling in misery in the nation's agricultural fields. I write *for Palestinians in the Gaza Strip, on the West Bank, and in East Jerusalem*. I write for Muslims and refugees who live under the terror of war in Iraq, Afghanistan, and Syria. And I write for all people who care about humanity. I believe that until Americans, especially Christians and theologians, can see the cross and the lynching tree together, until we can identify Christ with "recrucified black bodies" hanging from lynching trees, there can be no genuine understanding of Christian identity in America, and no deliverance from the brutal legacy of slavery and white supremacy.[45]

Like many other Black religious personalities today and Black Lives Matter leaders acutely aware of the twenty-first century intersectionality of liberation struggles—the "single garment of destiny" of which King spoke—Cone was not afraid of encountering political pushback from embracing the Palestinians' struggle and including them and so many others of the voiceless in his litany of the oppressed. Cone knew that no one would be free until all are free. As the spiritual and theological leader and the fighter for justice that he was, he gave inspiration and courage to a younger generation of Black liberation activists.

We have discussed Black theologian Barbara Holmes's paean to the "joy unspeakable" of Black spirituality. This spirituality and the theology of Black freedom, which have sustained the Black community through four centuries of slavery and racist cruelty, continue to be sung in this new century by virtually every Black religious and civil rights leader and every Black writer and artist. Holmes opens the preface to the second

---

45. Quoted in Hedges, "Heresy of White Christianity." Emphasis added.

edition of her book, *Joy Unspeakable*, with a quote from the writer Touré that calls forth an army of Black mystics and liberators: "If the Ghost Hunters snuck up behind me as I was trying to write," says Touré, "they might see a universe of slave liberators, political agitators, Baptist preachers, exuberant orators, beloved writers and incomparable musicians—so many musicians—arrayed around me all in chorus, urging and cajoling and daring me to somehow dig a little deeper."[46]

Dig a little deeper—keep going, never give up. The Black liberation journey in the United States, marked throughout its history by almost unimaginable suffering and pain, and still marked today by gross injustice, has always sought solace and inspiration in tight bonds of community and an undying, mystical faith in God. And, not coincidentally, Black liberation activists, whether obviously spiritual or not, have been the group perhaps most acutely aware of the suffering of other oppressed peoples. They are the liberation allies most clearly aware of Palestinian suffering and the allies most closely connected to the Palestinians; the Black Lives Matter movement has openly embraced the Palestinian struggle, in the belief that the freedom and human rights struggles of all oppressed people are interconnected. Although she does not mention the Black-Palestinian connection, Barbara Holmes notes that the newly emerging generation of young people in movements like Black Lives Matter uses "the language of faith" and employs contemplative practices that harken back to "the lineage of black communal and church traditions"—traditions that constitute a common mystical spirituality outside the confines of any one denomination. Holmes speaks of a shared "religious imagination" by which Black people sustain each other through suffering and "journey together toward joy despite oppressive conditions."[47] That common religious imagination among members of the Black church, recognizing Palestinians as allies and fellow strugglers for freedom, increasingly links with them in solidarity.

The renowned Black activist Angela Davis invokes the Black-Palestinian connection very strongly. She believes in fact that it is now "virtually impossible to talk about the Black movement in the US without also considering the ties with the movement for solidarity in Palestine." Recalling during a ten-year anniversary event the experiences of a delegation of Black, Indigenous, Asian, and Latina feminists from the United

---

46. Quoted in Holmes, *Joy Unspeakable*, ix.

47. Holmes, *Joy Unspeakable*, xiii.

States that visited Palestine in 2011, Davis credits this group with making a large contribution to "the trajectory that has transformed" how Palestine is viewed in the United States. Black and other activists of color have striven for years, she says, to guarantee that justice for Palestine would come to be viewed as "an organic element of agendas for social justice."[48]

Although there is a history of Black ties to Palestine going back to the civil rights era, these connections began to flourish anew, and more concretely, in the wake of the long-running 2014 protest in Ferguson, Missouri, over the police shooting of a young Black man, Michael Brown. The protest was a seminal event that marked the rise of the recently emerged Black Lives Matter movement in the United States and that happened to coincide with a massive Israeli bombing assault on Gaza. Palestinian activists, long experienced in how to cope with teargas fired during their protests against Israel, passed on their practices for avoiding the worst effects of teargas to Black protesters in Ferguson. Black-Palestinian solidarity intensified when a young Black group, formed initially to fight mass incarceration, the Dream Defenders, began sending delegations of Black activists to Palestine to witness to Palestinian oppression and interact with Palestinian activists in both secular and religious realms.[49]

Increasing numbers of Black congresspeople have also begun openly criticizing Israel in a forum where such criticism has long been verboten. This new generation of Palestinian-sympathizing congresspeople, both Black and White, makes up only a tiny minority in the House of Representatives, and those who are Black do not even constitute a majority of Black House members, but this group has gained attention precisely because their outspoken stance inside Congress in criticism of Israel is so unusual and is a possible harbinger of greater change. In May 2021, in the midst of Israel's bombing assault on Gaza that month, four Black House members joined seven other Democratic members (including the one Palestinian in Congress and three Hispanics) in a "special order" session on the floor of the House, speaking out in a collective criticism of Israel that was unprecedented in the history of Congress.[50] One of these Black

48. Abdulhadi and Musa, "Virtual Reunion."

49. Kane, "Black-Palestine Solidarity."

50. The four Black congresspeople were Ilhan Omar of Minnesota, Ayanna Pressley of Massachusetts, Cori Bush of Missouri, and André Carson of Indiana. The other congresspeople were Mark Pocan of Wisconsin, Betty McCollum of Minnesota, Jan Schakowsky of Illinois, the only Palestinian member, Rashida Tlaib of Michigan, and Hispanic members Alexandria Ocasio-Cortez of New York, Jesús Garcia of Illinois,

representatives, André Carson of Indiana, later spoke emotionally to an interviewer from the Israeli newspaper *Haaretz* about the Palestine issue as something "deeply personal" to him because of his concern for the oppressed. Noting that he was relieved to be able now to speak openly in Congress in criticism of Israel, he said he was "heartbroken" over the reality that for so long the United States "has looked the other way as Israel has engaged in this horrific campaign against Palestinians."[51] Carson continues to pursue Palestinian issues actively, most recently leading sympathetic House Democrats in pressing the US government for an independent investigation of the Israeli killing of Palestinian-American journalist Shireen Abu Akleh.

Missouri Representative Cori Bush, identifying herself strongly with this new group of congresspeople and evoking the intersectional, anti-colonial connections in justice politics today, has told an interviewer, "I know we [Black people] are on the right side of history when we stand up for human rights across the country and the globe—and that's only possible because of the power of our intersectional movements for justice and liberation." Recalling Black-Palestinian cooperation in 2014 in Ferguson, a district she now represents in Congress, Bush said that standing up for Black lives means also "standing against state violence, oppression, and the militarized police occupation of our communities— no matter where it takes place. And when we stand in solidarity with the Palestinian struggle for human rights and liberation, we rise in a strong tradition of Black-Palestinian solidarity to dismantle apartheid."[52] In the wake of Israel's May 2021 attack on Gaza, which Gazans themselves and knowledgeable commentators almost universally characterized as more intense and cruel than previous Israeli attacks—and which evoked a rare surge of sympathy with the Palestinians even among media typically hostile to the Palestinian viewpoint—political commentators increasingly began to draw a link between anti-racist protests in the United States and the Palestinians' struggle for justice. Commentators widely remarked on and analyzed the phenomenon that the nationwide Black Lives Matter protests that arose in the wake of the police killing of George Floyd in May 2020 had created a new atmosphere of sympathy and understanding for Palestinians.

---

and Joaquín Castro of Texas. See Rod, "Democratic Split on Israel on Display in Competing House Speeches."

    51. Samuels, "For This Congressman."

    52. Kane, "Black-Palestine Solidarity."

This manifestation in Congress of solidarity between people of color and Palestinians is fragile—fragile not in the sense that the feeling of solidarity is diminishing, but rather because the candidacies of all progressive politicians, and especially of any who are persons of color, are in danger generally from the pro-Israeli US right wing and specifically from pro-Israel political action groups like AIPAC and others that have recently been exerting a concerted effort to defeat these candidates and submerge criticism of Israel. The struggle in the political arena is acute, but it remains true that solidarity from the Black community in general is a growing phenomenon.

This Black solidarity has played out in the realm of liberation theology in recent years through the sponsorship of Friends of Sabeel North America (FOSNA), the US arm of the ecumenical Palestinian Christian liberation theology organization in Jerusalem, Sabeel, which we will encounter later. FOSNA has sponsored several online discussions and webinars—including a joint worship service with noted Black pastor and Poor People's Co-Chairman the Rev. William Barber, who has spoken out frequently on behalf of oppressed Palestinians[53]—that highlight Black Christian connections to Palestine and that have been a forum from which Black Christian leaders have promoted support for the Palestinian struggle in their congregations. One of these webinars, pointedly titled "Tied in a Single Garment of Destiny," featured five young Black Christian clergypeople and scholars discussing the shared realities of Black and Palestinian oppression. These Black leaders spoke passionately about the role of the church and of liberation theologies in the Black and Palestinian freedom struggles. Pointing to the Black struggle against what Martin Luther King called the "giant triplets" of racism, economic exploitation, and militarism, they drew a direct link to the Palestinian people, because Palestinians "face these giants as well, under Israeli occupation."[54]

One scholar-activist, the Rev. Nyle Fort, recalling his first awakening to the Palestinian issue during the 2014 Ferguson protests, in which he took part, and Israel's simultaneous assault on Gaza (using US-made weapons), said that Ferguson "made me cry over the sin of American racism, while Palestine made me cry over the sin of American imperialism." Theologically, these activists invoked the Exodus story of Israel's escape from Egypt's oppression—long a spiritual inspiration for Black

53. Kuttab, "William Barber Preaches."
54. FOSNA webinar.

churchgoers—but added a dose of reality to the story by making it clear that the ancient Israelites who sought freedom millennia ago bear no resemblance to the modern state of Israel that oppresses Palestinians: "the new Israel has become the old Egypt," Fort asserted.

Another speaker, social justice activist Ash-Lee Henderson, challenged the church for perpetuating racialized class and caste systems: if we move in the world and in the church acting as though these systems should continue to exist, she said, "we are not moving in the way of Christ." Movement work, liberation work to free all people, including Palestinians, Henderson affirmed, is "praise and worship"; she said she is angry with any church and any person identifying as a faith leader who would disagree with this. "Every day I show up in a kheffiyah, I'm praising and worshipping my God. Every day I work for the liberation of the Palestinian people, I am a manifestation of the love that God has for [God's] creation."[55] Henderson is the first Black woman to serve as Co-Executive Director of the Highlander Research and Education Center, a well-known grassroots social justice leadership training school in Tennessee founded ninety years ago by noted educator and social justice advocate Myles Horton. Henderson has also recently joined the advisory board of Adalah Justice Project, a Palestinian-led justice advocacy organization in the United States.

Still another speaker, the Rev. Erica Williams, emphasized that, although Jesus called on us to "set the captives free," we have been asleep for too long, ignoring present-day empires that continue to enslave the oppressed, and "God is not happy that the church has been playing the role of 'chaplain of empire.'" The time has come to set the captives free, she said, because none of us is free until the Palestinians are free. Henderson spoke emotionally for all panelists when she asserted that it is "our duty, our absolute responsibility" to fight in solidarity with the Palestinian people because "that is the absolute perfect will of my God." As so many liberation theologians do today, these leaders referred to Jesus as "the brown-skinned Palestinian Jew."[56]

This new awareness and embrace of Palestinian suffering inevitably recalls Gustavo Gutiérrez's remark that conflict and movement are at the heart of human existence. He was commenting on the failure of theology through the ages, as well as of the institutional church, to reflect on the

55. FOSNA webinar.
56. FOSNA webinar.

reality that conflict—among individuals, social classes, countries—is part of the nature of human history and that human existence has long been characterized by movement arising out of conflict: "the passage from the old to the new person, from sin to grace, from slavery to freedom."[57] This human progression has not been unbroken or as consistently positive in its direction as Gutiérrez implies; it has often been interrupted and shattered, something true of all liberation struggles. But the rise of liberation theology in this modern age has been a promising movement toward not only spiritual and theological, but also political, "wokeness"—to use a newly coined, utterly secular term indicating a keen critical awareness of social problems and injustice. This new mutual wokeness is nowhere more applicable than in the emergence of spiritual and theological solidarity between so many in the Black community and Palestinians.

Among the several liberation theologies that have addressed, and specifically cried out for relief from, state-imposed and often church-assisted oppression, none stands out more clearly than the "prophetic theology" formulated in 1985 by South African theologians and expressed in *The Kairos Document: A Radical Challenge to the Church in South Africa*. No theological statement has better described the pain of living under a racist theology constructed by the state to justify its own power and its oppression and dehumanization of the racially marginalized. Probably no liberation struggle has been more closely linked to the Palestinians' resistance than the South Africans' struggle against apartheid, and no people has been more aware and more understanding of what the Palestinians endure than the South African people. South Africa continues to speak out for Palestinian self-determination and in condemnation of Israel's apartheid policies—most recently in a resolution on Israeli apartheid presented to the World Council of Churches General Assembly in September 2022 and, during the same month, in an address to the UN General Assembly by the South African minister of international relations.

The *Kairos South Africa* document was a major inspiration for a similar ecumenical document that we will discuss in depth in Chapter 3: *Kairos Palestine*, issued in Palestine several years later, in 2009. *Kairos South Africa* was a classic liberation theology manifesto. Drafted by a group of more than fifty Black pastors from Soweto township in Johannesburg and

57. Gutiérrez, *Theology*, 23.

signed by one hundred and fifty additional clergy and lay people, both Black and White, from throughout the country, it was a grassroots statement, a self-described "people's document," that expressed what South African theologian John de Gruchy has termed the "agonized thinking" of an oppressed people in crisis. The document was addressed *from* the people, not only to the apartheid state, but especially to the churches of South Africa in criticism of their failure to oppose apartheid seriously and stand up for the rights of the oppressed. Rejecting church efforts to remain neutral and in the middle between government and people, the document insisted that the church identify clearly with the struggle for liberation and justice. *Kairos* stands, de Gruchy writes, as a "witness to a living God at work in transforming history."[58]

The *Kairos* document was so named for the Greek word meaning, as this *Kairos* statement framed it, "the moment of grace and opportunity," a time of crisis in which God issues a challenge to decisive action. The document analyzed what it defined as three separate theologies: a *State Theology*, a *Church Theology*, and a *Prophetic Theology*. Defining *State Theology* as "the theological justification of the status quo with its racism, capitalism and totalitarianism," the *Kairos* document charged that the apartheid state abused Scripture and theology, even blaspheming the name of God, in order to advance and justify its own political purposes. The state "blesses injustice, canonises [sic]the will of the powerful and reduces the poor to passivity, obedience and apathy." The preamble to the White South African government's constitution invoked God's name as the nation's savior—turning the God of Jesus' gospels into what the *Kairos* theologians denounced as a "sinister and evil" idol, "a god who exalts the proud and humbles the poor."[59]

Church Theology in South Africa, *Kairos* charged, was superficial, uncritical, and essentially empty, calling inanely for "reconciliation" in all conflicts and all matters of dissension, no matter their nature. In fact, the *Kairos* theologians maintained, not all conflicts occur between two equal sides, in terms of either morality or power. Critically, there are conflicts "that can only be described as the struggle between justice and injustice, good and evil, God and the devil." Advocating reconciliation in such conflicts is a distorted application of the true Christian concept of reconciliation and, more importantly, is "a total betrayal of all that Christian faith

58. de Gruchy, "Foreword."

59. *Kairos Document*, 16–17, 22–23.

has ever meant. Nowhere in the Bible or in Christian tradition has it ever been suggested that we ought to try to reconcile good and evil, God and the devil." Pointing to a guiding principle of liberation theology, *Kairos* declared, "We are supposed to do away with evil, injustice, oppression and sin—not come to terms with it."[60]

This *Kairos* rejection of neutrality in situations of injustice is a critical principle that must govern all liberation struggles. As these South African theologians made clear, there is absolutely no parity between justice and injustice, and so there can be no middle ground between them. Archbishop Desmond Tutu has repeatedly emphasized this reality. "If you are neutral in situations of injustice," he has famously said, "you have chosen the side of the oppressor. If an elephant has its foot on the tail of a mouse, and you say that you are neutral, the mouse will not appreciate your neutrality." In South Africa—and, it must be added, in Palestine and wherever the oppressed fight for their liberation—the notion of advocating for reconciliation and peace before current injustices have been ended is unacceptable. Any such plea, *Kairos* affirmed,

> plays into the hands of the oppressor by trying to persuade those of us who are oppressed to accept our oppression and to become reconciled to the intolerable crimes that are committed against us. That is not Christian reconciliation, it is sin. It is asking us to become accomplices in our own oppression, to become servants of the devil. No reconciliation is possible in South Africa *without justice*. What this means in practice is that no reconciliation, no forgiveness and no negotiations are possible *without repentance* (. . .). Reconciliation, forgiveness and negotiations will become our Christian duty in South Africa only when the apartheid regime shows signs of genuine repentance.[61]

Finally, the *Kairos* authors affirmed, formulating a *Prophetic Theology* meant demonstrating clearly that throughout the Bible, in the Hebrew Scriptures as well as in the New Testament, God identifies with the oppressed. It also meant recognizing when a regime, even a Christian government like South Africa's apartheid regime, is tyrannical and when that tyranny, because of its fundamental nature, is irredeemable and "irreformable"—which meant in turn rejecting the regime and struggling against it, although without resorting to hatred or violence. In the end,

60. *Kairos Document.*

61. *Kairos Document*, 25–27. See pp. 28–36 for a further description of the *Kairos* critique of South Africa's "Church theology." Emphasis in original.

a Prophetic Theology must be a theology of hope. Declaring their belief that "God is at work in our world turning hopeless and evil situations to good" and that tyranny and oppression cannot last forever, the *Kairos* authors pleaded with church leaders to join the oppressed struggling against injustice by giving these oppressed a strong message of hope: "hope needs to be confirmed. Hope needs to be maintained and strengthened. Hope needs to be spread. The people need to hear it said again and again that God is with them."[62]

The *Kairos South Africa* theologians' emphasis on the true nature and requirements of reconciliation, and their condemnation of the tendency among so many church officials and would-be peacemakers to *talk* earnestly about reconciliation without understanding what is involved, highlight the essence of liberation theology, of any liberation struggle, and indeed of any pursuit of justice. This misunderstanding of the fundamental nature of reconciliation applies to the Palestinian situation as well and to pressures always exerted on the Palestinian leadership to "reconcile" with Israel, "sit together with Israelis in dialogue" without preconditions, "be a partner for peace"—pressures that demand no reciprocity and ignore any thought of finding the truth or of establishing justice.

Whether the resolution of a conflict, any conflict, is called reconciliation or peace or some other term, it can be none of these things unless it is accompanied—in fact, preceded—by justice. Reconciliation is a difficult concept, not least because of what the South African *Kairos* document criticized as the church's unthinking—one sometimes wants to say mindless—application of the term. What is true reconciliation? Controversy surrounded the concept in South Africa from the time the *Kairos* statement was conceived in 1985, throughout the period later in the decade of the 1980s that saw the formal ending of apartheid, and throughout the years of the Truth and Reconciliation Commission (TRC) hearings in the late 1990s.

Theologian John de Gruchy delves into this controversy in depth in his 2002 book about the Truth and Reconciliation Commission proceedings, *Reconciliation: Restoring Justice*, and concludes that reconciliation, as the subtitle indicates, "is about restoring justice" first and foremost. But reconciliation "also pushes us to deeper than structural levels, to interpersonal and social *healing* and the *restoration of humanity*." In a world beyond South Africa that is riven by conflict, true reconciliation,

---

62. *Kairos Document*, 37–46.

de Gruchy makes clear, must go well beyond individual interpersonal relationships and even beyond personal communion with God, for it has broad social and political consequences: as the gospels affirm, true reconciliation involves "overcoming alienation and estrangement between God and ourselves, between us and others, and between all of us and creation." It would be "a theological travesty," he emphasizes, to limit the Christian doctrine of reconciliation to the personal and the individual: "If there was ever a theological theme that had to be developed in relation to the world in all its agony and hope, this is that theme." The TRC hearings not only functioned as a way of revealing the difficult and supremely painful truth of past abuses, but also served, precisely by dealing deeply with such issues as justice, guilt, morality, and moral symmetry on the way to reconciliation, as a forge for future peace and national unity. The need for reconciliation, de Gruchy asserts, "is something that is pertinent in every human community where alienated and estranged people cry out for healing and a reason for hope."[63]

It is in this framing of a broad future vision of healing humanity that the reconciliation process most clearly enters into the realm of theology; this is indeed the universal context of all liberation theologies. True reconciliation involves seeing, recognizing, listening to as well as hearing the "Other"—ultimately seeing and treating that Other as human—in order to survive in a peaceful future of human unity. It is made up of love and grief. For the oppressed, it means justice, freedom from the burdens of anger and hatred, freedom from domination; for the oppressor, forgiveness, grace, freedom from the burdens of guilt and hatred: in other words, remorse and the acknowledgement of guilt, against forgiveness and the acceptance of remorse, together leading to the rendering of justice. De Gruchy settles on a mixed description that deems reconciliation both "a human and social process that requires theological explanation, and a theological concept seeking human and social embodiment."[64] Elsewhere, he cites Jürgen Moltmann, whom we encountered early in this exposition of liberation theologies, as saying that the "open acknowledgement of guilt and an inward turning away from the ideologies of violence, the forgiveness of guilt, and the beginning of a new shared and just life" are together a "sign of the new humane politics."[65]

---

63. de Gruchy, *Reconciliation*, 1–2, 12–13, 25. Emphasis added.

64. de Gruchy, *Reconciliation*, 20.

65. Quoted in de Gruchy, *Reconciliation*, 174.

In a purely South African context but one that has universal application, the late Archbishop Desmond Tutu—spiritual leader of South Africa's anti-apartheid struggle, chairman of the TRC and shepherd of its healing grace, imaginative formulator of South Africa's liberation theology—preached and practiced and had at the core of his being the African theology of *Ubuntu*. Ubuntu, in Tutu's own words,

> speaks of the very essence of being human (. . .). It is to say, "My humanity is caught up, is inextricably bound up, in yours." We belong in a bundle of life. We say, "A person is a person through other persons (. . .). I am human because I belong, I participate, I share." A person with *ubuntu* is open and available to others, does not feel threatened that others are able and good, for he or she has a proper self-assurance that comes from knowing that he or she belongs in a greater whole.[66]

Tutu's spiritual biographer, theologian and US Episcopal priest the Rev. Michael Battle, identifies Tutu as a mystic and explains Ubuntu as a uniquely Black African version of Christian mysticism in which, unlike Western Christian mysticism, the mystery of turning toward God in community "cleanses self-awareness to be able to contain the awareness of the other." In this conception, Jesus' command to "love the Lord your God with all your heart, and with all your soul, and with all your mind" and to "love your neighbor as yourself" (Matt 22:37–40, NRSV) means that by loving God, one *cannot help but* love one's neighbor.[67] Liberation theologian and South African Anglican priest the Rev. Edwin Arrison, whom Tutu mentored and ordained and who has served for years as General Secretary of the *Kairos Southern Africa* organization, vividly describes this compulsion to love God and neighbor equally by likening it to breathing: the acts of breathing in and breathing out are both absolutely and equally essential, one following the other inseparably, neither more important than the other.[68]

Battle further explains that Tutu believed strongly that anyone who has an encounter with God must be passionately concerned for his or her neighbor, for "to treat anyone as if they were less than children of

66. Tutu, *No Future Without Forgiveness*, 31.

67. Battle, *Desmond Tutu*, 46–49.

68. Arrison, Zoom interview. Arrison now heads the Desmond and Leah Tutu Legacy Foundation in Cape Town, South Africa.

God is to deny the validity of one's own spiritual experience."[69] It is from this African belief in the importance of community and the deep sense of being cocooned in the mutual love of community—a belief and philosophy of life radically different from Western, particularly American, individualism—that Tutu drew perhaps the most critical feature of the TRC's path to reconciliation: forgiveness. Rather than fostering anger, or a desire for revenge, or even a sense of competitiveness, Ubuntu emphasizes forgiveness. "To forgive is not just to be altruistic," Tutu wrote. "It is the best form of self-interest. What dehumanizes you inexorably dehumanizes me."[70] Forgiveness is a central part of this process in another sense as well: as Battle says, "the purgative experience of becoming like God" makes it possible to rise above differences that seem irreconcilable and to cleanse "the wound between Creator and creation." Tutu himself said, "When you look at someone with eyes of love, you see a reality differently from that of someone who looks at the same person without love, with hatred or even just indifference."[71]

Tutu's spiritual vision of a future life of love and community did not, of course, play out perfectly in the real life of the TRC hearings, or in the years since. But the objective of reconciliation based on the restoration of justice set a course from the beginning of the hearings and established a vision—theological, spiritual, political—that continues to inspire. Some believe in fact that the TRC process was ultimately more positive and inspiring under the tutelage of a pastor and confessor like Tutu than would have been the case if the Commission had been chaired by a judge or politician.[72] Tutu himself remarked on the "heavy spiritual and indeed Christian religious emphasis" of the TRC, which he believed contributed immeasurably to the reconciliation process. Thinking theologically, he said, kept him always mindful that, however evil the act revealed during the Commission hearings, the act "did not turn the perpetrator into a demon. We had to distinguish between the deed and the perpetrator." For one thing, giving up on the perpetrator as an irredeemable monster would have eliminated any prospect of achieving accountability and uncovering the truth. But more importantly, "Theology said they still,

69. Battle, *Desmond Tutu*, 278.
70. Tutu, *No Future Without Forgiveness*, 31.
71. Battle, *Desmond Tutu*, 48–49.
72. de Gruchy, *Reconciliation*, 41.

despite the awfulness of their deeds, remained children of God with the capacity to repent, to be able to change."[73]

Everything about the South African story—the familiarity of its struggle against apartheid, the model of the *Kairos South Africa* document, the entire truth-and-reconciliation process, the witness and spiritual leadership of Desmond Tutu and other anti-apartheid leaders, South Africa's contextual theology—comes together to serve as a key inspiration to Palestinians and particularly to Palestinian liberation theology. South Africans of all faiths and of none are natural political and spiritual allies of Palestinians and, since achieving their own freedom, have been testifying to the similarities between their struggle and the Palestinians'. Tutu spoke out repeatedly against what he called "the systemic humiliation of Palestinian men, women, and children" by Israeli security forces. Citing Israeli checkpoints, roadblocks, and home demolitions, he likened the injustice and inequality that Palestinians face to what Black South Africans faced when they were "corralled and harassed and insulted and assaulted by the security forces of the apartheid government." And, like the liberation theologian he was, he reminded the powerful that God has a "litmus test" for them: "what is your treatment of the poor, the hungry, the voiceless? And on the basis of that, God passes judgment."[74]

The leader of South Africa's struggle for freedom and its first democratically elected president, Nelson Mandela, often linked the South Africa and the Palestine struggles, in a way that pointed to that "single garment of destiny" and recognized the common humanity of all oppressed peoples. During an international day of solidarity with the Palestinians in 1997, Mandela invoked the concept of Ubuntu and declared that South Africans "know too well that our freedom is incomplete without the freedom of the Palestinians." South Africans know well, he said, "that we are part of a humanity that is at one."[75]

"We know apartheid," Edwin Arrison declared to a small gathering of church-goers in the United States—"and this [Palestine] is worse! Palestinians are going through hell; the forces arrayed against them are huge."[76] Arrison knows whereof he speaks: as the leader of the *Kairos Southern Africa* organization, he became closely involved with the

---

73. Tutu, *No Future Without Forgiveness*, 82–83.

74. Jerusalem Post Staff, "Desmond Tutu," and Tutu, "Apartheid in the Holy Land."

75. Mandela, "Address by President Nelson Mandela."

76. Arrison, Zoom interview.

Palestinian theologians who created the *Kairos Palestine* document in 2009. In a lengthy recorded conversation with a Palestinian-South African academic, Farid Esack, Arrison described the start of his involvement with Palestinian issue. Although he had rarely even heard the term "Palestine" during his theological studies in the late 1980s and early 1990s, and even later, and knew virtually nothing about the situation there, he and several other South African clerics were invited to Bethlehem in 2009 to work with a group of Palestinian Christian theologians to listen to and comment on a theological statement being developed on Palestine similar to *Kairos South Africa*. The meeting clearly established an immediate spiritual bond; "we drew off each other's energy," Arrison says, pointing out that the Palestinians had been inspired by *Kairos South Africa*, and that the South Africans were "reinspired by them." That energy grew out of an instantaneous recognition of each other as people who had suffered or were still suffering under oppression. "We didn't have to ask very much" about the Palestinians' experience, Arrison says, "because we could smell and sense apartheid when we were there. They didn't really have to explain to us." He was shocked by the restrictive Israeli practices he witnessed, but he recognized them immediately as part of a system of apartheid.[77]

Arrison went on in the discussion with Esack to explain what he feels is the obligation of all Christians, in South Africa and throughout the world, to stand with the Palestinians. As Christians, he emphasizes, "if you're going to move toward the ideals of Jesus" and uphold the principles of non-discrimination among people, it is absolutely necessary to stand specifically on the side of the oppressed—"and the oppressed people at the moment are the Palestinians." Moreover, he says emphatically, "there is no struggle in the world where the Bible is so deliberately used as the justification for a people's oppression." He is referring not only to Israel's distortion of the Hebrew Scriptures to claim that God gave the land of Palestine exclusively to the Jews but also, more specifically, to the scriptural manipulation employed by Christian Zionists to support so-called Jewish chosenness and justify Israeli oppression of the Palestinians.[78] (We will examine Christian Zionism in greater depth in Chapter 6.)

Arrison's sense of theological solidarity with, and responsibility for, the Palestinians is striking. He speaks passionately when he declares

77. Arrison, "Palestine Israel."
78. Arrison, "Palestine Israel."

that, because of these biblical distortions, "the integrity of the Christian faith, the integrity of the Bible, the integrity of all that we do is at stake. Even the gospel is at stake!" And, because the integrity of the gospel is at stake, Christians cannot turn aside and dismiss the Palestinian struggle as simply a conflict between two groups of people. "It's not. We are providing the software. We, the Christian church, we are primarily—we are *primarily* responsible," he says with emphasis—"for what is happening to the Palestinian people. It's our responsibility." He names the Vatican, the World Council of Churches, and other Christian organizations, saying these groups "must come to the party and say, 'We will not allow the gospel to be compromised.'" And, speaking more passionately as he continues, he demands true conviction and compassion from all Christians in this endeavor: it is the conviction with which "we speak that will allow us to break free from our current 'neutrality' and our current apathy to move toward action." He emphasizes, "I say this very strongly—we're talking about *people* here (. . .). We're talking about the suffering children in Gaza. We're talking about people who are God's own creation; they have the breath of God within them. And if we cannot see that and we allow the Israeli oppression to be on the Palestinians' necks, then we should not call ourselves Christians who stand on the side of the oppressed."[79]

Arrison points out that his mentor Bishop Tutu—the Arch, as he is still familiarly referred to—always had a disciplined prayer life, one centered on deep contemplation leading to action. Tutu and his colleagues referred to this practice as "silence and solidarity." Tutu was able to hold on to his faith by maintaining this tension between silent contemplation and action in solidarity with others. And, Arrison explains, this is the South African path: connecting contemplatively with a God of justice, maintaining faith and solidarity with Palestine and, following Dietrich Bonhoeffer, taking action to put a spoke in the wheel of injustice.[80]

79. Arrison, "Palestine Israel." Emphasis in original.
80. Arrison, Zoom interview.

2

Palestine

A Lived Theology

*The spirit of the Lord is upon me, because he has anointed me,
to bring good news to the poor. He has sent me to proclaim
release to the captives and recovery of sight to the blind, to let the
oppressed go free, to proclaim the year of the Lord's favor.*

—LUKE 4:18–19 (NRSV)

*If I have prophetic powers, and understand all mysteries and all knowledge,
and if I have all faiths, so as to remove mountains, but do not have love, I am
nothing (. . .). Love (. . .) does not insist on its own way; it is not irritable or
resentful; it does not rejoice in wrongdoing, but rejoices in the truth (. . .).*

—1 CORINTHIANS 13:2,4–6 (NRSV)

*Love is patient; love is kind; it does not envy; it does not boast,
it is not proud, it is not rude. It is not self-seeking, it is not easily
angered, it does not keep a record of wrongs. It does not celebrate
injustice, but rejoices in the truth. Love never gives up, never loses
faith, always hopes, always endures. Love cannot be conquered.*

—AGAPE CREED

PALESTINIAN LIBERATION THEOLOGY ARISES from a context centered on a century of colonial domination, first by Britain and for seventy-five years by Israel's settler-colonial system. But, while the source of Palestinian oppression differs markedly from that of other liberation theologies, this theology is identical to the others in that it addresses a people's suffering. It is essentially, like the others, resistance to injustice.

Before delving more deeply into the origins and context of Palestine's liberation theology, it is important to know something about the psychological impact on Palestinians of their society's near destruction and their consignment to political oblivion in the rush to shower attention on their oppressor. In the wake of the Holocaust and the post-Holocaust romanticization of Jewish identity and notions of Jewish redemption—which have occurred at the expense of the Palestinians' own identity, indeed at the expense of the sanctity and security of their very existence—Palestinians have been forced to plead their legitimacy as a people in their own right. Recovery from this trauma, and Palestinian redemption, form a large part of what Palestinian liberation theology is about. As if Palestine had always been, or had even ever been, solely a Jewish place, Palestinians must still "prove" their indigeneity and argue their legitimacy as natives who have inhabited Palestine for millennia, and as a people comprising the diverse ethnicities and cultures of all Palestine's civilizations.

In that light, it is important to hear an informed Palestinian perspective on what it means to Palestinians to be the targets of a focused campaign of extinction. Jews, of course, were the victims of just such a campaign—which might have made them understanding of the Palestinian perspective, but which in fact, perversely, rendered a great many Jews totally unable to identify with the oppression Palestinians are enduring. The Palestinian perspective that follows, from the late Palestinian-American intellectual Edward Said, is a secular intellectual perspective that does not deal directly with theology but that sets a moral tone for the Palestinian-Israeli struggle.

Said chronicled the Palestinian condition of exile probably more eloquently than any other Palestinian writing in the English language. Preeminent scholar of colonialism and its impact on subjugated peoples everywhere, Said was able to diagnose the Palestinian condition intellectually, as well as from his heart. He was always keenly aware not only of Palestinians among themselves, as Palestinians, but also of how Palestinians have acted and been perceived in the world. In his extended personal essay *After the Last Sky*, written in the mid-1980s at one of many low points in modern Palestinian history, when Palestinians were more than usually scattered—literally, throughout the Arab world and beyond; metaphorically, without agency or an achievable purpose and without a central narrative that the world recognized as legitimate—Said lamented that the Palestinian condition was "miscellaneous (. . .). Without a center. Atonal." A situation partly the result of the Palestinians' own failure of initiative, he made clear, but primarily one utterly beyond their control, because of the "seriously incontrovertible" reality that they had for so long been "in the grip of Israeli power" and wrongly portrayed by Israeli propaganda.[1] His description stands as one of the most pointed, and poignant, descriptions of the impact on Palestinians of the physical and psychological campaign over decades to deny their legitimacy and existence.

The first "incontrovertible" fact of Palestinian existence, Said saw, was that "we have been regarded as a population that is essentially disposable," colonialism's classic inferior race. His second incontrovertible fact was that, although the Palestinians' dispossession had been enabled by Israel's alliance with and continuing support from the United States, this existential disaster remained generally unknown to the world because Israel had launched "the most powerful public relations apparatus (. . .) ever invented." (Forty years ago when Said wrote, the fact of Israel's ethnic cleansing of the Palestinian population in 1948, even the term Nakba, were indeed almost totally unknown, vigorously denied by that Israeli "public relations apparatus" and rarely spoken of, in English, even by Palestinians.) There was, he wrote with complete accuracy, "an almost total official American opposition to us as a people, as a society, as a cause," which ultimately amounted to "*the prohibition of our political identity*." Said explained this situation in a tone of almost open-mouthed amazement: "You can scarcely imagine what it means to a Palestinian," he emphasized, when you have to "watch one American political, cultural, or religious figure after another in an endless series declaring his or her allegiance to Israel."[2]

Said's third factor underscored the first two realities and spoke powerfully to the tragic irony for Palestinians of thus having their existence profoundly "othered," if not completely negated, their victimization by the twentieth-century's ultimate victims totally ignored, and of always being seen not as a people in their own right, but only in relation to the suffering

1. Said, *After the Last Sky*, 129–30.
2. Said, *After the Last Sky*, 130, 133–34. Emphasis added.

Jews of the Holocaust. "There has been no misfortune worse for us," he wrote in a kind of astonishment, "than that we are ineluctably viewed as the enemies of the Jews. No moral and political fate worse, none at all, I think: no worse, there is none." Because the Holocaust was such a frequent topic of discussion, he said he was always "centrally aware of the fact of the destruction of European Jews, an abomination." But, he wrote,

> I find myself saying that a generation later the Holocaust has victimized us too, but without the terrifying grandeur and sacrilegious horror of what it did to the Jews. Seen from the perspective provided by the Holocaust, we are as inconsequential as children on a playground; and yet—one more twist in the reductive spiral—even at play we cannot be enjoyed or looked at simply as that, as children playing games that signify little. Just by virtue of where we stand, every playground is seen as a "breeding ground for terrorists," every pastime a "secret plan for the destruction of Israel," as if our own destruction was not a great deal more probable. Something either pernicious or negligible can be attributed to us, no matter what we do, wherever we are, however we think or act.[3]

Continuing in a kind of rush, boring in on the pain, trying as if in a last desperate effort to make the Palestinian pain vivid and clearly understood, Said explained again: "What I have been saying is that we ourselves provide not enough of a presence to force the untidiness of life into a coherent pattern of our own making." Palestinians could only be read "against another people's pattern, but since it is not ours—even though we are its designated enemy—we emerge as its effects, its errata, its counternarratives. Whenever we try to narrate ourselves, we appear as dislocations in *their* discourse."[4]

Said was not a liberation theologian, although he was a Palestinian Christian and, in many ways, he spoke the plaintive, desperate language of liberation theology. His assessment of the Palestinian condition under Zionist Israeli domination was identical in its essentials—and in fact as we will see, coincided in its timing—with the thinking of the theologians who formulated Palestinian liberation theology in the 1980s. Forty years later, the Palestinian condition is the same in its broad outlines, despite substantial changes in many aspects. Because of the Oslo "peace process" of the 1990s and its long and utterly futile quarter-century aftermath, the

3. Said, *After the Last Sky*, 134.
4. Said, *After the Last Sky*, 140. Emphasis in original.

Palestinian struggle does now have something of the "center" that Said believed was lacking: both a geographic center precisely in Palestine and a more centered and focused resistance. Palestinians can no longer quite be categorized as "miscellaneous" or "atonal"—nor indeed are they quite as universally ignored as was true when Said wrote. The Palestinian narrative is actually increasingly well-known at the grassroots level amidst the growing awareness in the United States and around the world of the plight of oppressed peoples everywhere. The full Palestinian narrative— exposing the Nakba of 1948 and the demand for the Palestinians' right of return to their homes, rather than only the story of Palestinians living under occupation in the West Bank and Gaza—is now far more widely known. Importantly, many more Jews, especially of younger generations, and especially outside Israel, support the Palestinians' freedom struggle and question Zionism's exclusivity.

That said, however, most of Said's laments remain generally true forty years later. While the main focus of the Palestinian struggle and of global attention has returned to the place of its origins in the land of Palestine between the river and the sea, huge portions of the Palestinian population, including millions in refugee camps, remain widely scattered throughout the Arab world and beyond, and are increasingly forgotten.[5] It is also the case that, despite the far greater grassroots awareness of the Palestinian narrative and the presence in the US Congress of a few younger representatives who openly support the Palestinians and criticize Israel, Israel's interests still hold sway at the level of policymaking in the United States, and Palestinian interests are ignored. It remains true, as Said wrote, that Palestinians are trodden under by Israeli power and still face the profound moral and political misfortune of being viewed as the enemies of the Jews. There continues to be, as he noted, "an almost total

5. Millions of Palestinians remain outside Palestine, living in refugee camps in Lebanon, Jordan, Syria, and Iraq. Although when Said wrote, these refugee communities were a focus of greater attention than were Palestinians in Palestine, they are today almost completely forgotten and ignored. Despite providing a political centering, the focus on Palestine has left Palestinians on the geographic periphery scattered and increasingly "miscellaneous," as Said would have it. Even inside the "center," Israel's canny manipulation of populations and the institution of movement restrictions, physical barriers, and a draconian permit system have kept Palestinians in various areas disconnected from each other. Those living inside Israel, as well as those in East Jerusalem, the West Bank, and Gaza are physically separated, denied access to each other by Kafkaesque allocations of citizenship rights, residency-without-citizenship rights, permits, denial of permits, checkpoints, massive concrete walls, areas under blockade and siege, and a segregated road network.

official American opposition to [Palestinians] as a people, as a society, as a cause." Where Said wrote that Palestinians appeared as "dislocations" in the Israeli narrative, this remains true today for Israeli officials and pro-Israel lobbyists who are always watchful to label any Palestinian discourse as antisemitic. At the highest official levels in Israel and the United States today, moreover, it increasingly seems that Palestinians no longer register at all in official narratives.[6]

The principal formulator of Palestinian liberation theology is the Rev. Dr. Naim Stifan Ateek, a Palestinian Episcopal priest. Like so many other liberation theologians, Ateek lives his theology. He has personally lived the seminal events of Palestine's catastrophic modern history, fleeing warfare as an eleven-year-old boy, enduring his family's dispossession by a conquering army, living even now through Israel's continuing effort to minimize and erase his people's existence. Ateek calls the events of his life growing up in Palestine a journey that shaped his faith and planted the seeds of his search for justice and liberation, and indeed his theology shines forth as the embodiment of what liberation, and liberation theology, mean for all Palestinians, no matter whether they are Christian or Muslim. Because he has lived the Palestinian story, Ateek's journey captures on an individual level the principal aspects of any theology of liberation: the oppression and its very personal impact on human lives; the spiritual crisis that living under injustice arouses; the grassroots struggle to overcome oppression; and the *cri de cœur* for justice, compassion, and love from God—for a reason to live and to hope.

For Ateek and all Palestinians, the oppression and injustice they face fundamentally originate from Israel's settler-colonial system and from having endured because of it the loss of homes, land, most political

---

6. This is written at a time when relatively new leaders in Israel and the United States, including President Joe Biden, although less abrasive personalities than their predecessors, President Trump and Prime Minister Benjamin Netanyahu, appear to be continuing the general thrust of those predecessors' policies. The policies involved a concerted Israeli effort, with an unprecedented level of US support, to cement Israeli control over the occupied territories, just short of formal annexation, by continuing to expropriate more Palestinian land, build more Israeli settlements, launch periodic devastating attacks on Gaza, allow attacks by Jewish Israeli settlers on West Bank Palestinian villages, undermine international efforts to aid the Palestinians, and reject efforts at conflict resolution in favor of a policy of maintaining the status quo by simply "managing" the conflict.

freedoms, and the recognized legitimacy of claims to national sovereignty. They have also, throughout the decades since the creation of Israel, faced a striking lack of international interest and support for their plight. Ateek's story is typical. Born into a Palestinian Christian family in 1937, the eighth of ten children, in what was then the colonial British Mandate for Palestine, Ateek endured the Israeli military siege of his town and the massive dispossession and ethnic cleansing that the Palestinian Arab population experienced when Israel was created in 1948.

This seminal event of dispossession and ethnic cleansing, along with the period of British colonialism and Zionist political consolidation that preceded it, have together constituted the defining experience of Palestinian existence and identity for more than a century. The catastrophe of dispossession itself began with the United Nations Partition Plan of November 1947—an internationally devised and mandated plan that, without the consent of Palestine's inhabitants, divided the land lying between the Jordan River and the Mediterranean Sea, allotting more than half of the land, 55 percent, to a "Jewish state" and 45 percent to an "Arab state." The UN dictated this division, astonishingly, despite the fact that the population balance at the time was approximately one-third Jewish and two-thirds Palestinian Arab, and Jews owned only 7 percent of the land. By the conclusion of the war that erupted over this international decision to partition Palestine, Israeli military forces had taken control of almost half again as much territory as the UN had designated for the Jewish state; by the war's end, the new state of Israel controlled 78 percent of Palestine. The remaining 22 percent was taken by two neighboring Arab states: Egypt controlled the tiny Gaza Strip in the south, and the territory that came to be called the West Bank, as well as East Jerusalem, came under Jordanian control. (Both of these territories were captured by Israel nineteen years later, during the 1967 war.)

The major catastrophe for the Palestinians, and what is still recalled as the Nakba, was the terrorized flight of approximately seven hundred fifty thousand Palestinians, well over half of Palestine's Arab population of 1.3 million at the time. The majority of these Palestinians were forcibly expelled in early 1948 by pre-state Jewish militias and, following Israel's declaration of independence in May, by the Israeli military forces formed from the militias; some Palestinians simply fled in the midst of the warfare around them, fully expecting to return. These people—Muslims and Christians, people of all ages from infants to the elderly, ordinary and sometimes extraordinary Palestinians, descendants of generations and centuries of people native to the land, who had been living there peaceably minding their own business—made up the vast majority of the original refugee population that ended up, and remains, in refugee camps in neighboring Arab countries.[7] Israel has never permitted more than a handful of refugees to return, despite the United Nations' passage of a resolution in December 1948, UN Resolution 194, calling for return of any refugees willing to live in peace in the Israeli state.

It is important, in order to understand the scale of the Palestinian catastrophe, to explain some of the terminology associated with the events of 1948. The term "ethnic cleansing," for instance, although coined only in the 1990s to describe the widespread expulsions and killings of specific ethnic groups during the Balkan wars, is now frequently applied retrospectively to the dispossession, expulsion, and in some cases killing of Palestinians in 1948. Israeli historian Ilan Pappé uses the term in the title of his 2006 book, *The Ethnic Cleansing of Palestine*, and cites evidence that Israeli political and military leaders in fact used the Hebrew word *tihur*, meaning "cleansing," to describe their expulsion of the indigenous Palestinian Arab population. This word, Pappé says, "means in Hebrew what it means in any other language: the expulsion of entire populations from their villages and towns," and it appeared "on every order the High Command passed down to the units on the ground."[8] Pappé based his research on declassified Israeli military archives, as well as on Palestinian and Israeli political narratives and, importantly, he examines in some depth the moral and psychological processes that entered into Israel's strategic planning and that deliberately shaped what he calls "the enormity of the crimes the Israeli soldiers committed."[9]

Another noted Israeli historian, Benny Morris, who has written extensively on the events of 1948, has put a less harsh spin on the expulsion phenomenon, but his overall assessment is essentially the same. Morris has not used the precise word "cleanse." Moreover, in an encyclopedia article written more than a decade after publication of his first history of the

---

7. The story of the fate of Palestine's Arab population during the Arab-Israeli war in 1948, when hundreds of thousands of Palestinians were expelled or fled, has been told by numerous Israeli and Palestinian historians, including (chronologically by publication date): Morris, *Birth of the Palestinian Refugee Problem*; Flapan, *Birth of Israel*; Shlaim, *Collusion Across the Jordan*; Masalha, *Expulsion of the Palestinians*; Tamari, *Jerusalem 1948*; and Pappé, *Ethnic Cleansing of Palestine*.

8. Pappé, *Ethnic Cleansing of Palestine*, 72.

9. Pappé, *Ethnic Cleansing of Palestine*, xv.

Palestinian refugee issue,[10] he contends, perhaps over-emphatically, that the Zionist leadership did not have an "actual, comprehensive, systematic policy" of expulsion. Later in the article, however, he acknowledges that there was "something like a consensus, especially among the military, in favor of *clearing the Palestinians out* of Israeli territory for both military and political reasons." He cites several instances during the 1948 war in which Israeli military commanders issued explicit expulsion orders.[11]

The Zionists had long dreamt of establishing—and laid plans for—a more or less exclusively Jewish state in Palestine. Zionist founder Theodore Herzl wrote in the nineteenth century of his vision of "spiriting the penniless [native] population across the border." Expulsion of the native Palestinian Arabs, who made up the overwhelming majority of Palestine's population but who as non-Jews seriously clouded the Zionist dream, thus became an essential part of Zionist planning. Nonetheless, despite the massive scale of the ethnic cleansing and its utterly catastrophic and traumatic impact on the victims, Israel was able to deny and essentially obliterate remembrance of the event so thoroughly that the world and even subsequent generations of Israelis forgot or never knew of it. In his examination of the political and psychological armor built up around the Israeli narrative of 1948, Pappé observes that the ethnic cleansing of so many hundreds of thousands of Palestinians has "been eradicated almost totally from the collective global memory and erased from the world's conscience."[12] Even generations of Israelis born in the 1940s and after— too late to have participated in the events of 1948—never knew anything about the expulsions until recent years.

Some knowledge of the Palestinians' fate has begun to emerge more widely in recent years. It has become somewhat more common for Israeli writers and analysts to acknowledge this huge atrocity, but now in many cases rationalizing and justifying it. Israeli correspondent Ari Shavit, for example, writing a memoir-cum-history in 2013, *My Promised Land*, frankly described but ultimately excused one instance of mass expulsion: in July 1948, Israeli military forces forcibly marched tens of thousands of Palestinian residents of the town of Lydda eastward out of the town and out of Israeli-controlled territory, on foot and without food or shelter from the summer heat. Those refugees who survived the long walk

---

10. Morris, *Birth of the Palestinian Refugee Problem*.

11. Morris, "Exodus." Emphasis added.

12. Pappé, *Ethnic Cleansing of Palestine*, 9.

ended up in the Jordanian-controlled West Bank, often in one of several West Bank refugee camps. Lydda soon thereafter became the Israeli town of Lod, a suburb of Tel Aviv, and is the location of Israel's Ben Gurion International Airport. Shavit calls this expulsion "the dark secret of Zionism" but rationalizes it by contending, without evidence beyond his own conjecture, that Zionism and Israel could not have continued to exist if the Palestinians of Lydda had been allowed to remain. He protests passionately that, had it not been for the Israeli forces that oversaw Lydda's death throes, "the State of Israel would not have been born. If it wasn't for them, I would not have been born. They did the dirty, filthy work that enables my people, myself, my daughter, and my sons to live."[13]

The eradication of memory that has rendered the consciences of many multitudes of Israelis and Israeli supporters around the world so easy and clear has of course not occurred for the Palestinians—for precisely the reason that they are the victims of Zionism's "dirty, filthy work" and they have not received redress or justice. In fact, in the absence of any kind of justice, more suffering and more dark memories have been piled on, and more generations of aggrieved Palestinians have grown up remembering. Far from leading to fading memories, Israel's continued, decades-long oppression of Palestinians continually plants new seeds of righteous grievance from which have grown decades of resistance and refusal to surrender. While there is a strong psychological impetus for oppressors anywhere (including in the United States with regard to the near-genocide of its native population) to forget their actions, memory is all too acute for the victims, especially so when there has been no reparation or healing.

Memory—of past history, past accomplishments, past suffering— looms especially large in this confrontation between two peoples who both claim an ancient heritage in the same land. Although Jews and Judaism originated millennia ago in ancient Palestine, and a small indigenous Jewish population lived there continuously over the millennia, Jews made up only 10 percent of Palestine's total population at the end of World War I, when Britain assumed colonial control over Palestine and began to welcome large numbers of Jewish immigrants from Europe. The Jews who migrated to Palestine from Europe in the twentieth century—in the 1920s and 1930s, as well as after the Holocaust and Israel's creation—arrived as settlers under a Zionist program designed explicitly

13. See Shavit, *My Promised Land*, 99–132, for the chapter on Lydda; 108 and 131 for quoted portions.

to build a Jewish-majority nation-state, absorbing the indigenous Palestinian Jewish population and displacing the indigenous Palestinian Arab population. The Zionist claim to the whole of Palestine for Jews and only Jews is a supremacist settler-colonial imposition, aided initially by a British colonial regime. It is from this imposition that Palestinian liberation theology, and Palestinians in general, seek liberation.

It is critical to keep in mind that, although Israel and Zionism claim to represent all Jews worldwide and although Zionism is often conflated with Judaism itself, there is a distinction between Israel as a state, on one hand, and Jews as people of a particular religious and/or ethnic identity, on the other. The two modern identifiers of Israel-the-state and Jews-the-people are not synonymous, despite considerable overlap. Israeli policies and actions are not the policies and actions of all Jewish people, despite Israeli claims; all Jews are not adherents of Zionism, and neither Zionism nor Israel is identical with Judaism.

By contrast with the vast majority of Israeli Jews, Palestine's indigenous population, the Palestinian Arabs, did not "settle" in Palestine, but rather has had a continuous presence there. Today's Palestinian Arabs are the descendants of all the ancient and modern peoples who have lived in, immigrated to, and conquered Palestine, including ancient Canaanites and Jews and successive immigrants and conquerors such as Egyptians, Assyrians, Greeks, Romans, European Crusaders, and Arabs. Since the seventh century when Islam arose, this population has been largely Muslim. But the Palestinian Christian presence—beginning with the Jewish contemporaries of Jesus and his followers who were Christianity's earliest followers—has been substantial since the first century CE. Christians made up approximately 10 percent of the Arab population at the end of World War I, although emigration has now brought that proportion down to 2 or 3 percent. Palestinians have always been "multi-ethnic, multi-religious, and multi-cultural," according to Naim Ateek.[14] Many other scholars have pointed out that Palestine has been a land of multiple passing civilizations.[15] Rifat Odeh Kassis, who in 2009 co-authored the major Palestinian Christian statement of principles, *Kairos Palestine: A Moment of Truth*, and has since then served as coordinator of the *Kairos Palestine Group*, notes with apparent irony that numerous peoples and civilizations "rose in our area of the world and fell in the same place."

14. Ateek, *Palestinian Theology*, 16
15. See Masalha, *Palestine*.

All left behind "elements of their cultures, civilisations [sic], ideologies, legends and theologies." Like all Palestinians, Kassis identifies himself as "a son of all this history."[16] The renowned Palestinian scholar Walid Khalidi, himself a Muslim and member of one of the most prominent scholarly Palestinian families of Jerusalem, notes that Palestinians in general are "acutely aware of the distinctiveness of Palestinian history" and indeed view themselves as the "heirs of its rich associations."[17]

Despite the Palestinians' own clarity about who they are, they have suffered for the last century and more from being viewed through a self-serving Zionist lens, either ignored altogether or deliberately portrayed for the popular imagination as, at best, "non-Jews" and vaguely "other"; at worst, as the enemy of the Jews. Britain's 1917 Balfour Declaration, issued during World War I as Britain's promise to Zionist leaders of its intention to take colonial control of Palestine after defeating Ottoman Turkey, expressed support for the establishment of a "national home for the Jewish people" in Palestine. Almost as an afterthought, the declaration affirmed that the "civil and religious [although not political] rights of existing non-Jewish communities in Palestine" would not be overridden. At the time of this declaration, Palestinian Arabs—identified according to what they were not, not Jews—made up 90 percent of the territory's population. This same strange wording was incorporated a few years later, in 1922, into the colonial mandate for controlling Palestine granted to Britain by the League of Nations.

Palestinian liberation theology is rooted in trying to escape Israel's colonialist designs. This Palestinian theology is unique among liberation theologies in that it plays out in the very land where Jesus Christ lived and Christianity was born. Because they are descended from the first Christians of Jesus' day, Palestinian Christians regard Jesus as "uniquely theirs," Ateek has affirmed, and they see him as "a fellow Palestinian": someone like them, with ethnic origins in Palestine, and someone who lived under foreign, Roman, occupation, as they do today. Jesus was killed "by the occupation forces in collaboration with the religious leaders of the day" and, for them, he is both "the paradigm of faith and [their] liberator."[18] Affirming the inspiring effect of this discovery of Jesus himself as a Palestinian, Cedar Duaybis, a Palestinian theological colleague

16. Kassis, *Kairos for Palestine*, 15.

17. Khalidi, *Before Their Diaspora*, 32.

18. Ateek, *Palestinian Theology*, 39.

of Ateek who worked with him in formulating liberation theology and founding the Sabeel liberation theology center in Jerusalem, writes that this new knowledge of Jesus made him seem "accessible to [Palestinians] in his humanity and his relationship to the land, the people, and the powers." Jesus became a "tangible person" for Palestinian Christians, she says, and his teachings began to emerge more clearly and with much greater relevance to Palestinians.[19]

Ultimately, the Palestinian-Israeli struggle is one between two peoples with ancient claims who put forth those claims in totally different legal and moral ways: while Israeli colonialism asserts a claim to superior Jewish rights despite being a latter-day colonizer, the perpetually oppressed Palestinians seek to maintain their native presence on the land and, because of this presence, to assert a right to political freedom, as well as to equality and human dignity.

Naim Ateek's story describes in microcosm the root of Palestinian grievances against Israel. It puts a stark human perspective on the little publicized and now largely forgotten Palestinian side of the often-romanticized story of Israel's creation in 1948: the side involving the total disruption and near-total destruction of Palestinian society, the Palestinian people's wide dispersion across borders, and the shattering of their national aspirations.

During the disastrous episode of the Nakba, Ateek's family, unlike the hundreds of thousands of dispossessed Palestinians who ended up in refugee camps throughout the Arab world, became internal refugees, displaced but remaining inside the Israeli state at the conclusion of the 1948 war. In May of that year, while the war was still in progress, Jewish Israeli military forces emptied Ateek's small Palestinian hometown of Beisan (later renamed Beit Shean and populated by Israeli Jews) of all of its six thousand Muslim and Christian inhabitants and, sending the Muslims out of Palestine into neighboring Jordan, bused the Christians to Nazareth, which became part of the state of Israel. The Ateek family was forced to abandon its home, and Naim's father his silver- and gold-smithing business, taking with them only what they could carry on a bus. They were forced to begin life again in a place now called Israel.[20]

---

19. Duaybis, "Palestinian Liberation Theology."

20. Ateek, *Justice and Only Justice*, 9–11.

As is evident from Ateek's family story, huge societal disruption and dispossession were not limited to those Palestinians who landed in refugee camps after being expelled from Palestine altogether by Israeli forces. Even the relatively small number of Palestinians who remained in what became the Israeli state, like the Ateeks, encountered life-changing disruption when they lost homes and businesses and were forcibly relocated. Approximately one hundred fifty thousand Palestinians remained inside the borders of Israel at the end of the 1948 war.[21] This minority of Palestinian Arabs who became citizens of Israel has consistently made up approximately 20 percent of Israel's total, majority-Jewish population over the last seven decades. By mid-2020, according to the Israeli Central Bureau of Statistics, the total population of Israel was 9.2 million—of whom 21 percent, or 1.9 million, were Palestinian Arabs.[22]

For millions of Palestinians like Ateek and later generations, the catastrophe of 1948 is no mere historical tale; all Palestinians live their lives in catastrophe's shadow, with no healing or restorative justice. As a result, as Ateek has observed, the events of the Nakba remain "imprinted deeply in my psyche and memory."[23] The impact on all Palestinians, of the original as well as succeeding generations, is incalculable; recall what we learned of Edward Said's trauma and memories. Indignantly referring to Israel's tangled system of designating Palestinians like his family who remained in Israel after the 1948 ethnic cleansing, Ateek still bitterly recalls that "they drove us out, and then they called us absentees!"[24]

For Ateek in particular, those first seeds of righteous grievance grew to form the foundation of Palestinian liberation theology. At the same time, other seeds of love and nonviolence grew from the example of his

21. See McCarthy, "Population," 329.

22. *Wikipedia*, "Demographics of Israel."

23. Ateek, *Palestinian Theology*, 3.

24. Within two years of its establishment, the new Israeli government came up with a system for retrospectively legalizing its seizure of Palestinian Arab property left behind when the Palestinian population fled or was ethnically cleansed in 1948. A 1950 Israeli law defined as an "absentee" any person who, between November 29, 1947 (the date of the UN partition of Palestine) and May 19, 1948, left "his ordinary place of residence in Palestine" and either left the country altogether or moved to a different place in what became the state of Israel. In this way were the tens of thousands of Palestinians like Ateek and his family who were expelled from their residences and forcibly moved elsewhere inside Israel rendered officially "absent" from their property and homes, and their property given to an Israeli "custodian of absentee property." Those "absentees" who remained inside Israel were designated, nonsensically, as "present absentees." See, Lustick, *Arabs in the Jewish State*, 173, 310n63.

father's life of faith. In fact, he credits his father's abiding faith and trust in God, even in the dark period of the family's dispossession, with helping maintain his own faith. His father believed that "God went out with us into our new life in Nazareth" and continued to believe in the goodness of God, despite the injustices Palestinians endured. Because he has been able to maintain his own faith, Naim Ateek has always been able to put his trust in "the God of love and peace, justice and mercy, liberation and reconciliation."[25] This love and sense of God's presence with us in suffering is the taproot of any theology of liberation.

Ateek's spiritual journey has been a straight path from victim of injustice to theologian of liberation from injustice. After traveling to the United States as a young man, where he received a university and theological education, he returned to Nazareth in 1966 to be ordained a deacon at Christ Church, the small Anglican church where he had worshiped while growing up. He writes pointedly of having been "empowered" and inspired to activism on behalf of the oppressed by the biblical passage, from Luke 4:18–19, inscribed in Arabic above his church's altar (cited in the epigraph of this chapter). This call—in which Jesus, reading at his own synagogue in Nazareth, quotes from Isaiah about having been anointed to bring good news to the poor, release to the captives, sight to the blind, freedom to the oppressed—was another seed planted for the theology Ateek would formulate years later.[26]

Yet another seed of his theology sprang up as Ateek began to witness the near hopelessness of the Palestinian Christians to whom he ministered. He was ordained to the priesthood in the Israeli city of Haifa in 1967. This year was coincidentally the year Israel captured and occupied the remaining portions of Palestine not already a part of the Israeli state: East Jerusalem and the West Bank, which had been under Jordanian control since 1948, and the small Gaza Strip, which had been held by Egypt. One hundred percent of all Palestine, comprising the entire area between the Jordan River and the Mediterranean Sea, now came under Israeli control. Although Israelis regard the absorption of these lands as redemptive because this area encompasses what they term "Eretz Israel"—the whole "Land of Israel," recalling the Jewish biblical heritage—for Palestinians, this event represented another massive loss, constituting another Nakba, which Palestinians in fact call the *Naksa*, the "setback."

25. Ateek, *Palestinian Theology*, 3.

26. Ateek, *Palestinian Christian Cry*, 3–4, and Ateek, *Palestinian Theology*, 43.

As Israel consolidated its control, and as the supposedly temporary occupation stretched on, now to more than half a century, Palestinians faced
more colonialism: more ethnic cleansing, more and more expropriation
of land for construction of Jewish-only settlements and roads, more and
always intensifying controls over everything about their daily lives, more
and increasingly dehumanizing human rights abuses and, for the majority of Muslims and Christians who were religiously devout, more spiritual doubt and concern that God had abandoned them.[27]

This sense of abandonment by God arose from the utterly ca-
lamitous nature of the Nakba, which Ateek points out has in fact been a
threefold catastrophe for the Palestinians: not only is it a human catastrophe, as has been shown, but it is also an "identity Nakba" and a "faith
Nakba." Regarding identity, Ateek notes, Palestinians who remained in
Israel in 1948 went from living peaceably in their homes and land one
day to being strangers in their own country the next. Israel has made a
strenuous effort over the years to erase Palestinian culture, history, and
memory—excluding Palestinians living in Israel from any part in Israel's
"national collective" and altogether undermining the "collective memory
of the Palestinian people." Tens of thousands of books were confiscated
from public and private Palestinian libraries soon after Israel took control; Palestinian history has been completely expunged from school text-
books in Israel and even the word Nakba removed from the curriculum;
any use of the words Palestine and Palestinians was banned for the first
many decades, until the Oslo peace process began in the 1990s; the name
Palestinian has even been erased from national identity cards, replaced
with the more generic designation Arab. Ateek describes this process as a
"colonizing" of the Arabic language and of Palestinian symbols.[28]

"Faith Nakba" is a term coined by Ateek's theological colleague, Cedar Duaybis. Referring to this phenomenon also as a "theological Nakba,"
Duaybis has written that this catastrophe "pulled the ground from under
our feet and added to our feeling of being utterly lost," like an unanchored
ship drifting aimlessly.[29] Too often, Duaybis contends, when Palestinian

---

27. For descriptions of how Israel's long-running occupation of East Jerusalem,
the West Bank, and Gaza has affected Palestinians and all aspects of their daily lives,
as well as the ways in which this occupation continues the oppression of Palestinians begun in 1948, see Christison and Christison, *Palestine in Pieces*, and Makdisi,
Palestine Inside Out.

28. Ateek, *Palestinian Theology*, 27–28.

29. Quoted in Ateek, *Palestinian Theology*, 28.

Christians needed consolation and assurance of God's love and closeness, the church in all its denominations stood apart, as if under "church arrest," its faith "under curfew," refusing to take a firm stand or any initiative for Palestinian rights. Duaybis's own children came to regard attending church services as a time and a place of estrangement, when they were made to wonder if God too, like Israel, regarded them as "non-people whose very existence in our land seems to be the problem."[30]

For Palestinian Christians, the church seemed almost not to have noticed that their lives had been turned upside down by Israel's creation in their land. The liturgy, Bible readings, sermons, hymns and, notably, the local church hierarchy, which at that time was primarily foreign and therefore not personally concerned by the implantation of Israel inside Palestine, all remained the same, even though Palestinians were in shock from "a seismic tremor of enormous magnitude." Apart from feeling spiritually abandoned, Palestinians were further shocked to hear the Bible that they revered being used by Israel to justify its claim that God had bestowed the land on Jews as a uniquely "chosen" people. Palestinian Christians began to question in their hearts how it could be that, if the Bible is indeed the word of God, it could become the instrument of their dispossession—and the church failed to provide an adequate response.[31]

Even though liberation theologians in other nations and other contexts see the Bible as a "dynamic source for their understanding of liberation," Ateek came to feel early in his journey toward formulating a theology for Palestinians that this same Bible comes across quite differently for Palestinians. For them, many parts of the Bible seem to offer only "slavery rather than freedom, injustice rather than justice, and death to their national and political life." How could the Bible have become part of the problem for Palestinians, used to condemn their national aspirations, when it should offer them a blessing? It thus became of critical importance for Palestinians to discern the will of God and what the message of the Bible meant in light of Israel's oppressive rule over Palestinians.[32]

This question became especially insistent for Ateek and, after several years of parish ministry, he began to think and write about a theology that spoke specifically to Palestinians. Although he did not initially call this liberation theology, he was searching for a way to free Palestinians

---

30. Duaybis, "Becoming Whole," 120–21.

31. Ateek, *Palestinian Theology*, 28–29.

32. Ateek, *Justice and Only Justice*, 75–77.

religiously and psychologically, giving them spiritual comfort and hope
based on the conviction that God stands with them because God's principal concern is always for those who suffer injustice. Ateek set out on a
new part of his journey to chart the way for justice, peace, and reconciliation in Palestine-Israel—in that order, as he is careful to say.[33] Justice
for Palestinians, and for Jews as well, must necessarily precede peace, and
real peace with justice is an absolute prerequisite for true reconciliation
between the two peoples.

Further preparing himself both spiritually and academically, although he acknowledges that he was unsure where the Holy Spirit was
leading him, Ateek spent the early 1980s working on a doctorate in the
United States, focusing his study on theological issues of justice. He believes theology is the only bridge between the Bible and the people, and
that the purpose of this bridge is to interpret the biblical message faithfully but contextually, making the Bible relevant to the people's situation and
bringing the people into relationship with God. It was while traversing
this bridge that he began to focus on the deep distress Palestinian Christians were enduring because of what appeared to be the biblical message
that Israel's creation at their expense, hailed throughout the world as
the fulfillment of Jewish biblical prophecy, was a manifestation of God's
will.[34] Speaking as one of those Christians in distress, Cedar Duaybis
vividly describes that theological bridge as having collapsed and left Palestinian Christians "caught in the crack, unable to go back to our former
theological thinking while groping to find a meaningful way forward."
The Bible, the anchor of Christian faith, was being used to block the way
forward, she says—used by Jewish Zionists as the scriptural justification
for injustices against the Palestinians, by Western Christians expiating
guilt over the Holocaust, and by Christian biblical literalists espousing a
Christian form of Zionism.[35]

Palestinians, wondering if indeed the Bible is the true word of God,
were questioning the very integrity of God, and Ateek sought answers for
himself and for them: "What is God's relation to the new State of Israel?
Is God partial only to the Jews? Is this a God of justice and peace?" When
Ateek returned to Palestine in 1985 to serve at St. George's Anglican Cathedral in East Jerusalem, he found a church establishment that was still

33. Ateek, *Palestinian Christian Cry*, 10.
34. Ateek, *Justice and Only Justice*, 78–79.
35. Duaybis, "Three-Fold Nakba," 8.

unable to help its congregants and that remained "impotent and helpless before these questions" about God's love and intentions and the verity of God's word.[36] The overriding reality of injustice was at the forefront of Palestinian existence: the injustices they had by then faced for nearly forty years since 1948—injustices greatly intensified after two decades in which Israeli control had extended to additional occupied Palestinian territories—had become "our daily ration of food," Ateek realized. Many Palestinian Christians had emigrated; some had simply left the church in despair; those who remained increasingly wondered about the nature of a God who could liberate one people at the cost of gross injustice to another. Ateek himself "felt the need for peace in my guts, agonized over the injustice, and prayed to God for an end to the oppression."[37] The need Ateek felt for a way to give despairing Palestinians hope and spiritual succor pressed in on him—the need for a way to bring Palestinians, in the depths of their oppression, to an understanding of God as a loving God who understands and *feels* the injustice and suffering they face and cares about them in their distress.

That burden of injustice that Ateek himself felt, and knew to be at the forefront of all Palestinian lives after decades of living under Israeli control, boiled over in late 1987 into a widespread popular uprising that brought Palestinians from all walks of life into the streets of Jerusalem, the West Bank, and Gaza to tell the world about their oppression. Called the *intifada*, meaning in Arabic "shaking" or "a shaking off," the uprising erupted as a spontaneous protest primarily against the innumerable Israeli human rights violations perpetrated in the occupied territories, but also against the world's continuing indifference to the Palestinians' dire situation. The United States was enabling Israel's oppression with massive grants of military aid and unquestioning support for all Israeli actions; the Arab countries that once acted to support Palestinian rights were doing nothing; even the Palestine Liberation Organization, severely weakened after years of struggle and exile, was unable to provide meaningful support or leadership for Palestinians on the ground actually living under occupation. Palestinians were essentially without a voice and without hope of support from anywhere. Palestinian children were on the front lines of this popular struggle, throwing stones at heavily armed Israeli soldiers. They represented, in the words of Palestinian American

36. Ateek, *Justice and Only Justice*, 78–79.
37. Ateek, *Palestinian Christian Cry*, 5.

intellectual Edward Said, "the very ground of the Palestinian protest: with stones and an unbent political will standing fearlessly against the blows of well-armed Israeli soldiers." Otherwise the uprising was unarmed and the Palestinians were unaided, but they won a great deal in moral terms. Said wrote at the time that the "United States, the other Arabs, even putative allies like the Soviet Union seemed paralyzed by that mixture of foregone hypocrisy and benevolent hand wringing that always contributed to sustaining the occupation still longer."[38]

It became clear that, even as Naim Ateek's frustration and the urgent pressures on him to act were growing, the endurance of the whole of Palestinian society had also reached the boiling point. This became a time of awakened consciousness—and, at least briefly, of hope—in which Palestinians gained a voice, gained agency, and were able to bring their case to international attention. And, for a while, the international community did listen. It is not an exaggeration to say that the Palestinian political struggle reached a new stage in this late twentieth-century period—finally, after multiple decades in which no one had listened. Simultaneously with the intifada, a new and more activist theology of liberation designed specifically for the Palestinian context also began to grow, from the pressures Ateek felt and began to transmit to fellow Christians.

The theological aspect of the struggle, the gathering together of Christians that Palestinian liberation theology evoked, began publicly with Ateek's detailed articulation of the resistance theology for Palestinians in his book, *Justice and Only Justice*, which was published in the United States in 1989 and was officially launched in Jerusalem in early 1990 at an event held at St. George's Anglican Cathedral and participated in by representatives of all of Palestine's numerous, and often previously divided, Christian denominations. This launch was followed by an international conference attended by a small number of theologians from around the world—including, from the United States, Roman Catholic theologian Rosemary Radford Ruether and Jewish theologian Marc Ellis.[39] (Sadly but not surprisingly—further testimony to how much Pal-

38. Said, "Intifada and Independence," 8. Said's mention of "the blows" of Israeli soldiers refers to an order given Israeli soldiers during the intifada to break the arms and legs of Palestinian youth caught throwing stones.

39. Ateek, *Palestinian Theology*, 129.

estine is ignored around the globe—no theologians from Latin America attended, only one attended from Europe, and only four came from Asia and Africa.[40])

These scholars and spiritual leaders worked together in conference to refine and further develop Ateek's initial blueprint, striving to "conscienticize" liberation theologians everywhere and bring them to an awareness of the dark, negative message delivered to Palestinians by what Ruether termed Israel's "theology of conquest," which employs biblical themes to justify Jewish supremacy and the oppression and colonization of Palestinians.[41] Not only was this critical Palestinian interpretation highly controversial politically, but it also stood as a challenge to most Western Christian theology. Ateek has written of the heavy burden involved in so dramatically changing even the perceptions of ordinary Palestinians, not to mention the foundational beliefs of theologians elsewhere. Even with the model of Latin American liberation theology before them, the conference participants in Jerusalem were uncertain of where they were headed. They prayed for guidance on "where the Holy Spirit was leading us," Ateek has said, and as a result, they were able to feel throughout the conference proceedings "that Christ was breathing the Spirit on those Palestinian Christians who were eager to learn and to witness to the power of justice and nonviolence."[42]

Justice and nonviolence were, and remain, the key objectives and guiding principles of this new resistance theology, and the Spirit still inspires it. Three decades later, Ateek still believes the Holy Spirit was at work in this confluence of a new radical theology and a popular political uprising, the first intifada. He likens Pentecost to the intifada: Pentecost was a time when the disciples, fearful and seemingly defeated by the end of Jesus' earthly ministry, were "filled with the Holy Spirit" (Acts 2:4, NRSV), inspired to proclaim the message of God, guided by the "Spirit of truth" (John 16:13, NRSV). Similarly, the intifada was a time when, in a period of despair and hopelessness, Palestinians were suddenly inspired to rise up and resist. Just as Pentecost changed and empowered the disciples, so did the intifada change and empower ordinary Palestinians. In both cases, fear turned to courage, emptiness became commitment.

40. Ruether, "Preface," xi.
41. Ruether, "Preface," xi.
42. Ateek, *Palestinian Theology*, 129–30.

Pentecost is a spiritual renewal; the intifada marked the beginning of a new, and continuing, resistance.[43]

What came into being at the 1990 liberation theology conference was a study center established in 1991 in East Jerusalem called the Sabeel Ecumenical Liberation Theology Center, now entering its fourth decade. The name of the center, Sabeel, has special significance: taken from the first recorded reference to the early followers of Jesus as people of "the Way"—a label given them by Saul of Tarsus before his conversion (Acts 9:1–2, NRSV)—*sabeel* is the Arabic word for "the way." A second meaning for sabeel is "a fountain or spring of living water," which recalls the words of Jesus in John's Gospel (7:37–38, NRSV): "Out of the believer's heart shall flow rivers of living water."[44] One of Sabeel's founders, Samia Khoury, writing after years of working on Sabeel's board of directors, has recalled those years as representing "a long Way, a fruitful and rewarding Way—and definitely a source for quenching the thirst of our faith."[45]

Sabeel's "purpose statement" affirms:

> Sabeel is an ecumenical grassroots liberation theology move-
> ment among Palestinian Christians. Inspired by the life and
> teaching of Jesus Christ, this liberation theology seeks to deepen
> the faith of Palestinian Christians, promote unity among them,
> and lead them to act for justice and love. Sabeel strives to devel-
> op a spirituality based on justice, peace, nonviolence, liberation,
> and reconciliation for the different national and faith communi-
> ties (. . .). Sabeel also works to promote a more accurate interna-
> tional awareness regarding the identity, presence, and witness of
> Palestinian Christians as well as their contemporary concerns.
> It encourages individuals and groups from around the world to
> work for a just, comprehensive, and enduring peace informed
> by truth and empowered by prayer and action.[46]

Sabeel defines Palestinian liberation theology as not just critical, analytical theology, but as theology that deals contextually with politi-cal reality, actively but nonviolently struggles against injustice and op-pression, and offers a vision of alternatives to the present unjust reality. Although it is a theology enunciated by Christians and seeks to unite the multiple Christian denominations in Palestine-Israel in a common

---

43. Ateek, speaking during an online Sabeel prayer session (May 27, 2021).

44. Ateek, *Palestinian Theology*, 130–31.

45. Khoury, "PLT: A Rewarding Way," 6.

46. Reprinted in Ateek, *Palestinian Theology*, 153.

struggle, it also, importantly, puts itself forth as an interfaith theology: in the land where peoples of all three Abrahamic faiths live together, Palestinian liberation theology seeks to bring them all—Jews, Christians, and Muslims—together "for justice and peace in this one land."[47] Its advocacy for justice embraces Muslims as compassionately as it does Christians, and its overriding objective is a just peace and reconciliation of Palestinians of all faiths with Jews.

One of this theology's unique contextual struggles, as we will examine in greater detail in Chapter 6, is its strong effort to counter the growing influence of Christian Zionism, particularly in the United States. Christian Zionism is a fundamentalist Christian evangelical theology that believes that God bestowed the entire land of Palestine on the Jews; that Palestinian Arabs are a people cursed because they are not Jews; and that Jesus' second coming will occur when Palestine is populated only by Jews. Sabeel's great concern is that, even among mainline, non-evangelical Christians, there is a "subtle and more diffuse theology" that accepts and justifies the supposed "chosenness" of Jews and their supremacy in the land at the expense of Palestinians—a subtlety that is ultimately leading to mainstream Christian silence and indifference or, worse, directly leads to Palestinian oppression.[48]

Sabeel's theological framework is bounded by ten guidelines, ten aspects that define its nature. These are guidelines that to one degree or another frame the essence of all liberation theologies.[49] The first of the guidelines is that this Palestinian theology is *contextual*, focusing specifically on the theological implications of the Palestinian life situation under Israeli control and attempting to answer the fundamental questions of what God expects of Palestinians and of how they must respond to injustice. The theology is a *liberation theology*, in that it seeks liberation for both oppressed and oppressor: Palestinian liberation from oppression by Israel, as well as the liberation of Israel from "the sin of oppressing Palestinians." It is a *grassroots theology*, developed from the local Palestinian community's Bible study and reflection on its situation through the eyes of faith. It is an *inclusive theology*, rejecting exclusivist concepts of God that dehumanize, subjugate, and exclude people. It is therefore both an *ecumenical theology*, referring to all Christian denominations, and an

47. See "Liberation Theology: The Theology of Sabeel," FOSNA website.

48. "Liberation Theology: The Theology of Sabeel," FOSNA website.

49. The guidelines that follow are enumerated in Ateek, *Palestinian Theology*, 139–41.

interfaith theology that reaches out not only to Christians but to people of other faiths, especially to Muslims and Jews. Founded on the belief that God's love and care embrace all and that all are members of the same human family created by God, this theology seeks "to relate to one another in love and respect for the dignity of every human being, to serve one another, and to work together for justice and peace for all people." This is the heart of the Palestinian theology.

In keeping with its inclusive nature, this theology is a *humanitarian theology*, championing the dignity of every human being, especially the poor and oppressed, the marginalized and disadvantaged. It is a *theology of nonviolence*, believing that Jesus preached peacemaking even when he lived under a brutal, oppressive occupation. Jesus taught everyone to love their enemies, to pray for those who harm them and, in order to be true children of God, to engage actively in peacemaking. It is a *prophetic theology* that demands that Christians, both clergy and laity, courageously speak truth to power, speaking prophetically against the evils of injustice and oppression that Power imposes on them. Finally, it is a *christological theology* in which Jesus Christ, in his human nature, is seen as a tangible person, like Palestinian Christians themselves, and becomes the paradigm and model of faith, the guide and the hermeneutic or lens through whose life the faithful can discern God's authentic word.

These qualities comprise the barest outline of the theology and may appear, simply because they are definitional, to be mechanical and lacking in substance. But in fact there is profound theological and political substance behind each aspect of this outline. Examining substance begins with in-depth study of the unique context for this theology.

Because the Hebrew Bible has been used directly by Israeli Zionists, and in recent decades by Christian Zionists in the United States and Europe, as a weapon against Palestinians—as a justification for Zionism's conquest of the land of Palestine and against the Palestinians' very presence in the land, their right to freedom and self-determination—Ateek and Sabeel have formulated a body of critical biblical exegesis to address this "weaponization" of Scripture. Initially, Ateek's analysis was intended for the guidance of Palestinian Christians confused and alienated by biblical passages calling explicitly for their extermination, but as further developed by Sabeel's theologians over the years, this analysis stands now as an important body of critical thought and theo-political insight not only for the faithful but for the (hoped for) edification of political leaders and theological scholars of all faiths.

For Palestinian liberation theology, Jesus, as the incarnation of God's love and justice, is the hermeneutical key, the criterion against whose preaching and message Palestinian Christians can determine the authenticity and authority of God's word as revealed in the Bible. "Is what I am reading," Ateek asks as a guide throughout the biblical text, "in line with the spirit of Christ and does it agree with the knowledge, nature, and character of God that has been revealed to us in and through Jesus Christ? (. . .). [Is it] in harmony with the love of God for all people?"[50] Importantly for this exegesis, Palestinian theology focuses not only on Jesus' divinity, which has always been the major emphasis of Eastern Christian liturgy, but now also on Jesus as fully human and as an historical figure who lived under foreign occupation just as today's Palestinians do and whose life and actions under that occupation were directed at shaping a world of justice and love. This emphasis brings the gospels into focus as living history and Jesus as an exemplar of this liberation struggle.[51]

While he raises up many Hebrew Scriptures that deepen Christian faith and spirituality, the principal focus of Ateek's exegesis is on key passages that are particularly troubling for Palestinians. These are passages that Palestinians cannot simply ignore, interpret away as unimportant, or gloss over as merely allegorical—for the critical contextual reason that Zionism uses them to claim that the Jewish people are the "chosen" of God and to justify Israel's conquest of the land of Palestine as supposedly having been divinely mandated. Liberation theology, Ateek says, must discard as having no authority any biblical texts that "do not pass the test of the Christ hermeneutic or the love hermeneutic," because in fact they are "morally and theologically offensive." They offend human dignity and the spirit of Jesus and in "no way (. . .) constitute a word of God for us." Jesus himself did not quote from objectionable Hebrew texts that advocate the expulsion and ethnic cleansing of indigenous peoples.[52]

Regarding the quote from the Gospel of Luke (4:18–19, NRSV) that so inspired his own ministry, as we have noted, when Jesus was in the Nazareth synagogue quoting from Isaiah about God's good news to the poor, he omitted Isaiah's line hailing "the day of vengeance of our God"

50. Ateek, *Palestinian Theology*, 44–45.

51. Ateek, *Palestinian Theology*, 42.

52. Ateek, *Palestinian Theology*, 47–49.

(61:2b, NRSV). "Jesus refused to read that sentence," Ateek notes; he read the words about justice and God's liberation but "refused to call for God's vengeance on [the Jews'] non-Jewish enemies" because the words reflected racism and bigotry."[53] The prominent Catholic theologian the Rev. Richard Rohr has also noted that Jesus freely omitted objectionable Scripture texts. Rohr observes that "Jesus doesn't quote from his own Scriptures when they are punitive, imperialistic (. . .) classist, or exclusionary. In fact, he teaches the exact opposite in every case." Our task as Christians, Rohr insists, "is to imitate Jesus!"[54]

Ateek's critical exegesis of the Hebrew Scriptures concentrates on passages, ranging from the murderous to the merely exclusivist, that show God to be an angry, unloving deity—passages that Ateek says Palestinians must reject. These include the passage in Numbers (Num 33:50–53, NRSV) in which God tells Moses to instruct the Israelites to "drive out all the inhabitants of the land [of Canaan] from before you (. . .) demolish all their high places (. . .) take possession of the land and settle in it." In a passage from Deuteronomy (Deut 7:1–3, NRSV), Moses tells the Israelites that when they enter and occupy the land, "you must utterly destroy [the inhabitants]. Make no covenant with them and show them no mercy."[55] Even several familiar stories, some of which Western Christians have grown up studying and even singing about, are horrifying to the Palestinian and the Arab ear. These include Joshua's story of the battle of Jericho, which includes God's injunction to "utterly destroy all in the city" (Josh 6:21, NRSV). Similarly, as Ateek points out, it is God who inflicts disease and plagues on the Egyptians (Exod 7–12, NRSV), God who kills every firstborn male in Egypt (Exod 12:29, NRSV), and God again who totally destroys the Egyptian army (Exod 14–15, NRSV).[56]

Ateek's particular concern about these and other similar texts and his reason for condemning them, beyond the obvious fact that they justify killing and expulsion, is that they are embraced in this modern era by religiously extremist Israeli settlers and the Western Christian Zionists who support them, both of which groups enjoy strong influence on Israeli and US policy. When liberation theology's Jesus hermeneutic and love hermeneutic ask critical questions—"Do these texts reflect the spirit

53. Ateek, "Sermon: Today the Scripture is Fulfilled," 2–3.

54. Quoted in Ateek, *Palestinian Theology*, 49.

55. Ateek, *Palestinian Theology*, 49–51.

56. Ateek, *Justice and Only Justice*, 83, 197n10.

of Christ (. . .) [or] mirror and express the love of God that we have seen in Jesus Christ?"—the clear and emphatic answer is "No." The texts, Ateek asserts, reflect a primitive tribal ethics and violate everyday human morality and decency. They show God to be not simply angry but vengeful and cruel.[57]

Coming to the New Testament, Ateek focuses on passages in which he believes Jesus opens new interpretations emphasizing God's universal love. He labels these the "great revolutions" of Jesus, all having to do with love. The "first great revolution of Jesus Christ" comes from Jesus' adaptation of the Jewish faith's foundational *Shema*: in Mark 12:28–34, NRSV, when Jesus is asked by a scribe which commandment is the first, he answers by reciting the Shema: "Hear, O Israel: The Lord our God, the Lord is one; you shall love the Lord your God with all your heart, and with all your soul, and with all your mind, and with all your strength." Jesus goes on immediately—unprompted—to say, "The second is this, 'You shall love your neighbor as yourself.' There is no other commandment greater than these." Noting that the second of these commandments, which appears in Leviticus 19:18b (NRSV), had never previously been applied beyond the Jewish community, Ateek argues that Jesus' pointed linkage of the two commandments marks the first time that love of neighbor was lifted up as universal and on a par with the command to love God— signifying that love of God cannot be separated from love of neighbor. Ateek characterizes this linkage as "the first revolution" of Jesus because in Jesus incarnated, we are awakened to the reality that God loved us before we could love God, before we could know that Jesus came to save us. Moreover, we cannot love God if we do not love our neighbor. This is Ateek's "second great revolution of Jesus": Jesus laid out this dictum when he said that those who hate their brothers and sisters, whom they can see, cannot possibly love God when they cannot see God (1 John 4:20–21, NRSV). The "third great revolution," finally, is Jesus' injunction to love not only our neighbor but also our enemy, a commandment Jesus makes explicit in Matthew's Gospel (Matt 5:43–45, NRSV) and illustrates through parables such as that of the Good Samaritan (Luke 10:30–37, NRSV).[58]

The theological and political/social implications for liberation theology of Jesus' focus on love of neighbor, universal love of all humanity,

57. Ateek, *Palestinian Theology*, 51. See 49–82 for the entirety of Ateek's Hebrew Bible exegesis.

58. Ateek, *Palestinian Theology*, 83–90.

are clear and are indeed "revolutionary." This insight is essentially a declaration that, if in fact the only way to love God fully is to love all those
created in God's image and likeness, then any oppression imposed on any
human population is theologically a sin and a repudiation not only of
the commandment to love God but of God's love itself. When the *Kairos
Palestine* document was issued by the Palestinian Christian community
in December 2009 (which we will examine in more depth in Chapter 3),
it was prefaced by a categorical statement that "we Palestinian Christians
declare that the military occupation of our land is a sin against God and
humanity," and the word "sin" is repeated throughout the document.[59]

Moving forward from the "great revolutions of Jesus Christ," Ateek
observes that Jesus is shown throughout the New Testament, especially
in the gospels and in Paul's letters, rejecting exclusivity as he proclaims
that God's salvation is intended for peoples of all nations and faiths. Jesus
rejects bigotry and racism by welcoming and healing not only Jews but
also foreigners and Gentiles, and he demonstrates through his own coming that God's love is inclusive and extends to the entire world. In an
unmistakable assertion of God's love for the entire world, Jesus declares
in John's Gospel (3:16, NRSV), "For God so loved the world that he gave
his only Son, so that everyone who believes in him may not perish but
may have eternal life."[60]

Ateek also provides a detailed interpretation of Paul's epistles that
emphasizes Paul's teaching that salvation and liberation need not come
through observance of the Mosaic Law, but can now be fulfilled through
faith in Jesus Christ. Using particularly the texts of Galatians and Romans, he cites Paul's assertions that God's promise to Abraham, made
before the Law was written, passed to Jesus as Abraham's offspring (Gal
3:6–9, 16–18; Rom 4:13–17, NRSV). He also highlights the well-known
passage from Galatians (Gal 3:26, 28–29, NRSV) affirming that "in Christ
Jesus you are all children of God through faith (. . .). There is no longer
Jew or Greek, there is no longer slave or free, there is no longer male and
female; for all of you are one in Christ Jesus. And if you belong to Christ,
then you are Abraham's offspring."[61]

The importance of these passages for Palestinian liberation theology
clearly lies in their declaration of universal inclusiveness for everyone as a

---

59. See *Kairos Palestine*.

60. Ateek, *Palestinian Theology*, 90–93, 104.

61. Ateek, *Palestinian Theology*, 93–95.

loved child of God and their affirmation of God's opposition to any kind of political or religious exclusivity—opposition specifically to the notion that Jews are eternally the "elected" or the "chosen" people of God and, in particular, that this so-called election gives Israel any political or religious justification for denying Palestinian rights and erasing them from the land. These passages stand out, as some biblical commentary notes with respect to Paul's letter to the Galatians, as a "rationale for a Christianity independent of its Jewish roots."[62] In addition, of equal theological, as well as political, importance for the contemporary Palestinian perspective, the passages also stand as a direct counter to Israel's claim to be an exclusively Jewish state—a claim acted upon through Israel's actions and policies throughout the century and more of Zionism' existence and, more recently, a claim made legally through Israel's adoption in 2018 of the "Nation State Law" granting self-determination only to Jews.

Speaking emphatically of the importance of the Bible and of scriptural exegesis for Palestinian Christians, Ateek insists that Scripture is fulfilled *only* when justice and liberation are proclaimed—as Jesus said in the Nazareth synagogue—"for all the people of the land regardless of their ethnic, racial, or religious background." Fulfilling Scripture "is to take a stand for justice and to struggle and confront injustice, racism, violence, discrimination and everything that corrupts and de-humanizes people." Fulfilling Scripture is also to condemn "any misuse of scripture that justifies (. . .) the oppression of the people of the land."[63]

Liberation theology for Palestinians involves justice preeminently—a justice that arises only out of the kind of universal, inclusive love flowing between God and *all* God's people. Ateek brings his theological blueprint to a conclusion by describing a theology of *justice, reconciliation, and forgiveness*. This rubric recognizes that reconciliation can only follow a healing acknowledgement of injustice committed and that only forgiveness can complete the reconciliation process.

Envisioning the multiple dimensions of what he calls "a Palestinian liberation theology of justice," Ateek describes this theology in seven aspects that render justice complete.[64] The "theology of justice" is first one

---

62. "Letter of Paul to the Galatians," in *The New Oxford Annotated Bible*, 310.

63. Ateek, "Sermon," 4.

64. Ateek, *Palestinian Theology*, 119–21.

of *justice with love*: the two qualities are inseparable, involving relationships defined by respect for the "other" and for the rights of the "other."
Specifically in the Palestinian context, Ateek notes that love seeks the
good of the other, not its destruction, and points out that even though Zionism does not look out for the good of indigenous Palestinians, through
liberation theology Palestinians do seek justice with love, even for their
enemy. It is a theology of *justice with mercy*. Because justice can be harsh,
it must be tempered by mercy and compassion: Palestinians must seek
restoration of their rights through international law but without seeking
revenge or retaliation against their enemy. It involves *justice with truth*.
Guided by Jesus' affirmation that "You shall know the truth and the truth
will make you free" (John 8:32, NRSV), Palestinians seek to overturn the
myths and falsehoods propagated about themselves and their land that
have for so long framed a distorted picture projected to the world. As
Jesus was led in confronting the oppressors of his day, Palestinians must
be led by the knowledge that "facing, speaking, revealing, and sharing
truth is liberating."

It is a theology of *justice and security*. Because true security is
achieved only when justice is rendered, Israel's pursuit of security for
itself through the use of force, while denying justice to Palestinians, produces not security, but only hatred, a desire for revenge, and insecurity.
Justice is nonviolence: this theology rejects, and shames, violence on both
sides. Nonviolence introduces a moral context, accepts suffering without
retaliating, seeks the rehabilitation of the aggressors, respects the humanity of both oppressed and oppressor, and promotes nonviolent kinds of
resistance, including boycott, divestment, and sanctions. It is a theology
of *justice and peace*, based on the conviction that justice is the first objective and must come before peace can be achieved, and that it is the essential, and only, foundation on which peace can be built. It is ultimately a
theology of *justice, reconciliation, and forgiveness*. Healing and reconciliation—full liberation—come through a process in which attitudes change,
injustice inflicted is acknowledged, and forgiveness is granted.

Echoing the mid-1990s South African Truth and Reconciliation
process, which helped bring justice and healing after South Africa's
apartheid system ended, Ateek imagines a "peace circle" that begins with
the doing of justice—nonviolently, supported by international law, and
rendered with mercy. This process brings peace, which in turn produces

security for both peoples, which then opens the way to forgiveness and reconciliation, which finally leads to healing.[65]

Liberation theology is about universal love—love of God, love from God, love of neighbor, love and equality among humanity. Theologically speaking, liberation is freedom from sin—sin committed and sin imposed. Put another way, liberation comes when sinner and sinned against have reconciled, when acknowledgement of sin and forgiveness have been exchanged. Full liberation comes when injustice is acknowledged and forgiveness is offered and received; at this point, Ateek says, "both parties are set free. The forgiver is set free from the burden of revenge, and the forgiven is set free from guilt."[66]

Liberation is freedom both to live and to love God and humanity. Fifty years ago, Gustavo Gutiérrez wrote that the fullness of liberation, which he called a "free gift from Christ," is "communion with God and with other human beings"; to sin "is to refuse to love one's neighbors and, therefore, the Lord." From this liberation, Gutiérrez wrote, a "new humankind and a qualitatively different society" will emerge—a vision of such fundamental transformation that simply imagining it reveals the scale of the change required and provides an understanding of what "is at stake in our times." What is at stake, everywhere, is nothing short of salvation founded on a radical transformation of humanity, a transformation that is in turn founded on love. As framed by Gutiérrez in his Latin American theological context, this must be a thoroughgoing change of society—including transformation at all levels, of sinners and sinned against—in which humanity's life together is altered qualitatively. It becomes a transformation in which everyone in society rejects the selfish turn inward upon the self and moves instead to openness and a going outside of the self in love. Society thus becomes broadly integrated in true community and mutual love. This becomes true reconciliation.[67]

For Palestinians and Palestinian liberation theology, the envisioned reconciliation and liberation will involve a similar theological and human process and, ultimately, a radical transformation of society, Israeli as well as Palestinian. Universal love is key here, as it is for the Latin American theology. Love and justice are inextricably linked: when we love God, we cannot but love our neighbors as well and do justice to them; conversely,

65. Ateek, *Palestinian Theology*, 122–23.
66. Ateek, *Palestinian Theology*, 121.
67. Gutiérrez, *Theology*, 24–25.

when love is missing, justice is also absent.[68] For all Palestinians, both Christian and Muslim, what "is at stake in our times," as Gutiérrez framed it, is very basically continued Palestinian existence, as a whole people and a coherent nation, practicing differing faiths but possessing a common inclusive heritage: a common culture, language, attachment to a territorial locus, and an ethnicity rooted in these commonalities and in love of each other. The vision of living as one people free from oppression is the same for Palestinian Christians as for all other Palestinians and takes on added significance and spiritual vibrancy because the land where this freedom is sought is the very land of Christianity's birth.

For Israeli Jews, this Palestinian liberation theology vision of living together in reconciliation would mean sharing the land, not exercising singular political control over it and over its inhabitants, but relinquishing exclusivity and recognizing human diversity: recognizing the importance, and the healing grace, of accommodating the equal presence of Muslims and Christians along with Jews, as well as the right of all to political and social equality. The challenge before everyone in Palestine-Israel, Ateek believes, is for people of all three faiths to establish a new relationship to the land: all achieving "a full expression of our religious life by sharing the land" because all are equal beings and equally loved.[69] The similarity of this vision to Gustavo Gutiérrez's vision of liberation through "communion with God and with other human beings," leading to "a new humankind and a qualitatively different society," is striking and testifies to the universality of love and of liberation. This vision is indeed the vision of liberation theology everywhere.

To the secular ear, talk of "love" may sound soft and sentimental, and highly impractical. But in fact love is a concept at the heart of a great many, if not most, critical justice struggles. Martin Luther King Jr. spoke often about love during the civil rights struggle. "When Jesus bids us to love our enemies," he said, "he is speaking of neither *eros* [romantic love] nor *philia* [friendship]; he is speaking of *agape*, understanding and creative, redemptive goodwill for all people." Believing that "power without love is reckless and abusive," King said that "power at its best is love implementing the demands of justice, and justice at its best is power correcting everything that stands against love."

68. Ateek, *Palestinian Theology*, 41.
69. Ateek, "Biblical Perspectives," 115.

Love is a universal concept. Mahatma Gandhi, a Hindu, saw no division between the practical and the spiritual, believing that each must be infused with the other, and he maintained that "power based on love is a thousand times more effective and permanent than [power] derived from fear and punishment." Malcolm X, an American Black civil rights leader and a Muslim—a contemporary of Martin Luther King who often disagreed with King on tactics—believed essentially the same thing about the power and the importance of love. "We need more light about each other," he said. "Light creates understanding, understanding creates love, love creates patience, and patience creates unity. How can anyone be against love? (. . .). Love transcends just the physical. Love is disposition, behavior, attitude, thoughts, likes, dislikes."

To a considerable extent, the intersectionality of today's diverse movement for social justice—the raised consciousness that motivates struggles against racism, colonialism, social privilege, and that drives cooperation and solidarity among groups struggling for justice—is guided by same transcendent love that past heroes of struggle have spoken of. Bill McKibben, public intellectual and preeminent climate activist, was asked a few years ago about what an interviewer saw as the "religious" tone of his most recent, very secular book, *Falter: Has the Human Game Begun to Play Itself Out?*, and he spoke of love in response: "For me, questions about being human come down to questions about human solidarity. Another name for solidarity is love." He said he believes that the "hyper-individualism" so prevalent everywhere on the planet has led to rising inequality everywhere and to a sense among the most powerful that they "have no need for solidarity with the rest of us." Solidarity—love—is the only thing, he feels, that builds social movements and can rescue humanity and the planet.[70]

Love at its fullest is liberation; ultimately, it can be transformation.

70. Heim, "Bill McKibben," 30–33.

3

Palestine's Christians
Theology Crying Out

*In the land of our Holy One, today the waiting of Holy Saturday is still felt.
Leading up to this day, we are still on our own way of the cross—crucified by
the combination of oppressive state power, the lack of courage of the world's
religious leaders, and those who claim Christianity but have forgotten the
faithful here in the land. We, like Jesus, have been on a painful journey—we
have experienced the Nakba, the taking of Jerusalem, occupation, apartheid,
and blockade. We have lost so many along this journey. And today we are still
trapped by COVID-19. Waiting. We don't know what tomorrow will bring.*

—OMAR HARAMY, Director, Sabeel Jerusalem[1]

*We (. . .) cry out from within the suffering in our country, under
Israeli occupation, with a cry of hope in the absence of all hope,
a cry full of prayer and faith in a God ever vigilant, in God's
divine providence for all the inhabitants of this land.*

—*KAIROS PALESTINE*[2]

1. Haramy, Prayer at Sabeel Holy Saturday Service.
2. *Kairos Palestine*, Introduction.

Justice is nailed to the cross every day in Palestine.

—NAIM ATEEK[3]

THE STORY DOES NOT end with Sabeel. Sabeel itself has continued its work, as have many long-established Palestinian Christian ministries. Many newer Palestinian Christian organizations have emerged to take up the prophetic work that Naim Ateek and Sabeel began in that symbolic Pentecost time in the 1990s. But the struggle is heartbreakingly difficult. Throughout these decades, as Palestinian Christians speaking Truth have gained in strength and unified purpose, publicizing the Palestinian Christian plight more broadly, the Israeli Power they confront has grown immeasurably in military strength, in numbers of extremist adherents inside Israel and abroad, in influence with, and military and political support from, the United States. "Justice is nailed to the cross every day" in Palestine, and the times are dark. Little support comes from the institutional church.

Palestinians are living in a time of "Sad Friday" or "Sorrowful Friday," as Good Friday is called in Arabic. "When one looks deeply into the lives of Palestinians," Ateek says,

> it is possible to see the crosses many people are carrying—the cross of the loss of their right to live in the city of their birth; the cross of becoming homeless because of the demolition of their homes; the cross which people carry when their land is confiscated and their property taken; and the crosses of humiliation and degradation which many people have to carry daily. Finally, there is the slow, creeping pressure of the Wall [the massive Separation Wall built by Israel inside Palestinian West Bank territory] leading to suffocation of villages trapped by it. Many Palestinians continuously live through the events of Good Friday. Their way of the cross has been long and harsh. Their journey of suffering seems endless and full of despair.[4]

As they wait from Sad Friday through Holy Saturday, Omar Haramy notes, speaking again, as above, at a Holy Saturday service in the uncertain time of waiting, "Jesus is in the grave, in the darkness of the tomb. He was not breathing. His spirit had left his body. These themes of

3. Quoted in Davies, "Longtime Friends," 6.
4. Sabeel, *Contemporary Way of the Cross*, 5.

pain, devastation, waiting, gathering, breath, death, and spirit are inter-twined." Solidarity and loving care are also intertwined. The believers in Jesus in those early days "came together to wait," Haramy says, "because they knew it was not good to wait alone. They wanted to be surrounded by their community, to care for one another. Following their example, in the face of catastrophe—of apartheid and pandemic—we respond by cultivating a community of care, worshipping together."[5] In the same spirit, Archbishop Atallah Hanna, the only Palestinian serving as a Greek Orthodox archbishop, preached of love and hope on Easter Sunday 2021. Inspired, he said, by the feast of the resurrection, he tells Palestinians, "Fear not, never surrender, and refuse to be forced into frustration, des-peration, and hopelessness. Keep up your morals high, your will strong, and love each other. Reject all divisions and be united in defending our cause, the cause of all free men and women in our world (. . .). This is the Day the Lord has made."[6]

Easter, with its message of hope, has always carried special meaning for Palestinian Christians. As Samia Khoury, a theological colleague of Naim Ateek and co-founder of Sabeel, has written, the greatest sacrifice occurs with Jesus' crucifixion, and "the maximum possibility of hope is derived from the empty tomb. *Al Masseeh Qam. Haqqan Qam!* That is how we greet each other on Easter Sunday. Christ has risen; He has risen indeed."[7] After the darkness and uncertain waiting of Holy Saturday, Easter's images—of the tomb now empty, of Jesus present with his follow-ers, of Jesus still bearing wounds but walking on this very land with those who suffer—are immensely important for Palestinians.

"The image of the suffering Christ is unique, and key to the Chris-tian faith," Sabeel writes. "The God who experienced and overcame

> the physical and psychological pain of oppression, torture and execution is a source of great hope and strength to those who continue to suffer today (. . .). For us the image of the cross with its affliction and pain, and Jesus' response of gentleness, non-violence, and ultimately resurrection, is one of comfort and in-spiration. As Christ himself identified with the suffering people and called on his followers to reach out to them in their need,

5. Haramy, Prayer.

6. Hanna, "Easter Reflection."

7. Khoury, *Memoir*, 111.

we too invite our brothers and sisters in Christ across the world
to join us as we search for God in the midst of our affliction.[8]

The unique intimacy of the connection between Jesus' experience of
suffering and the Palestinian Christians' experience of suffering is both
a particular source of pain for Palestinians and a special source of solace and expectation. The knowledge that they carry their personal and
collective crosses in the very land where Jesus carried his cross—that
he suffers with them in a continual "Sad Friday" and that they wait for
rescue and liberation in the darkness and liminality of a "Holy Saturday"
reality—creates a spiritual bond, with Jesus and with each other, that is at
once unbearably painful and also "unspeakably joyful" and comforting,
as Black theologian Barbara Holmes would have it. Messages of suffering and of hope, always recalling themes of pain and waiting, as well as
of solace, are preached among Palestinians not only at Easter, the most
important holy day in the Christian calendar, but throughout the year.
The themes are a paradox, are indeed what liberation theology is about:
despair and hope, suffering and redemption living intertwined in the
hearts of Palestinian Christians and of all Palestinians.

The particular mission of Sabeel, as Omar Haramy has indicated,
is to cultivate and sustain a sense of community among Palestinian
Christians and to reach out for support from Christians around the
world—creating a community of care, of love, of worship. Among Sabeel's projects is the organization of several contextual Bible study groups
in Arabic for Palestinian Christians. Sabeel supports more than thirty of
these groups throughout the West Bank and in Israel, designed to teach
and interpret the rich biblical tradition in the Hebrew Scriptures and the
New Testament, as well as talk about the problematic passages in these
texts. The intent is also, and in particular, to educate Christians in their
struggle for freedom by pointing to biblical teachings on justice, truth,
and nonviolence. For its local and international followers, Sabeel maintains contact through a weekly prayer service in English, now online, and
simultaneously issues a global "Wave of Prayer." This is a prayer ministry
addressing local and regional events of concern; the expectation is that,
as communities lift these concerns in prayer at noon on the same day
in time zones around the world, a "wave of prayer" will wash over the
world. Sabeel also educates the faithful for nonviolent resistance through
an advocacy initiative called *Kumi Now* (Rise Up Now), which connects

8. Sabeel, *Contemporary Way of the Cross*, 3.

with over sixty Palestinian, non-Zionist Israeli, and international secular and religious organizations that work to keep Palestine and Palestinian identity—both its Muslim and its Christian identity—alive. These initiatives are designed to organize and inspire Palestinian Christians in areas where the church has failed spiritually and concretely.[9]

Beyond these organizational initiatives, as we will see, a younger generation of Palestinian Christian clergy and lay educators and activists has arisen in recent decades to continue spreading the story of Palestine and the theology of liberation. A new generation of indigenous Palestinian church leaders—who identify directly with Jesus Christ as a Palestinian himself who lived under foreign occupation—has also emerged to succeed the generations of Europeans who formerly led local church hierarchies and who, however caring their ministry, were essentially foreign colonialist administrators. New activists are born every day: secular and religious, Muslim and Christian, with a raised consciousness of the critical role that each individual, and the Palestinian community together, play in maintaining the character and the very existence of the Palestinian people as a nation. Palestinian political divisions remain, political leadership is crippled, its inertia still disappoints. But the struggle for justice and freedom continues through the people's resilience; their nonviolent resistance; their social and political justice work; their determination to maintain *sumud*, steadfastness, in the face of Israel's efforts to erase Palestine and the Palestinian people.

Although much of the Western institutional church remains dismayingly aloof from Palestinian concerns, Palestine solidarity networks have arisen in many Protestant denominations to work with and support the Palestinian struggle and to educate church members and leaders about the Palestinian plight—speaking *to* although not *for* their denominations. Sabeel itself has established "Friends of Sabeel" solidarity organizations in many countries that spread the message abroad; in the United States, FOSNA, Friends of Sabeel North America, works energetically not only to educate about the Palestinians but to link the Palestinian struggle intersectionally with other social justice struggles, such as Black Lives Matter, and also to counter the destructive influence of American Christian Zionists. Sabeel also has "Friends" organizations in Canada and in the UK and several other European countries.

9. Much of this information is taken from the Sabeel publication *Cornerstone*, no. 83 (Summer 2021). For more on *KumiNow* activities, see KumiNow website.

Perhaps most importantly, in December 2009 Palestinian Christian leaders, including bishops, clergy, and lay people, overcame long-standing divisions among the multiple Eastern and Western Christian denominations represented in Jerusalem and elsewhere in Palestine, to speak out together in one united, genuinely Palestinian voice through the *Kairos Palestine* document. This seminal document—*A Moment of Truth: A Word of Faith, Hope and Love from the Heart of Palestinian Suffering*—speaks the Truth of injustices facing Palestinians to the Power of governments, particularly Israel's, as well as of churches and the international community, which have for so long ignored Palestine. The *Kairos Palestine* group of authors has established an international movement, the "*Kairos* for Global Justice Coalition," to work with churches and other Christian organizations in the hope of gaining broad support for the Palestinian struggle from Christians throughout the world. The leaders who signed *Kairos Palestine* over a decade ago also issued a second, tenth-anniversary document restating the plea for justice. We will examine these seminal documents more deeply later in this chapter.

Palestinian Christians call themselves the "living stones," in contrast with the hard stones of churches and memorials honoring Jesus Christ. The term recalls Jesus' remark upon entering Jerusalem, when the Pharisees told him to silence the disciples singing his praises; the Gospel of Luke cites Jesus as responding, "I tell you, if these were silent, the stones would shout out" (Luke 19:40, NRSV). Palestinian Christians are those stones shouting out today—the living, breathing inheritors bearing witness to Jesus' legacy in the land of his birth. As we have seen, Christians native to Palestine have been a presence there since the days of Jesus and his first followers. With Palestinians of all faiths, they make up Palestine's indigenous population, descended without interruption from all the peoples and conquerors who have lived in and traversed Palestine through the ages.

Almost every Palestinian Christian meeting a Westerner ignorant of Palestinian history has been asked, "When did you convert?" and they are forced to explain that, as Latin Patriarch Emeritus Michel Sabbah has said, "We were all born here in Jerusalem on the day of Pentecost." Originally, he says, "We spoke the same language as Jesus—Syriac or Aramaic (. . .). Then we spoke Greek, with the Byzantine Roman empire. Then we spoke Arabic after the Muslim Arab conquest" in the seventh century. Contrary to the widespread impression that all Palestinian Arabs are Muslim, Sabbah, the first native Palestinian Roman Catholic leader in Palestine, emphasizes that Christian Palestinian history is the history of all Palestinians, whether Christian, Muslim, or indigenous Jew. Many of today's Muslims are descended from the same Syriac and Greek Christians who converted to Islam centuries ago. "The history of each is the history of all because all Palestinians belong to all of Palestine."[10]

Although in modern times Palestinian Christians have always been an important part of Palestine's business, professional, education, and scholarly communities, they have long comprised only a small minority among the overall Palestinian population, probably since the advent of Islam. Their proportion of that population, moreover, has fallen steadily over the last century and more—in part because of a higher Muslim birth rate, but primarily because Christians have been emigrating at a high rate. When a new nationalist consciousness began to arise in Palestine during the last days of the Ottoman Empire in the early twentieth century, Christians were prominent among delegates to Ottoman legislative assemblies and were among the founders and editors of newly emerging newspapers and political journals. But emigration had already begun on a sizable scale. Large numbers of both Christian and Muslim Palestinians emigrated to North and South America for commercial reasons during the late Ottoman years and also to escape Ottoman conscription during World War I. Christians, who were subject to conscription along with Muslims, were additionally drawn to the "new world" by the rising popularity and marketability of crafts such as olive wood carvings from the Holy Land. Some estimates are that more than 10 percent of Palestine's Christians left Palestine in the decade between 1907 and 1917, and that Bethlehem, then a largely Christian town, lost half its pre-World War I population of twelve thousand in these years.[11]

Census figures from the 1920s and 1930s, when Britain controlled Palestine, indicate that the Christian proportion of the Palestinian Arab population held steady at about 11 percent, even during the period when Jewish immigration to Palestine began on a significant scale. Despite the sharp rise in Jewish immigration during these decades, which brought a significant statistical drop in the Christian proportion of Palestine's

10. Sabbah, "Future of Christian Palestinians."
11. Raheb, "Palestinian Christians"

overall population of all faiths—down to about 8 percent—the balance between Christians and Muslims in the Arab population, excluding Jews, remained consistently at 11 percent Christian to 89 percent Muslim through several British censuses up to the mid-1940s. Although the substantial Jewish influx through the mid-1930s provoked an increase in Palestinian Christian emigration, this steady Christian-Muslim balance indicates that Christian emigration was not so great that it was not compensated for by natural increase in the overall Palestinian population.[12]

This situation changed dramatically, however, following World War II and Israel's establishment. It is believed that more than one-third of Palestine's Christians—some estimates even double this percentage—fled the country or were expelled during the Nakba in 1948, a massive loss out of a pre-1948 population of only about one hundred thirty-five thousand. Moreover, Christians were no better able to return to their homes than were their Muslim neighbors; Israel refused to permit any but a very minimal return of Palestinians who fled during the Nakba. In the ensuing three-quarters of a century, Christian emigration has remained a common phenomenon, for a range of reasons, most related in one way or another to Israel's increased control over and restrictions on Palestinian lives.

Although Israeli propagandists have long tried to promote the notion that Christians feel threatened by Muslims, this is decidedly not the case, as we will see later. Israel's restrictive policies and human rights violations, which impact Christians and Muslims equally, are the primary impetus for Christian emigration. Many Palestinians of both faiths resettled in Jordan and the Gulf Arab states during the early post-Nakba years, helping to build those young states. Additional numbers of Christians emigrated after Israel captured the remaining portions of Palestine in 1967. Christians are more easily able to emigrate than their usually rural Muslim compatriots, primarily because Christians have the financial resources to move and their commercial enterprises transfer more readily to new locations than do rural enterprises. As a result, they are readier to leave Palestine when Israeli restrictions make life difficult. As Christians, they also more easily fit in with North and South American cultures.[13]

12. Statistics in this paragraph compiled from various sources, including McCarthy, "Population," 325; Raheb, "Palestinian Christians"; and *Survey of Palestine*, 140–44. Tables on these pages show British Mandate figures for Muslim, Christian, and Jewish populations from six censuses between 1922 and 1944.

13. Ateek, "Israeli Occupation and Theological Thinking"; Raheb, "Palestinian Christians"; and Cook, "Palestinian Christians," 4–5.

Overall, the Palestinian Christian population between the Jordan River and the Mediterranean probably amounts now to little more than 2 percent of the total population of about fourteen million, including all faiths. A survey conducted by the Rev. Mitri Raheb, a long-established Lutheran pastor born and raised in Bethlehem who founded Dar al-Kalima University in that city, put that percentage at 1.7 percent as of late 2019.[14] Although it is difficult to arrive at a precise total of Palestinian Christians because overall estimates vary and concentrations of Christians vary according to particular areas, the true total is probably something under two hundred thousand. Whatever the variations, the number is strikingly low.

Inside Israel, where Palestinian Arabs make up 21 percent of the total population, Palestinian Christians are said to number about one hundred twenty thousand—6 percent of the total of Palestinian citizens, but just over 1 percent of the total population of Jews and Palestinians. Best estimates of Christians in the West Bank are around fifty thousand.[15]

14. Raheb, "Palestinian Christians."

15. Palestinian towns that had been traditionally Christian, such as Bethlehem and Ramallah in the West Bank, were emptied of a large proportion of their Christian populations in the wake of the Nakba. One demographic study indicates that, in the first decade and a half after Israel's creation, even before its capture of the West Bank, large numbers of Christians left that area, emigrating probably primarily from these two historically Christian towns. Emigration in those early years brought the Christian West Bank population down from forty-two thousand six hundred to twenty-nine thousand four hundred in the mid-1960s, a drop of about 30 percent. In Bethlehem, according to one source, Christians numbered eight thousand before Israel's creation and made up 85 percent of the town's population; the remaining 15 percent were Muslims. Today, those proportions have been reversed, Christians now accounting for only 15 percent and numbering seven thousand—fewer than their total when Israel was established. The situation is similar in the other historically Christian town of Ramallah, said to have been settled several centuries ago by seven brothers and their progeny, but the city and its suburbs are now largely Muslim. Not only have Christians emigrated from Bethlehem and Ramallah, but in both cases the towns' Christian majorities were reduced when large numbers of Muslims expelled by Israel from the coastal towns of Lydda and Ramle in a major ethnic cleansing operation in July 1948 were forced to walk great distances out of territory that became Israel and into the West Bank. Today, Palestinian Christian émigrés from Bethlehem, Ramallah, and several small neighboring towns like Beit Jala and Bir Zeit live in numerous large clusters throughout the United States and South America, altogether numbering in the tens and perhaps hundreds of thousands. There is some sense of Palestinian nationalism among these clusters of Bethlehemites and Ramallites, as they call themselves, but these Christians are essentially lost to Palestine and the land of Christianity's birth; the majority are probably likely to remain in the Americas even if Israel's occupation ends. These population clusters tend to be fairly insular, most often marrying within

Gaza's two million-plus population includes only about one thousand Christians. In East Jerusalem, where Palestinians have an anomalous status imposed by Israel that differs from that of Palestinians in the other occupied territories and also from that of Palestinian Israelis who are citizens, a recent estimate places the number of Palestinian Christians at about sixteen thousand; it is possible that this estimate includes foreign Christians who are not Palestinian.[16]

Palestinian Christians belong to a multitude of denominations, which are generally grouped into four principal church communities or "families": Eastern Orthodox, a separate group of Oriental Orthodox, Catholic, and Protestant. The Greek Orthodox Church is the largest in numbers of faithful and is the leading sect in the Eastern Orthodox family, which also includes other sects such as Russian and Rumanian Orthodox. A Greek Orthodox patriarch resides in Jerusalem and shares guardianship of the Church of the Holy Sepulchre with two other Christian denominations. The Oriental Orthodox family of churches includes, principally, the Armenian Orthodox, as well as Coptic Orthodox and Syrian or Syriac Orthodox. Each of these has a patriarch or archbishop situated in Jerusalem.[17]

The third family of churches is led by the Latin or Roman Catholics, whose patriarch is in Jerusalem, and it includes the Melkite or Greek Catholic church and the Maronites, both of which are in union with the Vatican and have an archbishop in Jerusalem. In addition, this family also includes Armenian, Syrian, and Chaldean Catholics. Finally, the Protestant churches include Anglicans and Lutherans, each led by a bishop or archbishop in Jerusalem. There are also numerous smaller Protestant denominations, including among others Baptists, Methodists, and Church of Scotland Presbyterians.[18]

The Christian depopulation over the last century and more is clearly a cause of great concern among local Christian leaders and the remaining Christian population itself. Not without reason, one hears frequent dire predictions of the total demise of Christianity in the very land of its

the group; their loyalties are more tribal than national; and they have lost most ties to Palestine. See Raheb, "Palestinian Christians"; Cook, "Palestinian Christians," 4–5; and Christison, *The Wound of Dispossession*, 102–23.

16. Cook, "Palestinian Christians," 12; Raheb, "Palestinian Christians"; and *Wikipedia*, "Demographic History of Jerusalem."

17. Kassis, *Kairos for Palestine*, 64–65.

18. Kassis, *Kairos for Palestine*, 64–65.

birth and warnings of the "museumification" of the Holy Land.[19] There is
some reason to hope, however, that the galvanization of Christian ener-
gies over the last few decades may be helping to slow the pace of emigration by inspiring multiple generations of Palestinian Christians to join
the *sumud* (steadfastness) struggle and continue nonviolent resistance.
It is important to note that Christians still play a key role in education
and medical care: several schools at all educational levels run by local
Christian churches still, as they have for decades, serve Muslim as well as
Christian students, and the local Lutheran and Anglican denominations
operate key hospitals and clinics in East Jerusalem and in Gaza. Furthermore, developments since the 1990s—including the formulation of a Palestinian liberation theology and establishment of Sabeel as a liberation
theology center; the continuing creation of new educational institutions
such as Dar al-Kalima University in Bethlehem; the rise of a new generation of local Christian leaders eager to spread the gospel to Palestinians
at home and broadcast the message of Palestinian Christianity abroad;
the adoption and issuance of major unified statements of principle such
as *Kairos Palestine* and its follow-up pronouncements; and the rise of
small but dedicated solidarity groups in a few Western churches—all are
having some effect in energizing and reassuring Palestinian Christians,
enfolding them in a broad community of care and compassion that can
be faith-restoring and hope-generating.

Latin Patriarch Emeritus Michel Sabbah expresses faith that Palestinian Christians will survive because Palestinians will survive. Palestinians are united by their history: "Christians and Muslims, we belonged
and we still belong to the same people and share the same history," he
says. Christians are simply Palestinians who believe in Jesus Christ, while
today's Muslims are descended largely from early Greek Christians who
converted to Islam following the Muslim Arab conquest. They are the
same people. Jesus said, "You are the salt of the earth" (Matt 5:13, NRSV),
Sabbah points out, saying he believes Palestinian Christians will remain
a small but important "ingredient of society, just as salt is wherever it is
used (. . .). When we need numbers, we find them in the nation, with all
the citizens." The struggle, against Israel and against the United States,
which Sabbah bluntly accuses of sowing war and death throughout the
area, will depend on all Palestinians cooperating with each other, and
having resilience and faith "the size of a mustard seed," which Jesus said

19. See, for example, Wagner, "Holy Land Christians and Survival," 44.

has the strength to move mountains (Matt 17:20, NRSV).[20] Sabbah has spent decades putting hard work behind his words, striving for well over a decade after his retirement as patriarch in 2008 to keep Palestinians and Palestinian Christians building together.

Several established Palestinian Christian missions have achieved a measure of international notice and brought some broader awareness to the Palestinian situation. Probably most notable is the ministry of Melkite Greek Catholic Bishop Elias Chacour. Chacour was born in the Palestinian Christian, largely Melkite, agricultural village of Biram in upper Galilee and was expelled at the age of eight with his family when Israeli forces took over the village in 1948 and drove all of its inhabitants out. Although some of the villagers fled to Lebanon, most of Biram's inhabitants were moved to a nearby village inside what became the state of Israel and ultimately received Israeli citizenship. Village elders struggled through legal means for years to obtain permission to return to their town and homes, and their repeated appeals to the Israeli High Court met with success. But, whenever villagers attempted actually to return, despite having legal approval, they were rebuffed by Israeli military forces. Because Biram was located very near the Israeli border with Lebanon, the Israelis assumed it would provide easy entry for cross-border infiltrators, so wanted it empty. In 1953, five years after the initial expulsion, Israeli forces actually bombed the village in air and artillery attacks, in order to forestall further attempts by villagers to return; only the local church was left standing. A nearby Christian village, Iqrit, met the same fate as Biram: although not as close to the border, Israeli forces expelled Iqrit's inhabitants in 1948 and several years later blew up every home in the village. Inhabitants from both villages and their descendants have continued their efforts to return for seventy-five years, but with no success.[21]

Elias Chacour himself thus grew up in exile, not from the land of Palestine like so many Palestinian refugees but from his native village. After showing an early inclination toward a vocation to the priesthood, he entered a seminary in Nazareth as a young teenager, later studied theology in Paris, and continued academic work in ancient languages

20. Sabbah, "The Future of Christian Palestinians."

21. Chacour's own story and that of the village of Biram are recounted in his autobiography. See Chacour, *Blood Brothers*.

and biblical studies at Hebrew University in Jerusalem, becoming the
first Palestinian to earn a degree there. Ordained in his mid-twenties, he
served a church in yet another Melkite village in northern Israel, Ibillin,
for decades before being named archbishop. During his years in Ibillin, he
worked to revive many fading Christian communities in northern Israel,
restoring churches, building schools and community centers, bringing
medical assistance and other services to underserved towns and villages.

Throughout his life and ministry, Chacour has striven to be a peacemaker, struggling against the disunity he found among Palestine's Christian communities, against the church's general neglect of Palestinian
Christianity, against the militancy of armed Palestinian guerrilla groups,
against the anti-Palestinian discrimination and prejudice he has found
and personally faced throughout the world, and against the "destructive,
oppressive force" Zionism has inflicted on his Palestinian people. Along
the way, his activism has gained him some renown, and brought the Palestinian Christian situation to greater attention throughout the world.[22]

Another Palestinian Christian mission that is helping raise awareness of the Christian situation internationally, in a very different way,
is the Tent of Nations. Calling itself an "educational and environmental
family farm," Tent of Nations reaches out both to local Palestinians and
to visitors from around the world, primarily from churches, who wish to
volunteer on the farm and witness to the conditions under which Palestinians live. Run by the Palestinian Christian Nassar family on a one
hundred-acre plot of land southwest of Bethlehem that has been privately
owned by the family for over a century, Tent of Nations sees its mission
as "building bridges between people, and between people and the land."
Brothers Daoud and Daher Nassar run the farm on land inherited from
forebears who have farmed it for generations. In addition to simply host-
ing visitors to tell the Palestinian story, the project works to reconnect
Palestinians to the land and promote environmental preservation. It runs
work camps throughout the year to teach volunteers to help with harvests
and on other projects. There are also children's educational programs
during the school year and children's camps in summer, as well as projects to educate and empower Palestinian women, all designed to better
connect Palestinians to the land of Palestine.[23]

22. Chacour, *Blood Brothers*, especially 114 for the quote about Zionism. See also
Chacour, *We Belong to the Land*.

23. See Tent of Nations website and its several subsites.

Tent of Nations and the Nassar family have been under legal and often physical attack for years. Although the family has owned the land through Ottoman, British Mandate, Jordanian, and now Israeli regimes, and has legal ownership documents, Israeli authorities and illegal settlers (from three Israeli settlements that surround the farm) have been attempting to force the family out since the 1990s, frequently bulldozing, burning, and otherwise vandalizing orchards, especially its olive trees. The family refuses to leave and has fought a long battle in Israeli courts to retain legal ownership. As has so often occurred in Christian villages like Biram, however, the Israeli military has ignored most legal court rulings affirming the Nassars' ownership, and Israeli settlers are lawless. The Nassars are dedicated to nonviolent resistance, noting on the Tent of Nations website that, although "faced with great injustice, we know that we should not hate, despair, or flee. We can refuse to be enemies and channel our pain and frustration into positive actions which will build a better future." Echoing a major liberation theology objective, they declare that a major goal of Tent of Nations is "to help the oppressed and marginalized realize that they are powerful. We all have a role in creating the future we want to see. At Tent of Nations, we seek to work with others to lay the foundations for a future Palestine, in the belief that justice and peace will grow from the bottom up."[24]

Working with others to build Palestine is the overriding philosophy of another Palestinian Christian organization, *Wi'am*: The Palestinian Conflict Resolution Center. A grassroots organization founded in Bethlehem in 1994 with the aim of providing psycho-social support for individuals and families enduring the stress and trauma of living under Israeli occupation, Wi'am strives in general to build community resilience by mediating disputes, reconciling personal and community differences, and building and reinforcing relationships. The organization runs education and activity programs for children, teenagers, and women of all faiths, holds children's summer camps, and conducts tours of the Bethlehem area for visitors.[25]

Wi'am is the Arabic word for "cordial relationships." The organization was founded and is run by internationally recognized nonviolence educator and mediator Zoughbi al-Zoughbi, a Palestinian Christian born and raised in Bethlehem. Zoughbi has been closely involved in

24. Tent of Nations website, and *Wikipedia*, "Tent of Nations."

25. Zoughbi and Zoughbi, "From the Chaos of Fear, Panic and Anger." Also see Wi'am website.

Bethlehem's civic life, serving on the city council, and was involved in the founding of Sabeel. Wi'am sees its major task as overcoming the social stigma in Palestinian society of seeking psychological counseling and, following this, as guaranteeing that help is available and effective. This means, as Wi'am pledges, providing "ways to uplift the people's spirits, enhance their steadfastness, and empower their resilience," teaching and demonstrating compassion and empathy toward each other.[26]

Rifat Odeh Kassis, one of the several authors of *Kairos Palestine* who later became coordinator of the *Kairos Palestine* Group, which maintains this critical document's policies and principles, has written about the difficulty of growing up a Palestinian Christian in a land under harsh Israeli occupation and wondering, like many of his co-religionists, how he could be "a good Christian and a good Palestinian at the same time," because what the institutional church offered him provided no solace for the profound difficulties he and all Palestinians were suffering. When he turned to the church as a young man seeking "answers to our misery as an occupied and oppressed people," he laments that he found "a place only for praying," not for answers. "The church had failed me (. . .) by failing to provide us with a vision and direction." Not only was the church failing Palestinians, but much of the Western church was giving "overwhelming and unquestioning support" to the Palestinians' oppressor.[27]

Kassis points to that generation of clergy newly emerging at the time of the first intifada as the ones who led to his own reconnection with the church after years of political activism: a group of younger, native Palestinian clergy who, he says, "put the people's interests at the forefront," identifying with and supporting the people's resistance to oppression and their steadfastness.[28] Several members of this generation, both clergy and lay, have worked with the *Kairos Palestine* generation especially in the last ten to twenty years to bring the situation of the forgotten Christians in Palestine to greater attention in Europe and the United States. These personalities include Alex Awad, an ordained Baptist minister and long-time professor at the Bethlehem Bible College, who has spoken about Palestine throughout the West; Jonathan Kuttab, a prominent attorney,

26. Zoughbi and Zoughbi, "From the Chaos of Fear, Panic and Anger."

27. Kassis, *Kairos for Palestine*, 18–19.

28. Kassis, *Kairos for Palestine*, 20.

writer, and speaker for Palestinian Christians, recently appointed as executive director of FOSNA in the United States; and Munther Isaac, Lutheran minister, pastor of the Christmas Lutheran Church in Bethlehem,
Dean of the Bethlehem Bible College, and author of several books, most
recently *The Other Side of the Wall: A Palestinian Christian Narrative of
Lament and Hope.*

The thesis of Isaac's book, whose title refers to the eight-meter-high
concrete Separation Wall built by Israel inside Palestinian West Bank territory, captures the heart of the existential problem that Palestinian Christians face and that indeed animates Palestinian liberation theology. In a
harsh indictment of the church, Isaac writes that Palestinian Christians,
like all Palestinians, are separated from the world, in reality as well as
metaphorically, so that a psychological barrier has always existed "in the
mind, heart, and theology of the Western church." This metaphorical wall
"has shielded [the church] from having to engage with us. Palestinians do
not exist in this theology and narrative about the land—a narrative that
chose to see an empty land and a two-thousand-year gap in history. Most
pilgrims come [to Palestine] having only learned one narrative about this
land—they see only Israel. In this version of the story, we do not exist,
or maybe we do not matter (. . .). [The wall] diminishes both our history
and our present."[29]

Another particularly prominent member of this group of Christian
spokespeople is Mitri Raheb, a Lutheran pastor and theologian from
Bethlehem. He preceded Isaac as pastor of Bethlehem's Christmas Lutheran Church and has dedicated himself to education for Palestinians,
not only writing prolifically and speaking about the Palestinian situation,
but also building a consortium of Lutheran educational institutions in
Bethlehem, including Dar al-Kalima University, open to students of all
faiths. Raheb has described growing up in Bethlehem in the 1960s and
1970s in a relatively small-town, close-knit culture: religion in a town
like this, he writes, creates an intimate bond, even between Christians
and Muslims, essentially because suffering is community-wide and everyone is involved. Returning in the late 1980s from years of study in
Germany, where he read German Lutheran theologians whom he found
to be deeply enriching in their rational and dialectic approach, Raheb
began his ministry as the first intifada was breaking out and discovered
that, unlike the rational approach of the German theologians, theology

29. Isaac, *Other Side*, 18.

for Palestinians is more emotional, formulated from the heart and sometimes on the street. It is contextual. The cross is a highly symbolic part of
this emotional, heart-centered theology, regarded by Muslims as well as
by Christians as a "paradigm for Palestinian suffering."[30]

Raheb has now been preaching, writing, participating in activism,
and "listening to where people are" for years, focusing his theology on the
cross and its particular meaning for Palestinians, seeking answers to such
questions as why there is so profound a correlation between the cross and
the Palestinian struggle, both for Christians and for Muslims. He also
writes about why Muslims, especially poets and artists, are so attached to
the cross and seem to find a special message in it. Raheb is awed by the
knowledge that, as he puts it, "there is something very deep, something
very existential in the cross that connects it to the struggle of our Palestinian people." He has written multiple books through the years as he
has delved into this "something"—this deep, existential connection—that
links the cross on which Jesus suffered and died with the contemporary
cross that Palestinians bear, individually and collectively, every day.[31]

Raheb has arrived at a theology that is intriguing in its originality.
It is a theology that in significant ways focuses less on the people—on
Palestinians themselves and their forebears—than on Palestine itself. He
describes the history of Palestine as a continuum from earliest biblical
times and in fact sees all the peoples of Palestine as themselves existing in
a continuum. The people, forged from a heritage spanning several millennia and encompassing a diversity of ethnicities and religions, have virtually always lived under occupation by one imperial power or another but
have never fully succumbed—always resisting, always understanding the
impermanence of empire, never forming an empire themselves. Because
of their long belief in one God, the people of Palestine have always, Raheb
maintains, been able to see that "there is something more powerful than
the empire," a necessary dose of skepticism that leads to a questioning
of empire: "God questions the omnipotence of the empire," and so do
God's people. Equally and perhaps more important, "seeing God on the
other side of the empire" challenges empire's morality, which weakens
it. Faith in God, he says, thus "becomes a strong factor in mobilizing

30. Raheb and Henderson, *Cross in Contexts*, 5–7.

31. Raheb and Henderson, *Cross in Contexts*, 5–7. Although Raheb names Jürgen
Moltmann as one of the several "rational" German theologians whom he studied during his years in Germany, he does not seem to link Moltmann's theology of the cross,
discussed in Chapter 1, with his own.

people against the empire," even to the point of sacrificing their lives if need be. Raheb sees the long and continuing reality in Palestine of this prevailing faith in God as the reason the Bible emerged from Palestine rather than from an empire somewhere else, and as the reason the three monotheistic religions took root in Palestine. "It is, in fact, this context of ongoing oppression, of forever living in the shadow of the empire, that brought about the birth of both Judaism and Christianity, and across the sea, Islam."[32] God is always present with the oppressed and disadvantaged because they are always seeking God.

Moreover, Raheb continues, without God, Palestine would never have become a central player in history; without God, Palestine would always have been of peripheral importance. But, "the moment God identified [Godself] with this land, everything changed. Who would have heard of the Jordan River if it were not part of the salvation history? And who would have heard of [Raheb's] hometown, the little town called Bethlehem (. . .)?" In Palestine, he says, there has always been the possibility, as empires have come and gone, of a new beginning after defeat and disaster, because God has always been steadfast, "showing solidarity and choosing to share [the people's] destiny." Ultimately, "Jesus revealed this God on the cross, in a situation of terrible agony and pain (. . .). The people of Palestine could then say with great certainty: 'For we do not have a high priest who is unable to sympathize with our weaknesses, but we have one who in every respect has been tested as we are' (Heb 4:15)." God is very personal in Raheb's telling—always there through the ages, "almost interchangeable with his people," present with them in defeat, through exile, through destruction. Whereas God might be gloriously visible elsewhere, the people of Palestine have been gifted with "the ability to spot God where no one else was able to see [God]" and, Raheb believes, in places where one would not expect God to be—without the glorious trappings of empire, in those places of defeat and sorrow. Raheb quotes Paul's paean to the power of the cross (1 Cor 1:21–24, NRSV): "For since, in the wisdom of God, the world did not know God through wisdom, God decided, through the foolishness of our proclamation, to save those who believe. For Jews demand signs and Greeks desire wisdom, but we proclaim Christ crucified, a stumbling block to Jews and

---

32. Raheb, *Faith in the Face of Empire*, 70–74, 85–86.

foolishness to Gentiles, but to those who are the called, both Jews and
Greeks, Christ the power of God and the wisdom of God."[33]

It is from this concept of the crucified Christ as signifying the power
of God in suffering that Raheb draws his symbolism of Palestine as "a
land on the cross" and its people, all its people throughout the ages, as
also on the cross. This is the context, he says, in which the Bible was written and the context in which Palestinians exist today. This reality is the
reason, he believes, that so many Muslim artists focus on the cross when
depicting Palestine. Jesus shares the Palestinian story and its destiny. In
Jesus, "we see ourselves; in his pain we feel our pain. In his wounds we
recognize our wounds." In the triumph of the cross and resurrection,
because these events occurred in Palestine, there is hope—great hope
particularly for Palestine, as well as for everyone.[34] In a concluding essay
in their book, *The Cross in Contexts*, Raheb and his colleague, theologian
Suzanne Watts Henderson, quote priest and mystic Cynthia Bourgeault's
belief that, significantly, hope is "a quality of aliveness" arising not from
a happy outcome, but "*at the beginning, as a pulse of truth that sends us
forth.*" They themselves conclude that the cross is one of these pulsating
symbols of hope. It is "a symbol not of tragedy but of hope, not of death
but of life," they say. It is also "a dialogue between first-century Palestine
and the Palestine of today," a sign that God is in the midst of the marginalized and silenced.[35]

Because Palestinian Christians themselves, and the role they play in
Palestinian society, their indigeneity, indeed their very existence, are so
widely misunderstood in the West, it is no surprise that the relationship
of these Christians with their Muslim compatriots is also profoundly
misunderstood. Most Westerners, including church leaders, who even
bother to think about Middle Eastern Christians tend to think that
Christians throughout the region are oppressed by Muslims and treated
as a kind of unwelcome alien implant. Israeli propagandists and many
anti-Muslim propagandists tend to promote this fiction. But in Palestine, it is no exaggeration to say that relations between Christians and

33. Raheb, *Faith in the Face of Empire*, 87–89.

34. Raheb and Henderson, *The Cross in Contexts*, 16–18, 119.

35. Raheb and Henderson, *Cross in Contexts*, 141–45. The quote from Cynthia
Bourgeault appears on 141. Emphasis added.

Muslims have been generally stable and amicable for centuries. Occasional interfaith tensions arise, and in recent years both Christian and Muslim Palestinians have been deeply concerned about the rise of radical Islamist groups like ISIS, operating militarily in Iraq and Syria. But it is safe to say that, with regard to Palestine, whatever Christian-Muslim tensions arise are no more serious, and in fact may be less serious, than the periodic differences among the several Christian denominations in Jerusalem, or the differences in Judaism between, for instance, Orthodox and Conservative denominations.

As Michel Sabbah has noted, all Palestinians, Christian and Muslim, share a common history; Christians are simply Palestinians who happen to believe in Jesus Christ. Palestinian Muslim anthropologist Ali Qleibo reaffirms this commonality, noting that people of the two faiths share a common heritage, and have for centuries. Some call it a "blood bond," he says[36]—something that may exaggerate the closeness of interfaith ties at the institutional level, but is not an exaggeration at personal levels. Christian-Muslim intermarriage is not uncommon, especially in cities and towns where people of both faiths live in the same neighborhoods and mix easily. Even in smaller villages with Christian populations, people of both faiths live intermingled and engage in common community activities and close personal interaction. In the village of Aboud near Ramallah, for instance, which dates back to Roman times, Muslims and Christians participate in each other's weddings and religious celebrations. Such interaction is common in many villages. During the Muslim holy month of Ramadan, Christian villagers help prepare the community *iftar*, the meal after sundown that breaks each day's fast, and Christians traditionally prepare breakfast before sunrise for their Muslim neighbors before they begin the daily fast. Christian and Muslim women occasionally act as wet nurses for each other's infants, and in the case of illness, Muslim villagers pray for healing at the village Christian church.[37] Qleibo recalls visiting a Muslim village south of Bethlehem and, upon being entertained inside the home of acquaintances for the first time, noticing a picture on the wall of the Virgin Mary and Jesus. The hostess explained that two brothers among her family's ancestors had come to Palestine with the Crusaders; one remained Christian while the other, her own maternal ancestor,

36. Qleibo, "Blood Bonds."
37. "Neighbors of Trees and Stones."

had at some point converted to Islam. "We used to be Christian," the woman explained; "it feels good to have the Virgin Mary."[38]

Muslims revere Jesus; he is considered a prophet in the Islamic faith, and many individuals honor him in prayer. The well-known Palestinian filmmaker Mohammad Alatar, who produced a short film in 2021 about former Latin Patriarch Sabbah, recounts a story about his own reverence for Jesus. Asked by one of his sons completing a homework assignment years ago who his hero was, Alatar recalls answering that it was Jesus. In response to the boy's surprise because the family is Muslim, Alatar explained that he considered Jesus, and still does, "the first human rights activist who ever existed" and regards the Sermon on the Mount as the best enunciation of human rights ever. Alatar says he focuses intensely on human rights himself, and he honors the subject of his film, Michel Sabbah, as someone who personifies "the way of Jesus and the justice, peace, and humanity for everyone" that Jesus preached. For Palestinians, who Alatar says have been "in a dark hole for so long," Jesus and his disciple Sabbah are a source of hope.[39]

As we have seen, Mitri Raheb has discovered that Muslim artists feel a connection to the cross, perhaps as deep a connection, under the circumstances in which they live, as Christians do. In 2002, the Church of Sweden approached Raheb requesting one or two paintings of Jesus from a Palestinian perspective for a planned exhibit of artwork depicting Christ from a range of international artists. Under difficult circumstances, since Bethlehem at the time was under a round-the-clock curfew imposed by Israel, Raheb and a colleague arranged a competition among Palestinian artists from throughout the occupied territories. To his surprise, ten of the sixteen paintings entered in the competition were done by Muslims, and all but one of these submitted a painting of the crucified Christ, whereas of the six Christian artists, only one chose to depict the cross. The message Raheb drew from this was that many Palestinians, including Muslims, see themselves in the crucified Jesus: "In his pain we feel our pain. In his wounds we recognize our wounds." When seeking a theme for their entries in the competition, Raheb believes, even the Muslim artists could find a sense of emotional comfort in portraying a

38. Qleibo, "Blood Bonds."

39. Statement by Alatar, *People's Patriarch*, sponsored by Sabeel Jerusalem (February 6, 2021).

righteous Jesus hanging on the cross, powerless just as they are; "they could see the power of that powerless Christ."[40]

That shared suffering is a powerful force inspiring Muslim-Christian cooperation among religious leaders, as well as at the grassroots level. Dr. Mustafa Abu Sway—a Muslim imam who holds the Imam Al-Ghazali Chair at al-Aqsa Mosque in Jerusalem and is also Dean of the College of Islamic Studies at Jerusalem's al-Quds University—works with Sabeel and other Palestinian Christian organizations, including the Holy Land Christian Ecumenical Foundation, in the struggle to preserve the Palestinian character of Jerusalem, and indeed the Palestinians' very presence in Jerusalem, against Israeli attempts to erase that presence from the city. Although as a scholar of Islam Abu Sway speaks from a Muslim perspective, he teaches a liberation theology for Palestinians that is identical to Christian liberation theology in its embrace of everyone oppressed by Israel's political system. Sabeel, he says, is a place where Palestinian Muslims and Christians "can get together, where we struggle together, but also where we can celebrate being Palestinians," even sharing Muslim Ramadan rituals "with our Christian brothers and sisters with whom we share this land." Liberation, he emphasizes, means "to be liberated from our own pigeon holes and reclaim the one human family. Any ideology, whether advanced by Muslims, Christians or Jews or whoever, that puts one group above another, is not loyal to this one human family."[41]

In frequent writing and lectures, Abu Sway harks back to the time before the advent of British and Zionist colonialism in Palestine, when this one human family actually existed and functioned well in Palestinian. Indigenous Palestinians of all faiths coexisted reasonably harmoniously. This was a time when a population of Palestinian Jews comprised an integral part of Palestinian society, living and working alongside Muslim and Christian Palestinians, in Jerusalem and elsewhere in Palestine.[42]

In a further striking example of the respect Christians and Muslims hold for each other, Tarek Abuata, the Christian Palestinian-American former director of FOSNA, has described how he once drew powerful inspiration and a sense of solidarity from a group of Muslims praying in difficult circumstances. "While I was living in Palestine," he wrote,

40. Raheb and Henderson, *Cross in Contexts*, 16–20.
41. Abu Sway, "Concerns of Palestinian Muslims."
42. Abu Sway, "Jerusalem."

I witnessed Israeli soldiers stopping a group of [Muslim] Palestinian men from marching in the village of Tuwani. Prevented
from moving forward, the men stopped, knelt, and prayed. The
scene was stunning: Men who appeared to be bowing to soldiers
were instead bowing past them to God. I looked upon them in
awe of their commitment to their land, their protest, their faith.
They set their gaze on their true purpose and lived by it regardless of the cost. I recognized the beauty of their resistance in
the face of worldly violence, and I joined them in protest. As a
queer Palestinian Christian, this I know is true: Jesus is multiple.
Jesus is Black, Jesus is a woman, Jesus is undocumented, Jesus
is poor. Jesus is vibrant in the same way this liberation movement is vibrant. That day, I felt the deep and enduring power of
this vibrance as I joined these men in defying the boundaries
of Israeli occupation. I know that the depths of our faith in action will determine the arc of justice. It is our conviction that
will transform the streets to our sacred spaces, just as these men
made their arrest the site of prayer. And it is our conviction that
will make churches the site of our protest, just as Jesus did when
he defied an empire.[43]

Liberation theology speaks for all the powerless, all the oppressed,
and can give all who share the pain of oppression an ineffable spiritual
comfort, no matter their faith. That spiritual bond arises from the pain
that Christians and Muslims equally experience living under the same
Israeli oppression. In fact, this shared political trauma accounts in large
part for a bond between the Christian and Muslim communities that is
unique to Palestine.

When Christians speak out about Palestinian suffering and political oppression, they speak about the situation of all Palestinians, Muslim as
well as Christian. The *Kairos Palestine* document issued in December
2009—*Kairos Palestine: A Moment of Truth: A Word of Faith, Hope and
Love from the Heart of Palestinian Suffering*—has been described by Rifat
Kassis, coordinator of the *Kairos Palestine* Group, as a call for freedom
for the entire Palestinian people, arising from the resistance of the people
rather than from any political leadership. Although composed by Christians as a Christian theological call, the document is broadly inclusive
in its objectives and its intended audience. The framers' intent, Kassis

43. Abuata, "Stand in Conviction."

affirms, was, and remains, to challenge the common misconception that the Palestinian-Israeli struggle is a religious clash between Muslims and Jews and to demonstrate instead that it is "political through-and-through: a conflict between the occupiers and the occupied, regardless of their faith."[44] The document affirms in fact that both Christian and Muslim Palestinians are natural inhabitants of the land: "Our presence in this land, as Christian and Muslim Palestinians, is not accidental but rather deeply rooted in the history and geography of this land" (2.3.2).[45] Conceived as a statement of faith in a just and loving God who speaks to Christians through Jesus but who is present in every human being, it reaches out to all Palestinians—Christians themselves, Muslims, and those of no religion—who struggle together for freedom and justice.[46]

The *Kairos Palestine* document has been called a living initiative: it describes an ongoing situation for Palestinians—an oppression—that endures, continuing to affect the Palestinians' very survival, and that has aroused an enduring resistance movement. The document in fact calls on Christian Palestinians to treat resistance as "a right and a duty" (4.2.3). *Kairos*-Palestine-the-movement was created to maintain resistance and, in Kassis's words, to add a new voice alongside the Israeli narrative that has dominated international discourse for so long. It offers "new intellectual and theological tools to use in the struggle against occupation." Among the movement's tools have been multiple international conferences on the Kairos theme designed to educate theologians, solidarity activists, and even tourists; books and articles by Palestinian theologians and dialogue with theologians around the world in a further educational effort; and the formation of an international movement, the "Kairos for Global Justice Coalition," which has established Kairos affiliates in twenty-five countries that work to mobilize churches and Christian organizations.[47]

The idea behind issuing *Kairos Palestine* as a *cri de coeur* at a time of crisis comes from the similar *Kairos South Africa* document of many years earlier, and during the drafting process the Palestinian authors invited the advice of several South African theologians, including the Rev.

44. Kassis, *Kairos for Palestine*, 10, 99.

45. Numbered references here and following are to paragraphs and subparagraphs in the *Kairos Palestine* document.

46. Taken from the *Kairos* Palestine website and from an undated explanatory booklet about the *Kairos Palestine* document, issued shortly after its passage and distributed by FOSNA.

47. Kassis, "*Kairos* Palestine," 58–62.

Edwin Arrison, whom we met in Chapter 1. The Palestinian theologians wanted at a minimum, according to Kassis, "to honour the legacy" of the South African call for justice, and they obviously hoped to be able to emulate the South Africans' success.[48] In an explanatory note appended at the end of the formal *Kairos Palestine* document, the signatories expressed hope that this document would be welcomed with the same kind of strong support that *Kairos South Africa* had received a quarter-century earlier, when that document "proved to be a tool in the struggle against oppression and occupation."

Although the Palestinian document was framed differently from its South African predecessor, it followed a generally similar outline in moving from a description of the abysmal reality on the ground for Palestinians, through a frank discussion of the church's betrayal of Christian theology in its apparent support for Israel's claims of chosenness, to a heartfelt expression of a desperate hope "in the absence of all hope," in the absence of "even a glimmer of positive expectation" (3.1). Both documents adopted a forthright tone in their criticism of the world's failure, particularly the church's, to support legitimate struggles against oppression and racist rule. The South African document comes across as harsher in tone, while the Palestinian document, because of its framing as a "word of faith, hope, and love," is more spiritual.

Kairos Palestine opened by briefly detailing the worsening situation on the ground for Palestinians (as of 2009), including: a separation wall constructed on occupied Palestinian territory; expanding Israeli settlements that "ravage" Palestinian land and resources; daily humiliation of Palestinians en route to work and school at military checkpoints; severe restrictions on access to holy places; abandonment of Palestinian refugees; detention of thousands of political prisoners; extensive home demolitions and other actions intended to diminish the Palestinian population, particularly in Jerusalem; and utter disregard for human rights and international law. Noting that international decision-makers were simply managing rather than resolving the crisis, the *Kairos* authors wondered pointedly what the international community, the Israeli and Palestinian leaderships themselves, and particularly the church were doing: this was a crisis, they cried, arising from Israeli policy and international disinterest, "in which human beings are destroyed." The "hearts of the faithful

---

48. Kassis, *Kairos for Palestine*, 99.

are filled with pain and with questioning," and this should "be of concern to the Church," although it clearly was not (Introduction and 1.1–1.5.1).

Out of this picture of existential desperation and threatened destruction, *Kairos* theologians nonetheless put forth their statement as a Christian expression of faith, hope, and love. They expressed *faith* in God because God is good and just and God's holy Word cannot possibly be the source of Palestinian destruction, cannot be used to support war or oppression or to legitimize Israel's occupation. The occupation is a "sin" because it deprives Palestinians of their basic, God-given human rights, and also because it distorts "the image of God in the Israeli who has become an occupier." Addressing the uniqueness and the theological centrality of the land and its people—meaning all its people—the document affirmed that the land has a "universal mission" based on promises made "to all of humanity." The promise of the land has never been a political program; nor has history been stagnant. Rather, God sent "the patriarchs, the prophets and the apostles to this land so that they might carry forth a universal mission to the world." The land, in fact, *Kairos* affirmed, is *God's land*, home to the three religions of Judaism, Christianity, and Islam: the presence of Christian and Muslim Palestinians is "not accidental but [is] rather deeply rooted," and Palestinians are connected as "a natural right." Indeed, "*God has put us [Jews and Palestinians] here as two peoples*" and given both the ability to live together in justice and peace. Referring to Zionists and especially Western Christian Zionists, the *Kairos* authors expressed a strong faith in God and God's Word against those who use the Bible to undermine and delegitimize the Palestinians' very existence. We know, they said, "that the word of God cannot be the source of our destruction" (2.3–2.5, emphasis added).

Palestinian *hope* remains strong, the document asserted, even in the face of the dire circumstances of Israel's oppression and especially in the face of its "growing orientation towards racist separation and the imposition of laws that deny our existence and our dignity."[49] By the reckoning of the *Kairos* theologians, hope means—very simply but with deep spirituality—"not giving in to evil," not forgetting injustices, but rather confronting injustice and maintaining steadfastness and resistance. Despite everything, "our hope remains strong, because it is from God." The

---

49. Although it would be more than a decade later that human rights organizations began openly to label Israel an apartheid state, most aspects of apartheid and of what *Kairos Palestine* called an "orientation towards racist separation" were evident in Israeli rule for decades before the *Kairos* document was issued.

document quoted Paul: "If God is for us, who is against us? (. . .). For I am convinced that neither death (. . .) nor anything else in all creation, will be able to separate us from the love of God" (Rom 8:31, 38–39, NRSV). In the land of Jesus' resurrection, *Kairos* affirmed, Palestinian Christians can do no less than remain strong and emulate Jesus' victorious rise over evil (3.1–3.5).

Despite the oppression Palestinians face, the *Kairos* document expressed—indeed, commanded—*love* among Palestinians, as well as by Palestinians for Jews: "Love is the commandment of Christ our Lord to us and it includes both friends and enemies (. . .). Love is seeing the face of God in every human being." This does not mean accepting evil. In fact, resistance is an obligation: "Resistance is a right and a duty for the Christian. But it is resistance with love as its logic (. . .) find[ing] human ways that engage the humanity of the enemy." Resistance must be nonviolent, engaged in through civil disobedience, including an economic and commercial boycott "of everything produced by the occupation," as well as other advocacy campaigns. Either the cycle of violence, consisting of Israeli injustice and the Palestinian terrorism that arises from it, *Kairos* declared, will "destroy both of us," or peace "will benefit both." Love is for the enemy also (4.1–4.3).

After its affirmation of the fundamental Christian values of faith, hope, and love, the *Kairos* document addressed its audiences at home and around the world, urging Palestinian Christians to remain steadfast in their faith and in the land, sending a Christian message of love, acceptance, and coexistence to Muslims and Jews, and especially issuing a heartfelt plea to the "churches of the world" to pay attention and help. Begging for understanding of the Palestinians' right to self-determination in their own land, the document asked fundamentalist churches—meaning, clearly, evangelical Christian Zionist churches—to rethink their theological positions. And to the general audience of churches, the plea was that they "stand alongside the oppressed and preserve the word of God as good news for all rather than to turn it into a weapon with which to slay the oppressed (. . .). God is not the ally of one against the other, nor the opponent of one in the face of the other. God is the Lord of all and loves all, demanding justice from all and issuing to all of us the same commandments" (6.1).

In a pointed appeal to the institutional Christian church, which as of the time over a dozen years ago when *Kairos Palestine* was issued, had noticeably distanced itself from its Palestinian Christian flock and placed the weight of its support and solidarity on Israel's side, *Kairos* said bluntly, "We ask our sister Churches

> not to offer a theological cover-up for the injustice we suffer, for the sin of the occupation imposed upon us. Our question to our brothers and sisters in the Churches today is: Are you able to help us get our freedom back, for this is the only way you can help the two peoples attain justice, peace, security, and love? In order to understand our reality, we say to the Churches: Come and see. We will fulfill our role to make known to you the truth of our reality (. . .). You will know the facts and the people of this land, Palestinians and Israelis alike (. . .). We call on you to say a word of truth and to take a position of truth with regard to Israel's occupation of Palestinian land (6.1–6.3).

Kairos Palestine had begun with a cry of near-despair: "We (. . .) Christian Palestinians, after prayer, reflection and an exchange of opinion, cry out from within the suffering in our country, under Israeli occupation, with a cry of hope in the absence of all hope." It ended as it began, with a similar cry from the depths of the Palestinian soul: "In the absence of all hope, we cry out our cry of hope (. . .). We believe that God's goodness will finally triumph over the evil of hate and of death that still persist in our land" (Introduction and 10).

Ten years after the release of *Kairos Palestine*, in December 2019, with no more reason for hope, and perhaps less, the *Kairos* movement called a conference in Bethlehem and issued an anniversary statement lamenting that the Palestinians' situation had deteriorated under Israel's ever "more aggressive and brutal" occupation and that "the global Church is failing us." The conference called out to the world in anguish, saying that Palestinians "are standing as if on the edge of a cliff, looking into an abyss," and pleaded for solidarity from around the world, for prayers, and for a global commitment to take action by calling out Israeli apartheid and condemning distorted theologies—such as Zionism itself and its Christian offshoot, Christian Zionism—that "justify the privilege of one people over another."[50]

Still later, in July 2020, a new coalition formed from *Kairos Palestine* and Global *Kairos* for Justice issued a formal statement, *Cry for Hope: A Call to Decisive Action,* reiterating and more urgently emphasizing the demands issued in the tenth-anniversary call, underlining the sense of desperation that Palestinians feel and the belief that the very integrity of

---

50. *Kairos Palestine, "Kairos Palestine* 10th Anniversary Conference Statement."

the worldwide church is threatened. The statement—signed by Patriarch Michel Sabbah and Rifat Kassis for all heads of local Christian churches in Jerusalem—was headlined, "We cannot serve God and the oppression of the Palestinians"; its central message was the blunt assertion that the "very being of the church, the integrity of the Christian faith, and the credibility of the Gospel [are] at stake. We declare that *support for the oppression of the Palestinian people, whether passive or active, through silence, word or deed, is a sin.*"[51]

The response from the Western Christian churches to which *Kairos Palestine* and its several offshoots around the world have repeatedly appealed was initially near-total silence—indicating, if not a continuation of the churches' clear support for Israel regardless of its policies toward the Palestinians, at least a continued disinterest in Israel's behavior and a reluctance to confront the pressure of pro-Israel lobby and Jewish community groups that constantly monitor the positions of political and religious organizations on Palestine.

Jewish theologian Marc Ellis has written often of what he pointedly calls the "interfaith ecumenical deal": an unspoken understanding, always hovering over Christian-Jewish dialogue and relationships, that Christians are the guilty supplicant pleading for forgiveness for centuries of church antisemitism, while Jews and Israel are morally innocent, never to be criticized or held culpable for Israel's oppression of Palestinians. As "Jewish culpability in the displacement and occupation of Palestine" has become obvious, Ellis says, "Jews demanded their Christian partners' silence." Unquestioned support for Israel is part of Christianity's continuing repentance, part of the "deal," and any criticism of Israel is—to an increasing extent—loudly called antisemitism.[52] Naim Ateek has described the "deal" as a kind of masquerade, the arrangement being "to have polite conversations and wonderful dinners with the Jewish establishment organizations, provided we remain silent about justice for Palestinians." It is an arrangement that looks wonderful on the surface, but in fact "it silences the prophetic and smothers the truth."[53]

51. *Kairos Palestine* and Global *Kairos* for Justice, "Cry for Hope." Emphasis added.

52. Ellis, *Future of the Prophetic*, 44.

53. Ateek, "Naim Ateek Responds."

This interfaith bargain—Christian silence for Jewish goodwill, and the ever-present threat of heavy pro-Israel lobby pressure on any church or organization that ventures to speak or act on behalf of the Palestinians—has clearly had a chilling, silencing effect on the church and its several denominations. Although the years following *Kairos Palestine's* 2009 appeal saw the growth of several subsidiary mission groups in US Protestant denominations that advocate for Palestinian rights, it was only after the Palestinians' 2020 *Cry for Hope* that any mainstream Protestant denomination in the United States responded with a church-wide stance criticizing Israel's apartheid policies. Fully twelve years after *Kairos Palestine*, in July 2021, the United Church of Christ adopted a resolution, by a greater than 80-percent favorable vote, naming Israel an apartheid state and decrying the continuing oppression of the Palestinians as a "matter of theological urgency"; this oppression, the UCC declared, is "a sin in violation of the message of the biblical prophets and the Gospel." The UCC action was presumably spurred not only by the *Cry for Hope*, but also by the B'Tselem and Human Rights Watch reports in early 2021 labeling Israel an apartheid state.[54]

A few months later, in February 2022, the Christian Church (Disciples of Christ), in a pastoral letter entitled *Compelled to Witness* and declaring that "the places of Israel and Palestine are dear to us as Christians," catalogued Israel's occupation and its injustices against Palestinians as policies inconsistent with "our understanding of God's vision of justice for all people, and therefore [constitutes] sin." The statement concluded as a result that "Israeli policies and practices that discriminate against Palestinians—Christians and Muslims alike—are consistent with the international legal definition of the crime of apartheid" and urged the United States, which it noted had done little to hold Israel accountable to international law, to take steps to prevent the use of US aid to Israeli military units that violate human rights. The pastoral letter was careful to note that the church's criticism was "legitimate criticism of the State of Israel's laws, policies, and actions," which it distinguished from antisemitic discourse and action, and it pledged to continue working against both antisemitism and anti-Muslim bigotry.[55]

In July 2022, the biannual Presbyterian Church (USA) General Assembly adopted a resolution, by a favorable vote of 70 percent, stating

54. Vail, "Synod Delegates Approve Resolution."
55. Christian Church (Disciples of Christ), *Compelled to Witness.*

that "the government of Israel's laws, policies, and practices regarding the Palestinian people fulfill the international legal definition of apartheid." Noting that for too long the "conflict between Israeli Jews and Palestinians" has been wrongly seen as one of two peoples who cannot get along, the PC(USA) declared that the "core of the conflict is not enmity between two peoples but an unjust structure of power that privileges one group of people over another, a structure that is reflected legally at all levels of society (. . .). We must name this unjust structure by its most accurate name—apartheid."[56] In a statement issued in advance of the General Assembly, ten former Assembly moderators urged passage of the resolution, noting that it would give hope to the more than one million Presbyterians in the Middle East. In addition, in anticipation of heavy criticism from the Jewish community and the pro-Israel lobby, the moderators' statement pointedly noted that the resolution is "about the laws, policies, and actions of the Israeli government and not about the Jewish faith or Jewish people." Not surprisingly, this statement has not in fact headed off criticism of the PC(USA) as antisemitic, even though no critics have offered any specific refutation of the apartheid charge.[57]

Almost simultaneously with the PC(USA) General Assembly decision, the Episcopal Church in the United States, holding its General Convention in July 2022, made a conscious decision to avoid discussion and a vote on the issue of declaring Israel an apartheid state. Because there was not enough time for discussion of a contentious issue during the Convention, which had been shortened by half because of COVID, a committee of Convention deputies and bishops formed to review proposed resolutions deferred debate about apartheid until the next Convention in 2024. Importantly, the full General Convention, including both the House of Bishops and the House of Deputies, did officially adopt a resolution that talks around the apartheid issue without using the word; this resolution condemned the oppression of the Palestinian people and urged the US administration and Congress to "take action to oppose Israeli laws and practices that result in unequal rights for two peoples." In another important move toward Palestinian rights advocacy, the Episcopal Church also expressed its opposition to the current widespread drive to criminalize

---

56. Presbyterian Church (USA), 225th General Assembly (2022), "On Recognition That Israel's Laws, Policies, and Practices Constitute Apartheid Against the Palestinian People."

57. Wright, "Presbyterian Church (USA) Adds Its Voice."

nonviolent boycott, divestment, and sanctions efforts, affirming the legitimacy of such efforts as a matter of free speech.

Despite adoption of these two resolutions, the Episcopal decision to dodge the specific issue of apartheid at a time when other churches and major human rights organizations were directly addressing apartheid, and at a time when the Episcopal Church itself is engaged in a concerted campaign to combat racism in the United States, demonstrated a clear lack of concern about the importance of justice for Palestinians and seemingly little awareness of the issue's urgency—as if delegates were oblivious to the plethora of recent declarations on this major moral issue. One of the principal expressed worries of the Episcopal delegates, evoking the unspoken interfaith "deal," was that passage of a resolution using the word "apartheid" might provoke and antagonize Jewish dialogue partners.

Over the last few years, importantly, the Episcopal Church and several other Protestant denominations have divested from some Israeli banks and corporations that operate in the occupied Palestinian territories. The PC(USA) has led the way on the issue of divestment for almost two decades, and other denominations have added their voices. There has also been considerable church activity at the grassroots level in most denominations. Despite the silence and slow action of denominational hierarchies, subsidiary mission groups that advocate for Palestinian rights but are not formally connected to the denominational hierarchy have, as noted, been active in each denomination during the last decade and more, speaking to the church hierarchies and carrying out solidarity actions in Palestine.[58]

During the period in 2022 when many churches and organizations considered the question of apartheid, the General Assembly of the World Council of Churches, the Council's highest governing body, met in Germany in September and addressed the issue from the perspective of a worldwide church body, representing three hundred fifty-two member churches from one hundred twenty countries. The issue—whether apartheid exists in Israel, whether even to mention the word in official WCC General Assembly documents, who was and was not allowed to address the issue during floor debates—was undoubtedly the most contentious

58. Another grassroots social justice and pro-Palestine activist, Anglican priest the Rev. Garth Hewitt in the UK, has been writing and singing tributes to Palestine for several decades. His most recent songs address the Palestinians' *Cry for Hope* and the issue of apartheid. See Hewitt, *Palestine is Calling*: "No. 2 Cry for Hope," and "No. 3, Standing Against Apartheid."

issue during the week-long meeting, which occurs only every eight years. Presented with a resolution from the Anglican Church of South Africa that described Israel's policy as one of apartheid, the WCC Assembly did engage in vigorous debate and, despite objections by the host German Protestant Church, did use the word "apartheid" in its final statement, although only to note that various international organizations have found Israel to be practicing apartheid. But the meeting opted for caution and maintaining church unity over making prophetic pronouncements and failed to reach an agreed position on the issue. While reaching no judgment on whether Israel practices apartheid—lamenting that "we are not of one mind on this issue"—the Assembly supported Israel's legitimacy by affirming its "rightful place" in the community of nations and attempted to deflect attention from Israel's human rights abuses by attributing them to extremists and "settlers," rather than to Israeli government and military forces. Ultimately, by deferring serious consideration of the apartheid issue to later study, this key world church body essentially failed to be prophetic.[59]

Kairos USA, the US arm of the global *Kairos* movement established after the release of the Palestinian document, was formed in 2012 by a group of theologians hoping, as a broad multidenominational advocacy group, to bring the *Kairos* message and awareness of the Palestinian plight to the institutional church in the United States. Like the other such grassroots responses to *Kairos Palestine* from around the world, the US response was both an expression of solidarity with Palestinian suffering and, in some ways more notably, an acknowledgement of guilt for church complicity: these responses were "the confessions of the complicit" about how churches have supported state oppression.[60] Importantly, however, this *Kairos* response must be seen as an unofficial theological response, not one coming from any part of the institutional church. The *Kairos* USA response was issued as a "Call to Action" intended, as its mission statement affirms, to "unify and mobilize American Christians—lay, academic and clergy—to respond faithfully and boldly to the urgent situation in Israel and Palestine," especially the dire circumstances of Palestinians.

In composing a "church confession," the US *Kairos* theologians recognized and addressed the church's failure of conscience, issuing a challenge that stands as a powerful and enduring prophetic message to the

59. See WCC, "Seeking Justice and Peace"; Wright, "World Council of Churches General Assembly"; and Palestine Portal, "Resolution on Israeli Apartheid."

60. Braverman, "Moment of Grace and Opportunity," 50.

church. Speaking in the first person as "the body of Christ in the United States," and as if in personal confession, the theologians begged forgiveness for their own and the church's complicity in the suffering of Palestinians. "It was in ancient Israel," the statement noted, "that the prophets called states and peoples to the core principles of God's rule: equal rights and justice for all, compassion for the most vulnerable and the unity of all humankind." Following after the prophets, they continued,

> Jesus proclaimed the reign of God as a present possibility and a demand to follow God's commandments to do justice (. . .). As the body of Christ in the United States, we confess that by not speaking truth to power we have failed to follow the call of Jesus to serve God with love and compassion for all people. We have failed to challenge our government's policies (. . .) that have brought suffering to Palestinians, continuing insecurity to Israelis and the declining prospect of a just peace. As individuals and as church institutions, we have supported a system of control, inequality and oppression through misreading of our Holy Scriptures, flawed theology and distortions of history. We have allowed to go unchallenged theological and political ideas that have made us complicit in the oppression of the Palestinian people (. . .). We have forgotten the difference between a theology that supports the policies and institutional structures of oppression and a theology that, in response to history and human affairs, stands boldly with the widow, the orphan, the poor and the dispossessed.[61]

In the transformative period when South African apartheid was nearing an end and *Kairos South Africa* was attempting to generate church solidarity for the work of that momentous change, South African theologian John de Gruchy wrote that any profound theological statement like *Kairos*, for the precise reason that "it is a witness to a living God at work in transforming history," would always be an evolving instrument, open to change through action on the ground and to continued discussion and reflection.[62] *Kairos Palestine* and the *Kairos* responses to it from around the world do indeed constitute a broad "witness to a living God at work," and the Palestinian testament remains a living document, its vision of

61. *Kairos* USA, "Call to Action."

62. de Gruchy, "Foreword."

transformation sustained by the enduring faith, hope, and love of Palestinian Christians and all other Palestinians who continue their resistance to Israeli oppression. But, where it is easy to see that the promise of *Kairos South Africa* has been fulfilled to a great extent, the promise of *Kairos Palestine* remains still a hope rather than an actuality. The "hope in the absence of all hope" expressed by the *Kairos Palestine* theologians is but a thin connection to that living God who works to transform history. Without the sustaining help of the church, God's church on earth, that connection of hope is in some danger of fraying.

4

Narrating with the "Eyes of the Heart"

Scripture as Liberation

I pray that the God of our Lord Jesus Christ (. . .) may give you a spirit of
wisdom and revelation (. . .) so that, with the eyes of your heart enlightened,
you may know what is the hope to which [God] has called you (. . .) what
is the immeasurable greatness of [God's] power for us who believe (. . .).

—EPH 1:17–19 (NRSV)

For us the image of the cross with its affliction and pain, and Jesus'
response of gentleness, non-violence, and ultimately resurrection, is one
of comfort and inspiration. As Christ himself identified with suffering
people and called on his followers to reach out to them in their need,
we too invite our brothers and sisters in Christ across the world to
join with us as we search for God in the midst of our affliction.

—SABEEL, *Contemporary Way of the Cross*[1]

IN HIS EARLIEST FORMULATION of Palestinian liberation theology, Naim
Ateek emphasized that the very heart of the biblical message, especially
the New Testament message, is the "liberating aspect of the Word of God."
The church and its theologians largely neglected this message through

1. Sabeel, *Contemporary Way of the Cross*, 3.

the ages, even in the land where the Bible originated and where Jesus, whom Ateek calls God-in-Christ, lived. But the new theology that he and his colleagues developed is helping to bring this liberating word—Jesus' word of justice—to the Palestinian faithful in their daily lives. This theology, based heavily on the books of the New Testament, speaks prophetically to the particular contextual situation of "oppression, suffering, and injustice" that Palestinians have so long faced. Indeed, Ateek says, God-in-Christ has "something very relevant and very important to say to both the oppressed and the oppressors."[2]

What Jesus teaches comes largely in the form of parables and stories that all speak in one way or another to the issue of justice for the oppressed. But so many of these stories have never been heard in the true fullness and depth of their meaning—never heard as what they truly are: tales in which Jesus *hears* the cries of the marginalized and the voiceless when no one else will listen and renders liberating justice. The renowned theologian and biblical scholar Walter Brueggemann—speaking in broad terms but also specifically of the Palestinians—has written that the oppressed need to demand their own right to narrate their stories and to be heard, and that the time has come for the church to listen. Brueggemann takes his theme of narration from a 1984 essay by the late Palestinian-American intellectual Edward Said in the *London Review of Books* entitled "Permission to Narrate,"[3] in which Said lamented the reality that Palestinians were usually denied the right to narrate their side of the Palestinian-Israeli conflict, while Israel enjoyed virtually unlimited narrative opportunities. Brueggemann describes some biblical stories that testify to profound "transformative experience" but that come to light only when the testifiers are granted "permission to narrate." He cites in particular the story of Bartimaeus, the blind beggar who seeks Jesus' mercy and continues to cry out to Jesus even when those around him attempt to silence him (Mark 10:46–52, NRSV[4]). Because Bartimaeus insists on being heard, Jesus listens, hears and understands his faith, and heals him.[5]

2. Ateek, *Justice and Only Justice*, 6.

3. Said, "Permission to Narrate."

4. Matt 20:29–34 (NRSV) and Luke 18:35–43 (NRSV) tell the same story of one or, in Matthew, two blind beggars near Jericho who call out to Jesus, but they do not name Bartimaeus.

5. Brueggemann, "Permission to Narrate." Brueggemann has written elsewhere about the Palestinian-Israeli situation. His book is *Chosen?* He has also written the

Jesus granted Bartimaeus "permission" to speak, but Brueggemann says that today it is the church that should be "the permission granting community so that those who have been silenced and denied their narrative have a secure place in which their narrative can be told, received, honored, and taken seriously." This is the essence of liberation theology in all its contexts. Theologians and preachers, among whom Brueggemann includes himself, should be able to understand and enter into the depths of the oppressive realities of today's world—for precisely the reason, he says, that "we see through the prism of the one crucified and risen," the one who was himself oppressed but defied the empire. Because the story of Jesus is "powerfully subversive" and conflicts with dominant interests in church and state, its relevance to the situations of oppressed populations today is too often silenced out of a misbegotten "prudence." The Palestinian story, Brueggemann declares, is clearly such a story, unwelcome and usually silenced in the West. Silence and prudence must no longer govern discourse, however; honest narration requires "the willful *violation of prudence* and the *transgression of silence*."[6] The time for these transgressions is now. We in the church "do indeed have a story to tell," he says. But, "the story we have to tell the nations is from below. It is a story occupied by slaves such as Bartimaeus. It is a story of *the urgency of mercy* that every time overrides the force of silencing culture. The truth for which the church has permission to narrate is subversive. Its telling, however, is likely the only ground for hope for our society amid its deep denial and its equally deep despair."[7]

The stories that Sabeel's theologians and Bible studies leaders, as well as other Palestinian Christian pastors and theologians, tell their Palestinian congregants are these "subversive" parables that Jesus told. These parables, and the entire biblical story of Jesus' ministry, carry as much meaning for Palestinians today, and for all those suffering oppression, as they did in Jesus' time; the "urgency of mercy" and the urgency of liberation are as great today as they were two thousand years ago and, as Brueggemann notes, these tales provide what may be the only "ground for hope" that exists today for Palestinians and the world.

---

forewords to Braverman, *Fatal Embrace*; Wagner and Davis, eds., *Zionism and the Quest*; and Ateek, *Palestinian Theology*.

6. Brueggemann, "Permission to Narrate." Emphasis in original.

7. Brueggemann, "Permission to Narrate." Emphasis added.

No biblical story better captures the physical and spiritual totality of Jesus' earthly life and mission—the suffering, the love, the glory and wonder—than the culmination of this human life in his crucifixion and resurrection. For Palestinians, who share the ethnic roots of Jesus and his first followers and who daily walk the same ground that Jesus walked, no story stands as more *real*. Any Christian anywhere in the world, listening to gospel stories on Sunday, or hearing them in Sunday school, or devoting a life to following them in religious orders can spiritually imagine, with the "eyes of the heart," being there with Jesus. But Palestinians actually *are* there; it barely takes any imagination for Palestinians to liken themselves to Jesus and his followers, who looked like them, lived a life and endured suffering nearly identical to their own lives despite the great span of time, and existed in the very place where they exist. As we heard from Sabeel's Omar Haramy, Palestinians "are still on our own way of the cross (. . .). We, like Jesus, have been on a painful journey—we have experienced the Nakba, the taking of Jerusalem, occupation, apartheid, and blockade."

Being able to walk the way of the cross where Jesus walked it, in the original location, on the same ground, is an experience unique to Palestine; it is a walk that has been going on for two thousand years. The first European to record making a pilgrimage on Good Friday in Jerusalem was a Spanish woman named Egeria, who joined local Christians commemorating the events of Good Friday in the fourth century. Later, tenth- and eleventh-century visitors to the Holy Land reported local processions and Good Friday commemorations in and around the Church of the Holy Sepulchre. The processional path began to be marked by "stages" and later by "stations," and Franciscan friars who came to Jerusalem in the thirteenth century and have remained as custodians of the holy sites established a fourteen-station Way of the Cross. Nine of the stations were taken directly from events recorded in the gospels; the remaining five were added from medieval European commemorations.[8]

Sabeel has designed a contemporary version of the Way of the Cross: a liturgy and act of worship that Sabeel asserts is "rooted in the land" where Jesus lived and that links the events of his suffering on Good Friday with the "very real and constant suffering of the Palestinian people" today. This liturgy, the Palestinian *Via Dolorosa*, attempts to provide a realistic image of the Palestinians' situation and suffering, "simply ask[ing]

8. Sabeel, *Contemporary Way of the Cross*, 3.

those who take part in this act of worship to listen, to pray for us and to pray with us." The image of "the suffering Christ is unique," Sabeel notes, and it is "key to the Christian faith."[9] Indeed, this perception that Jesus' suffering is linked with and is a part of the suffering of Palestinians and of all oppressed people today is the essential tenet, the hermeneutic of Palestinian and all other liberation theologies. Recall German theologian Jürgen Moltmann's belief that the only "liberating" and "truly Christian" theology is one that sees God—or God-in-Christ, to use Ateek's imagery—as suffering *with*, participating fully in and feeling, the pain and suffering of all the oppressed. This is the animating force of all liberation theologies, as we have seen.

Sabeel's liturgy links each traditional Station of the Cross with a contemporary station that tells the story of some aspect of Palestinian oppression. Each station includes a Scripture citation, meditations and prayers, testimonies by Palestinians, sometimes a poem. The entire liturgy of the Contemporary Way of the Cross is designed to be used in a multitude of ways, individually or in community: for instance, reciting several of the stations during each week of Lent or one or two each day of Holy Week; following the entire contemporary way on Good Friday during worship or in a dedicated workshop; or teaching the contemporary stations in Sunday school or in a Bible study program. The contemporary stations can also, most vividly, be followed and recited in Jerusalem's Old City, at the multiple spots along winding market alleyways where each station of the traditional Way of the Cross marks an actual spot on Jesus' journey of agony.

The traditional First Station depicts the moment when Jesus is condemned to die; Sabeel's contemporary First Station deals with the Palestinian Nakba of 1948—the catastrophic ethnic cleansing campaign that Israel intended as the effective death sentence of the Palestinians as a people. The opening meditation begins, "Just as Jesus was condemned to die, so the actions of 1948 passed a death sentence on more than 500 historic Palestinian villages that were completely destroyed across the country. We remember that pain of losing community, family networks and a sense of place." The Scripture reading is from Ps. 69:1–3 (NRSV): "Save me, O God, for the waters have come up to my neck, I sink in deep mire, where there is no foothold; I have come into deep waters, and the flood sweeps over me. I am weary with my crying; my throat is parched.

9. Sabeel, *Contemporary Way of the Cross*, 3–4.

My eyes grow dim with waiting for my God." The heartbreak of the Nakba is further brought alive with testimonies from a man who experienced the ethnic cleansing of his village as a terrified eleven-year-old boy, as well as from the well-known Palestinian Melkite Greek Catholic priest, later archbishop, Elias Chacour, whose Christian village was attacked by Israeli soldiers in 1948. The brief reflection by Chacour, taken from his book *Blood Brothers*, is about a visit to his still-empty village years after he and his family and neighbors had been forced by Israeli soldiers to flee, when he feels at once "dumb-struck, nearly overcome by the sense of desolation" and also awed by "a deep sense of life," as if he were actually hearing conversation and laughter, children singing hymns at church—when he realized the sadness of the situation but also knew that nothing could ever "fully destroy such reverence for God and life and the land as we had felt there." It is a story of death and hoped-for resurrection. Worshippers are urged at the end of this station to pause and personally reflect on the deep meaning of the destruction of villages like Chacour's: thinking about the human lives lived in such villages, and how profoundly and permanently these hundreds of thousands of Palestinian lives were changed, and are still being changed, by having been so totally uprooted.[10]

Other contemporary stations along Jesus' agonizing route to the cross describe stages in Palestine's journey: the 1967 occupation is likened to Jesus' first fall, Station 3; Israel's wanton practice of demolishing Palestinian homes, to Jesus' second fall, Station 7; Israel's construction of the massive, suffocating Separation Wall, to Jesus' death on the cross, Station 12, which is described as his surrender and feeling of abandonment to overwhelming power. Occasional good moments on Jesus' path—Station 5 when Simon of Cyrene carries his cross and Station 8 when Jesus meets the women of Jerusalem—are likened, respectively, to the help Palestinians receive from numerous international advocacy and solidarity organizations, and to the support rendered to Palestinians by several women's groups, particularly the Israeli groups Women in Black and Machsom Watch, which monitors the behavior of Israeli soldiers at checkpoints.[11]

The last of the traditional stations—Number 14, Jesus is laid in the tomb and is raised from the dead on the third day—is labeled in the contemporary stations "Hope in the Absence of Hope," from the *Kairos Palestine* document, which concludes that "We believe that God's goodness will

10. Sabeel, *Contemporary Way of the Cross*, 8–10.
11. Sabeel, *Contemporary Way of the Cross*, 8–46.

finally triumph over the evil of hate and of death that still persist in our land."[12] No story of Jesus' life is more human or more intimate than the story of his passion and death, and nothing connects us more closely with him spiritually and emotionally than following his path, either in spirit or in actuality, on Good Friday. In the same way, walking Jesus' path with intentionality, following this uniquely Palestinian, very gritty liturgy, takes us far more intimately into the Palestinian story than is possible from visiting the many churches built over the places of Jesus' ministry.

The Bible, of course, is filled with relevant tales of justice and mercy rendered to the oppressed, but too often these are not recognized as the moral lessons for all humanity that they were meant, and continue, to be. A key but little-heralded passage in John's Gospel (John 1:35–51, NRSV), telling a story of Jesus' effort to gather disciples, is an emblematic tale about the importance of witness and narration that Palestinian Christians put forth today. For these Palestinians, the central theme of this passage—"Come and see," meaning look closely, hear Jesus and engage with him—stands as a reminder to a generally ignorant world that Palestinians and specifically Palestinian Christians exist, a small attempt to attract the attention of Christian pilgrims and indeed of the Christian church.

Early in Jesus' effort to gather disciples, this gospel passage relates, two people, intrigued by John the Baptist's statement that Jesus is the Lamb of God, follow curiously and, when Jesus tells them to "come and see" where he is living, recognize him as the Messiah. One of these men is Simon Peter's brother Andrew, and he soon brings Peter to see Jesus. Others of the apostles also follow, including Philip and Nathaniel. A skeptical Nathaniel wonders what good could come out of Jesus' small hometown of Nazareth (1:46, NRSV), but he is urged to "come and see." Each time, new followers are beckoned with the same words, to come and see Jesus where he lives and learn who and what he is. Ultimately, each one is convinced: "We have found him about whom Moses in the law and also the prophets wrote, Jesus son of Joseph from Nazareth" (1:45, NRSV). In each case, Jesus hears them; in each case, they become believers.

Today, the land where Jesus lived is still there, the descendants of those followers of Jesus are still there. But close-up knowledge of the land and of the Palestinian people who have lived there for millennia is sadly

---

12. Sabeel, *Contemporary Way of the Cross*, 47–49.

lacking. Seeing is believing, and Palestinians of all faiths eagerly wait and hope for visitors to "come and see"—to go there and learn what Palestine is all about. Sabeel's principal ministry is precisely narration—narrating the gospel and Jesus' message to Palestinian Christians themselves and to the broader church and the world. One of its principal missions has been training Bible study facilitators from various parishes in Palestine, who work with their churches to form Bible study groups in the community. These groups, and Sabeel in all its ministries, practice liberation theology by bringing Jesus' suffering alive to Palestinians who are today suffering as did Jesus himself and those to whom he ministered.

A passage from the Gospel of Mark (Mark 5:21–43, NRSV) is foundational to Sabeel's work of narrating and raising up the Palestinian story. This passage, describing Jesus' healing of a synagogue leader's dying young daughter and of a woman suffering from hemorrhages for twelve years, demonstrates vividly that Jesus always hears the pleas of the suffering, just as he did for Bartimaeus. These stories show three dimensions of healing, Naim Ateek notes: hope, agency, and liberation. Hope based on faith is central: even when all seems futile, when Jairus, the synagogue leader, learns that his daughter has died and the hemorrhaging woman knows that all medical efforts have failed to help her, they nonetheless persist, and Jesus heals in both cases. Jesus tells Jairus, "Don't be afraid; just believe." The injunction to keep hoping is essential to sustain "steadfastness [*sumud*] in continuing to seek liberation." The woman had faith and persisted in her hope and conviction that simply touching Jesus' garment would liberate her from years of suffering. When members of Jairus's household tell him that his daughter is dead and he should give up and not bother Jesus anymore, Jesus does not give up; he says the girl is only sleeping and tells her to rise: *Talitha Kumi*, the Aramaic words for "Little girl, rise up."[13]

This passage also speaks to agency: it is a push, an impetus, for Palestinians to work on their own behalf, taking the initiative as the two supplicants in Mark's Gospel did. Although it may be foolish, Ateek says, for Palestinians to hope that they can end Israel's occupation, "by God's grace, here we are nonetheless, proclaiming that where there is death, we see only slumber. What appears to be dead can rise up. We are committed

13. Ateek, "Bible Study on Mark."

to remaining steadfast in our hope." Both of Mark's stories challenge Palestinians to continue working "to liberate the people living in this land, both Palestinians and Israelis." Like Jairus and the woman in Mark's Gospel, Palestinians "are taking the initiative to act based on our faith that the impossible can be made possible."[14]

In 2018, inspired by this story of Jesus raising the little girl from death with the command *Talitha, Kumi,* Sabeel launched a new initiative called *Kumi Now* (rise up now), which it dubbed an "inclusive call for nonviolent action to achieve a just peace." Kumi Now invited the cooperation of several local (both Palestinian and Israeli) and international individuals and organizations, secular as well as faith-based, that all work nonviolently in various types of activism to expose Israeli injustice and narrate the Palestinian situation and the search for justice, to the end ultimately of achieving the dismantling of the Israeli occupation. "The ugly reality of the present situation has created a feeling of hopelessness for many Palestinians," Ateek explained in launching Kumi Now. "In our attempt to stand firm in the face of oppression, many believe that we have no chance of success and rightfully feel that we have reached rock bottom (. . .). We are disheartened by the current reality." But hopelessness is not an option, as it was not for Jairus and the hemorrhaging woman—or for Bartimaeus—who all simply ignored the negative put-downs of those around them because they knew they had permission to narrate.[15]

Activism through initiatives like Kumi Now, along with prayer, are Sabeel's principal missions. Well before Kumi Now was launched, Sabeel began sending out to an international audience a weekly "Wave of Prayer" that enables friends of Sabeel and of Palestinians everywhere to join in prayer for Palestinian concerns. For years before the COVID-19 pandemic set in, Sabeel held a Eucharist service every Thursday in Jerusalem—now converted to an international online prayer service—and the Wave of Prayer is intended to unite Sabeel's network of supporters in a "wave" as each community lifts the prayers every Thursday at noon in its respective time zone. The intent is for a "wave of prayer" to "wash over the world."

The prayers, which are sent in a dozen languages to an email list of thousands, are always devoted to concrete incidents and issues that

14. Ateek, "Bible Study on Mark."
15. Ateek, "Invitation to Kumi Now."

confront Palestinians in their daily lives. During the second week of
January 2022, for instance, several prayers in the "wave" concerned
unprovoked Israeli assaults on Palestinian Bedouin individuals and
communities. The first concerned Suleiman al Hathaleen, an elder and
community leader from the West Bank village of Umm al-Khair, who was
known for his nonviolent protests against Israeli assaults on the village.
He was hit and run over by an Israeli police tow-truck as he protested
Israel's removal of vehicles from his community. Haj Suleiman, as he was
known because he had performed the Haj pilgrimage to Mecca, was left
without help on the road, according to Sabeel's prayer, "in a coma with
head injuries, along with spine, rib, and hip fractures." He was taken
to a hospital by village residents and remained unconscious for almost
two weeks before he died. Before his death, Sabeel prayed for Suleiman's
recovery, and asked God to "Grant strength to the communities of the
South Hebron Hills [in the West Bank] as they struggle daily with threats
from [Israeli] settler communities and oppression by Israeli authorities."

A prayer the following week also concerned Israeli actions against
Bedouin communities located inside Israel, where Israeli soldiers and
settlers have recently stepped up attacks on rural Bedouin agricultural
and herding communities. Sabeel prayed this time for villagers, in this
case citizens of Israel, whom Israeli forces had injured during a protest
against a project initiated by the Jewish National Fund to plant an entire
forest on land where a Bedouin village sits and where farmers always
plant wheat. This is part of a long-term Israeli plan to displace Bedouin
populations throughout southern Israel and the southern West Bank in
order to turn the land over to Jewish settlement.

As week after week passes in which the Waves of Prayer call out to
God for relief and liberation from Israeli human rights violations, and
as weeks turn into years, Palestinians never seem to lack for reasons to
petition God. There are prayers for Palestinians whose homes have been
demolished; for rural villagers whose olive groves have been ravaged and
property pillaged by government-supported Israeli settlers; for children
arrested in middle-of-the-night raids or shot to death by Israeli soldiers;
for detainees held without charge for lengthy periods; for Gazans enduring a years-long Israeli siege interspersed with deadly Israeli bombing
assaults; for the hundreds of nonviolent protesters killed and seriously
injured during what Gazans called the Great March of Return in 2018
and 2019; for Israeli solidarity groups that help Palestinians; even for

enlightenment for Israeli military forces, that they might see how unjustifiable their killing of civilians is.[16]

The prayers offered in these weekly waves are impassioned, intimate pleas to God for help. One of the most powerful, a prayer that addressed the fundamental injustice touching every Palestinian everywhere in the world, was recited on an anniversary of the Nakba. Others are prayers simply of grief, or collective anxiety, or frustration and anger, along with pleas to maintain Palestinians' steadfastness.

- *On the Nakba anniversary in 2017:* God of love and justice, as we commemorate the Palestinian Nakba (May 15) this week, our hearts break with the grief of 69 years of different forms of injustice and suffering in Palestine. Though our hearts break, please do not let our hope die. Keep our courage and resilience strong, and renew within the Palestinian people the will and the hope for strategic peaceful resistance to on-going abuses. Lord, we cry out that the continuing Nakba of Palestinian dispossession and suffering must end! We pray for all Palestinians (. . .). How long, O Lord, will this continue?

- *Following Israel's demolition of a number of Palestinian homes:* Lord Jesus, we come before you with hearts full of grief as we think of the Palestinian families forced to watch the destruction of their own homes. Lord, you experienced a harsh life under occupation during your ministry on earth, with nowhere for you to lay your head (Matt 8:20 NRSV). We pray for an end to this deplorable practice of home demolition.

- Lord, we come before you ready to lay our anxieties and fears at your feet and ask that you would guard our hearts with your peace which surpasses all understanding.

- *Following Israel's killing of sixty unarmed protesters in Gaza on one day in May 2018:* Lord, we confess that we feel overwhelmed with anger. We pray that your Spirit will work in our hearts to help us continue working for justice and to persevere in our efforts to call for peace and reconciliation.

- Lord, we continue to suffer humiliation at the hands of the powerful as they force us to choose between charity [love] and justice. Grant our people the courage to withstand coercion and to carry the cross towards liberation from the Israeli military occupation.

16. Each week's *Wave of Prayer* can be found on Sabeel website.

Sabeel's hope is that these prayers will "wash over the world." Walter Brueggemann might call them narrations intended to wash over the church as well: stories from below of "the urgency of mercy" for the oppressed that should override the force of silencing culture. Jesus always gives permission to narrate and hears the story. The plea still goes out to the church.

Sabeel's weekly prayers often highlight the hundreds, even thousands, of Palestinian children abused by Israeli authorities, many shot to death, orders of magnitude more detained in Israeli military prisons. "Lord Jesus, you rebuked your disciples and told them to let the little children come to him and not to hinder them (Matt 19:13–15, NRSV)," one prayer began after an Israeli settler had attempted to run down three Palestinian children crossing a road near Hebron. "We bring before you the children of Hebron and elsewhere in the West Bank who suffer harassment, violence and arrest on a daily basis under the Israeli occupation. We long for an end to this nightmare and for a better future for them to live in a land of justice and peace." Other prayers are for the hundreds of Palestinian children detained on average every year in Israeli military prisons. Citing another gospel passage in which Jesus urges his disciples to allow the children to come to him, this one from Luke's Gospel (18:16, NRSV), this prayer calls to Jesus for compassion: "We pray that in your compassion, Lord, you will see how Palestinian children are treated by the Israeli occupation forces in the West Bank. We pray for all those who are trying to support and protect them"—including in this instance an international nonprofit organization, Military Court Watch, that monitors treatment of Palestinian children—"and we pray for the dismantling of the Israeli military court system which has such a corrosive effect on the communities in Palestine."

One Thursday in the last week of the year 2020—a day coinciding with the church's Feast of the Holy Innocents—during a weekly online prayer session with Sabeel followers from around the world, Naim Ateek led a discussion about modern Israel's treatment of Palestinian children, based on the story of the Holy Innocents in the Gospel of Matthew (2:13–18, NRSV). This horrific biblical story is well-known: following Jesus' birth, an angel appeared to Joseph telling him to take the child and the family to Egypt because King Herod, having been informed by the Wise

Men of Jesus' birth, viewed the infant as a threat and intended to kill him. When Herod later discovered that Jesus' family had fled, he ordered that all children in the Bethlehem area aged two years and under be killed.

We do not know with certainty that this story is true. It appears only in Matthew's Gospel, and there is no other record of the Holy Family's flight into Egypt. But the story is, and was undoubtedly intended to be, profoundly symbolic: as the story of Herod's murderous rampage against any perceived threat to his rule, even from an infant, the story symbolizes the unlimited oppressive power that earthly systems of governance wield over the powerless, voiceless, vulnerable populations who exist at the mercy of those systems. And as the story of the challenge Jesus posed to Herod, it is a harbinger of the kind of spiritual power that Jesus' ministry of love and compassion for the downtrodden poses to all oppressive rule.

This gospel story's analogy to today's context in Palestine is striking, and the discussion with Ateek that followed its reading dwelt on its contextual relevance to the situation in Palestine. Here were children, the most innocent of humanity, slaughtered millennia ago at the whim of a leader bent on maintaining his hold on oppressive power, while today in Palestine children are arrested, and too often murdered, by Israeli soldiers usually without cause except at most for stone-throwing—simply because they exist and are easy targets and because Israel allows no challenge to its power and control to go unanswered. These Palestinian children pose no physical threat to the soldiers' or particularly the Israeli government's power, but their innocence in standing up for the Palestinian right to exist, armed most often with nothing but their presence, poses a psychological and a public relations threat to Israel's carefully crafted image, only very recently beginning to be tattered, as a benevolent democracy struggling for its own survival against supposed rampant "security" threats.

The Israeli military detains an average of five hundred to seven hundred Palestinian children under age eighteen every year; these children are held in adult military prisons, denied due process, subject to harsh interrogation and often torture, forbidden contact with parents and attorneys and, if they come to trial, prosecuted in a military court system in which the conviction rate for Palestinians of all ages is over 99 percent.[17] During 2020, Israeli soldiers shot and killed six Palestin-

17. Numbers of arrests and other data are taken from a bill submitted in 2019 to the 116th US Congress by Rep. Betty McCollum, a Democrat from Minnesota: H.R. 2407, "Promoting Human Rights for Palestinian Children Living Under Israeli

ian teenagers in the West Bank and injured more than one thousand. United Nations reporting indicates that between 2014 and 2020, Israeli forces killed a yearly average of over twenty Palestinian children under age eighteen. In only three instances were indictments issued against the responsible Israeli military personnel.[18] The year 2021 was particularly devastating for Palestinian children. Among a total of over three hundred Palestinians killed by Israeli security forces and in Israeli military attacks, according to the Israeli human rights organization B'Tselem, more than seventy were children: seventeen were teenagers in the West Bank and East Jerusalem, and fifty-four were children in Gaza slain during Israel's air assault on that territory in May 2021.[19]

The conflict resolution center Wi'am bases its reconciliatory philosophy, and its entire healing, relationship-building mission, on the passage from Paul's first letter to the Corinthians (1 Cor 12:12–27, NRSV), in which Paul teaches the concept of humanity as one body—one body in Jesus Christ—with many differing members:

> For just as the body is one and has many members, and all the members of the body, though many, are one body, so it is with Christ. For in the one Spirit we were all baptized into one body—Jews or Greeks, slaves or free—and we were all made to drink of one Spirit. Indeed, the body does not consist of one member but of many. If the foot would say, "Because I am not a hand, I do not belong to the body," that would not make it any less a part of the body (. . .). God has so arranged the body (. . .) that there may be no dissension within the body, but the members may have the same care for one another. If one member suffers, all suffer together with it, if one member is honored, all rejoice together with it. Now you are the body of Christ and individually members of it.

Military Occupation Act," which would prohibit the use of US military aid to Israel for "the military detention, interrogation, abuse, or ill treatment of children in violation of international humanitarian law." The bill was a successor to similar legislation submitted in 2017 to the 115th Congress, H.R. 4391. The earlier bill had thirty co-sponsors in the House of Representatives; H.R. 2407 gained only twenty-two co-sponsors. In the 117th congressional session beginning in 2021, McCollum introduced yet another iteration of this resolution, H.R. 2590.

18. Office of the High Commissioner for Human Rights, "UN Experts Alarmed."

19. B'Tselem, "2021 Was the Deadliest Year Since 2014."

In this spirit, Wi'am teaches that all humankind is part of one body: all of humanity, and in particular all Palestinians, belong to that one body. "We may be oceans apart, and separated by many degrees of freedom and rights," Zoughbi has written, "but we are all connected through our humanity and one world." Palestinians are crying out to the body—to the world and the body of Christ—with the most important plea of liberation theology, "proclaim[ing] to our body: We are hurting and have been suffering." Palestinians are resilient and steadfast, Wi'am preaches, holding firmly to the belief that "no injustice will last forever" and to the hope that the body of Christ, humanity, "will soon awaken to the suffering of some of its parts."[20]

Any serious activism or advocacy on behalf of justice for the disadvantaged and marginalized—however nonviolent and innocent, no matter whether a protest against Israeli oppression or an action to help those afflicted by that oppression—poses a threat on some level to the smooth functioning of oppressive rule. The Palestinian children held in detention by Israel are innocents because they are young, hapless victims of Israel's harshly oppressive rule and children whom Israel can use to intimidate other youth who might challenge that rule. Wi'am is also an innocent, standing up nonviolently against the suffocating effects of Israeli domination. But advocacy for justice and the rights of the oppressed and marginalized is not only a political imperative; it is a critical theological imperative laid out clearly in the gospels by Jesus himself. The examples are legion of Jesus' call for justice for everyone—not only for the downtrodden but, because they are so often forgotten and ignored, especially for them, and most especially for innocent children. The mission of love and compassion, justice and mercy for the poor—the poor as defined most broadly—is the role and provenance of liberation theology.

Jesus himself, of course, posed a considerable threat to the smooth functioning of oppressive rule, as Herod foresaw from the beginning, that first Christmas. This message is usually lost in the noise and bustle of Christmas preparations and festivities, even sacred celebrations, but the biblical Christmas story in fact provides the theme for numerous liberation stories, well beyond the sacred tale of a blessed babe in a manger. The Rev. Alex Awad, a now-retired Palestinian Methodist missionary and

---

20. Zoughbi and Zoughbi, "From the Chaos of Fear, Panic and Anger."

scholar from Bethlehem, has taught about Christmas as an event that revealed a "collision of forces" between the divine power of God's work on earth and the forces of darkness represented by the oppressive secular power of Herod and his Roman overlords, who pursued and oppressed Jesus from the time of his birth. Awad notes that Mary foretold this "collision" when she sang the Magnificat, praising God for looking with favor on herself and all the lowly. Mary proclaimed: "His mercy is for those who fear him from generation to generation. He has shown strength with his arm; he has scattered the proud in the thoughts of their hearts. He has brought down the powerful from their thrones, and lifted up the lowly; he has filled the hungry with good things, and sent the rich away empty" (Luke 1:50–53, NRSV).[21]

Identifying Mary's words as the description of a successful revolution, one still to come upon the birth of her son, Awad also cites the prayer of Zechariah as foretelling a revolution, another "collision of forces," that would save and liberate the people from oppression. Zechariah, the father of Jesus' cousin John the Baptist, was a priest of the Temple, but he had been struck dumb when he expressed doubt that he and his wife Elizabeth could be expecting a child at their advanced ages. His speech was restored at the birth of his son John and, filled with the Holy Spirit, he spoke this prayer and prophecy:

> Blessed be the Lord God (. . .). He has raised up a mighty savior for us in the House of his servant David, as he spoke through the mouth of his holy prophets from of old, that we would be saved from our enemies and from the hand of all who hate us. Thus he has shown the mercy promised to our ancestors, and has remembered his holy covenant (. . .) that we, being rescued from the hands of our enemies, might serve him without fear, in holiness and righteousness before him all our days. And you, child, will be called the prophet of the Most High; for you will go before the Lord to prepare his ways, to give knowledge of salvation to his people by the forgiveness of their sins. By the tender mercy of our God, the dawn from on high will break upon us, to give light to those who sit in darkness and in the shadow of death, to guide our feet into the way of peace (Luke 1:68–79, NRSV).[22]

21. Awad, "Colliding Forces."
22. Awad, "Colliding Forces."

The collision of forces about which Awad speaks continues two thousand years later. Awad is preaching the central message of liberation theology when he notes that millions around the world still "yearn for freedom from poverty and political oppression, and hundreds of thousands of activists are demanding justice for all members of humanity." This is graphically demonstrated, of course, in Palestine, the very place of Jesus' birth—where Palestinians daily endure gross atrocities and human rights violations at the hands of today's "imperial occupier," Israel's apartheid regime.[23] Christmas can thus be a time of lamentation as well as of hope and joy for Palestinians. A recent issue of *Kairos Palestine's* annual Christmas message carried a plaintive prayer and cry to God for rescue, coming not from the gospels but from Isaiah, written at a time of turmoil for the Jews:

> Look down from heaven and see, from your holy and glorious habitation. Where are your zeal and your might? The yearning of your heart and your compassion? They are withheld from me [us] (. . .). You, O Lord, are our father (. . .). Our Redeemer from of old is your name (. . .). O that you would tear open the heavens and come down, (. . .) so that the mountains would quake at your presence—as when fire kindles brushwood and the fire causes water to boil—to make your name known to your adversaries, so that the nations might tremble at your presence! (Isa 63:15–16, 64:1–2, NRSV).[24]

But in the midst of turmoil and lamentation, as Awad shows, Christmas also brings hope: hope that, even as Israeli apartheid collides with every aspect of Palestinian life, Palestinians themselves and a growing number of human rights advocates—not only Christians, but secular activists of all faiths, including Jews and Muslims—are challenging that system. The gospels, especially the Gospels of Matthew and Luke, still carry "stories of hope for the hopeless." God comes "to collide with the powers (. . .) that oppress the poor [in order] to bring them freedom and peace." The incarnation narratives demonstrate that God anoints ordinary men and women to do God's own "work of salvation, rescue and liberation."[25]

23. Awad, "Colliding Forces."
24. *Kairos Palestine*, "Kairos Palestine Christmas Alert 2020."
25. Awad, "Colliding Forces."

Few New Testament stories are as well-known, or as directly relevant to Palestinians, as the story in Luke's Gospel (2:8–20, NRSV) of the angels' appearance to a few lowly shepherds on a hillside near Bethlehem: ordinary people selected to receive extraordinary news, the kind of news that actually set them on a course apart from Empire and Power. Just as God shares the pain of the oppressed and marginalized, those who most need spiritual succor, so does God share "good news of great joy for all the people" with ordinary people, those who feel inconsequential and who most need hope and messages of joy.

These shepherds were Palestinians, most likely in those days Palestinian Jews, but clearly the native people of Palestine. The hillside on which they were spending the night with their flocks is now the town of Beit Sahour, today a mostly Christian town adjacent to Bethlehem. Palestinian Christians are proud to be the descendants of these shepherds of two thousand years ago. The "grandchildren of the shepherds," as a Palestinian church official calls today's Christians, "are still here." These grandchildren are the Christians of Palestine, says Yusef Daher; they are Palestinians of all faiths who have faced military occupation for centuries but who see Palestine "as an inclusive country where all are equals," Palestinians who today nonviolently resist Israel's illegal settlement and occupation. And they are the Palestinian Christians who composed *Kairos Palestine* as a "word of faith, hope and love in the midst of the Palestinian suffering." The shepherds are still here, Daher reiterates, "carrying the message from the angels: Glory to God in the highest heaven, and on earth peace to those whom God favors!"[26]

26. *Kairos Palestine*, "Kairos Palestine Christmas Alert 2020."

5

Jewish Liberation Theology Allies

Exceptionalism has become a monstrous fantasy of Jewish nationalism.
The things I love about Judaism, the things that made me, are
today often disdained as signs of weakness. And look around you,
communities everywhere are trying to overcome their own crumbling
ideas of exceptionalism in an era of globalized discrimination,
inequity and climate crisis. The old ways don't serve us anymore.

—PHILIP WEISS[1]

I realized the most Jewish thing I could do was stand with the Palestinians.

—RABBI BRANT ROSEN[2]

If Christian triumphalism as expressed in supersessionism led to
the ovens of Auschwitz, then Jewish triumphalism as expressed in
political Zionism has led to the ethnic cleansing of Palestine.

—MARK BRAVERMAN[3]

1. Weiss, "Addressing the Role of my Community."
2. Rosen, Lecture, "A Jewish Perspective." Rosen was speaking about Israel's assault on Gaza, Operation Cast Lead, December 2008–January 2009.
3. Braverman, *Fatal Embrace*, 114.

THREE QUARTERS OF A century past Israel's massive ethnic cleansing of Palestinians and well into its existence as a self-declared, exclusivist "Jewish state," more than half a century after its conquest of all the remaining land of Palestine between the river and the sea, few would deny that Israel's Zionist narrative on the Palestinian-Israeli issue dominates global public discourse, eclipsing the Palestinian narrative almost completely. This is true in the media, in churches and Christian religious circles, certainly in synagogues and Jewish religious circles, in centers of political power, in think tanks and government sectors wherever public policy is made. We saw the late Palestinian-American intellectual Edward Said's eloquent lament about the eclipse of the Palestinian narrative in Chapter 2. Zionist narrative domination is a reality that has existed in fact for more than a century—from the time when the Zionist movement began to gain influence and its aggressive political campaigning to thrive, well before the state of Israel was established.[4] The narrative has dominated the making of policy from the time over a century ago, in 1917, when the author of Britain's post-World War I colonialist plan for Palestine, Foreign Secretary Lord Arthur Balfour, issued the colonialist memorandum known as the Balfour Declaration expressing Britain's support for establishment of a Jewish "national homeland" in Palestine. This declaration referred to the Palestinian Arab population of Palestine—an indigenous people, making up 90 percent of Palestine's population at the time—merely as "non-Jews." Two years later, in Paris for the postwar peace conference, Balfour again wrote off the Palestinian Arabs, declaring with astonishing directness in a recorded interview that Britain had no intention of consulting Palestine's Arabs about its colonial plans, because "Zionism, be it right or wrong, good or bad, is rooted in age-long traditions, in present needs, in future hopes, of far profounder import than the desires and prejudices of the seven hundred thousand Arabs who now inhabit that ancient land."[5]

This is not the place to rehearse at any length the by-now well-documented history of Zionist Israel's long and continuing effort, buttressed by the active support and propaganda of Israel's supporters in Europe and the United States, to erase Palestinians and their narrative

4. For an analysis of the ways the Zionist narrative has captured political discourse in the United States, particularly how it has framed the thinking and decision-making of US policymakers for the last century and more, see Christison, *Perceptions of Palestine*.

5. "Interview in Mr. Balfour's Apartment."

from the political scene. The evidence of this effort to "disappear" Palestinians physically from the land Israel calls "Eretz Israel" and claims as its
own, and politically from the Zionist narrative has been crystal clear for
some time despite the continuing vigorous denials of Israel's supporters.[6]
By now, the narrative as formulated by the most ardent Zionists and ac-
cepted in much of public discourse around the world, goes something
like this: Jews are indigenous to the "land of Israel" and are the only
indigenous population; despite being dispersed for millennia, they are
merely returning to their homeland; far from being a colonialist state,
Israel is merely reestablishing its governance in its own and the Jewish
people's "native land." This particular exclusivist narrative is just one of a
multitude of arguments in a Zionist rhetorical arsenal produced by Israel
and its supporters, and turned into a staple of public discourse, that is
designed to "prove" that Palestinians are not native to the land; that they
are simply part of a broad conglomeration of indistinguishable Arabs
who have no rights in their own land, which is not their own land in any
case, and who are motivated solely by hatred of Jews; they are terrorists,
uncivilized and unworthy of democratic freedom, who wish to "throw
Jews into the sea."

Neither is this the place to examine the Jewish psyche to discern the
motivations for this Zionist effort to erase the Palestinians, whether this
effort arises from trauma and pain over centuries of persecution culmi-
nating in the Holocaust or from the sheer ruthlessness of racial suprema-
cism, or from a combination of these and other factors. Whatever the
underlying impetus, the general tenor of public discourse about Israel
and the Palestinians as molded by Zionist propagandists and *hasbara*[7]
specialists and their allies has been always to paint Israel in a bright light,
never acknowledging flaws or imperfections, and either to ignore the
Palestinians altogether or to attack them as terrorists with no legitimacy
in the land and no cogent reason for hostility toward Israel except hatred
of Jews.

Without intruding into the psychology or the passion of Jewish and Zionist thinking, it is important to be aware that there is today

6. The literature detailing this anti-Palestinian Zionist effort, and the Palestinian
struggle against it, is massive. See the several sources cited in preceding chapters, as
well as in the Bibliography.

7. The Hebrew word *hasbara* can be rendered in English more or less literally as
"explaining," although it is most often translated somewhat delicately as "public diplo-
macy." One might also call it "propaganda."

considerable open, and increasingly intense, debate within the Jewish community at grassroots levels in both the United States and Israel over the moral condition of the Jewish body politic, at least of that part of the community that identifies specifically as Jewish and is actively supportive of Israel and its existence. This debate is exposing more and more of those flaws and imperfections that have previously been considered off-limits for discussion outside the Jewish "family," as well as more and more doubts among the family about Zionism's moral compass.[8] In Israel, the Israeli human rights monitor B'Tselem, which has published a steady stream of reports through the years on an array of Israeli atrocities against Palestinians, began the year 2021, as we have seen, by issuing its breakthrough report labeling Israel a Jewish supremacist, apartheid regime throughout the entire territory under its control, both inside the state and in the occupied Palestinian territories. Also in Israel, there is a small core of media correspondents, writers and activists, and a growing number of alternative blogs and activist groups that help Palestinians and actively protest Israeli government and settler actions against them; all, importantly, stand in solidarity with Palestinians, even though some remain politically Zionist. In the United States, several anti- or non-Zionist organizations, along with a few prominent writers and several alternative websites, blogs, and media organs stand out as outspoken—and, in view of the usually angry response they receive, courageous—questioners of Zionism and as supporters of Palestinian rights against Israel's abusive actions and policies. There are enough of these individuals and organizations that attempting to name all of them here risks doing a disservice by inadvertently omitting some.

8. The notion of *ahavath Yisrael*, or love for the Jewish people, appears to be at the center of the current intra-Jewish debate. It is discussed in some depth in Angel, "Responsa: On Loving Jews." Angel, the *Jewish Currents* editor-in-chief, writes about finding herself and the publication "mired in an intracommunal argument about tribalism and humanism": on whether Jews must unquestioningly follow *ahavath Yisrael*, on how "affiliated American Jews" who are attached to organized Jewish life understand their Jewishness, and ultimately on her own personal belief that "Jewishness must mean justice for the Palestinian people or nothing at all." Angel also discusses the issue separately with *Jewish Currents* Editor-at-Large Peter Beinart in a podcast, during which they talk about the intellectual and emotional struggle they and many American Jews on the left have in trying to balance, on the one hand, a sense that all Jews have an "obligation" of loyalty to other Jews—the belief that "there really is no Judaism without following this imperative to love your fellow Jew"—versus, on the other hand, trying to meet what many have come to believe is an urgent moral imperative to support Palestinian freedom. See Angel, "Use and Abuse of 'Jewish Peoplehood.'"

Sadly, however, none of these, either individually or collectively, has yet been able to turn many US politicians and or any US political leaders or policymaking officials away from total and unquestioning support for Israel. Despite the considerable emotional debate inside the Jewish community over degrees of familial and political attachment to Israel, and despite the growing reality that a younger generation of American Jews is speaking out against their elders' zealous support for Israel, very little of the discourse has yet had enough of an impact to alter policy, either in the Israeli circles or at the official US political levels where policy is formulated.

Not surprisingly, with respect specifically to Palestinian liberation theology, what little Jewish reaction to this contextual theology exists has been highly negative. During the 1990s and the first decade-plus of the twenty-first century when Sabeel's US arm FOSNA sponsored hundreds of local conferences around the country to give exposure to the Palestinian and Palestinian Christian perspective on the struggle with Israel, local Jewish Federations and other Jewish organizations mounted strident efforts to oppose and, occasionally successfully, to close the conferences, always labeling Sabeel as antisemitic. Among Jewish theologians, only a very few have devoted any study to the Palestinian theology and how Judaism and Jewish theology relate to it. As we examine these Jewish theologians, those opposed to liberation theology, as well as those who support it, it will be important to keep in mind the moral debate going on within the grassroots Jewish community, as a measure against which Jewish attitudes toward Palestinian liberation theology can be judged. An intense moral tension now increasingly frames the Jewish debate: a conundrum between, on the one hand, remaining in unquestioning loyalty to and love of the Jewish people, and on the other hand, facing what many see as an urgent moral imperative to support Palestinian freedom and equality.

If British colonialism provided the secular political underpinnings of the Zionist project in Palestine, significantly enabling the vision of Jewish statehood in the early decades of the twentieth century, the Holocaust and the profound anguish that it laid on all Jews provided the theological underpinnings and rationale for Zionism's perceived need to pursue Jewish national exclusivity later in the twentieth century. It is important to understand the huge impact that so-called Holocaust or post-Holocaust theology—as scholars refer to Jewish theology in the aftermath of the Holocaust and of Israel's establishment—has had in shaping discourse *in* Israel, *about* Israel throughout the world, and about Jews in general. It is equally important, although far less of global interest, to study how this theology has affected perspectives on the Palestinians, who became the victims of the Holocaust's victims. One assertion by a leading Holocaust theologian will suffice for now to set the scene: Emil Fackenheim, a Holocaust survivor himself, wrote voluminously in the decades following the Holocaust and powerfully reasserted the notion of Jewish "chosenness" and exceptionalism, which he viewed as the Jews' only possible response to their collective suffering. The Shoah (as the Holocaust is often called), he declared, "compelled" Jews "to *accept themselves as singled out* by the most elemental moral necessity (. . .) [to reaffirm] the age-old doctrine of the divine covenant with Israel."[9]

The self-absorbed Jewish- and Zionist-centric perspective that this declaration speaks to and endorses seems to render the many Jews who embrace it incapable of coping with a world that does not center on them and their attachment to Israel. More to the point here, it appears to render those who share this perspective incapable of understanding the Palestinian-Israeli struggle from other than this Jewish-centric perspective.

As almost any Jewish thinker will loudly assert, Jews are not monolithic, nor is Jewish thinking. But the Zionist policy that disadvantages and abuses Palestinians *is* monolithic, for the very reason that it is official state policy. Unquestioning support for that policy from friends of Israel renders the policy still broader, more unitary, and to all appearances unchanging. There exists, of course, a massive amount of Jewish theological commentary around Jewish support for Zionism and its policies in Israel, but little of the commentary deals with Palestinian theology. It is thus helpful—and, as it happens in this case, reflective of a broad sampling of general Jewish thinking—to examine the views of one theologian, Amy-Jill Levine, who comments specifically on Palestinian liberation theology and is highly critical of it. Levine's commentary is indicative of a common viewpoint informed by a Zionist-centric lens. Later, we will examine the positions of other Jewish theologians with totally different viewpoints, theologians who are in fact closely engaged from their Jewish perspectives with Palestinians and the Palestinian theology. An examination of Levine's thinking provides a tableau against which to credit those Jews

9. Quoted in Braverman, "Theology in the Shadow," 151. Emphasis in original.

who are able to view the Palestinian-Israeli struggle not only from their own Jewish vantage point, but from a Palestinian perspective as well, and against which to apply moral standards.

In a 2006 book entitled *The Misunderstood Jew*, about modern Christian church teachings about Jesus and their implications for Jews today, Levine, a noted scholar of the New Testament, sets the scene for her study with the astonishing declaration in the book's Introduction that in "the churches" today—presumably meaning, because she adds no qualifiers, all churches—"Christian ministers and laity alike depict his [Jesus'] Jewish background as the epitome of all that is wrong in the world." Although it might be thought that the "misunderstood Jew" of Levine's title is meant to be a kind of Jewish everyman representing Jews today, misunderstood by the Christian world, it is actually Jesus who Levine believes is misunderstood. Her thesis is that Christian teaching typically fails to remind us that Jesus was a Jew and remained so to his death and that, because of this imagined misidentification, all teaching about Jesus' goodness comes across as an indictment of a Judaism that is supposedly bad. In a leap of logic, Levine argues that, if Christian teaching asserts that "Jesus preaches good news to the poor," this means that Christians believe "'the Jews' must be preaching good news to the rich. If Jesus welcomes sinners, 'the Jews' must have pushed them away."[10] And so on, *ad absurdum*.

Although she makes it clear that she does not worship Jesus, Levine says she is personally rather taken with him, and she actually seems to feel a bit proprietary about him: "I find Jesus reflects back to me my own tradition, but in a new key. I also have to admit to bit of pride in thinking about him—he's one of ours." But Christian teaching too often, by her lights, "turns Jesus away from his Jewish identity and makes him into a liberal Protestant," a transformation she believes is antisemitic. Antisemitism, she feels, tends to arise when the history of Jesus' Jewishness is not known.[11]

Much about Christian church history is indeed condemnable: the church clearly did, through much of history until the end of the Holocaust, shamefully misappropriate Jesus' name and spirit as a blessing on Christianity's centuries of antisemitism. And, as we have seen, the church has long been, and remains, closely allied with empire and entwined with

10. Levine, *Misunderstood Jew*, 9.
11. Levine, *Misunderstood Jew*, 8–9.

the power of secular oppressors. Christian practice in modern times is replete with imperfections, perhaps most of all, as noted repeatedly, in its general failure to aid or act in solidarity with oppressed and marginalized populations. But Levine is not complaining about church collusion with empire, and her complaint about the church's failure to honor Jesus' Jewish background is what we might today label "fake news." Her generalization that all Christianity portrays Jesus' Jewish background as the "epitome of all that is wrong in the world" is startling: startling both because it is so blatantly pejorative—such sweepingly critical generalizations, if spoken about Jews or Judaism, would rightly be denounced as antisemitic—and because it is increasingly inaccurate as a characterization of Christian liturgy, teaching, and belief. Levine is apparently unaware of how closely in fact Jesus is identified with his Jewish roots in modern Christian seminary teaching and in church liturgy. She might also be surprised, and her broad charge against the church seriously undermined, if she knew that, in today's reality of increased racial consciousness, many progressive Christians (though not institutional church leaders) refer to Jesus with affection as "the brown-skinned Palestinian Jew."

Levine's assertions about Christianity in general and how it depicts Judaism display the kind of self-absorbed field of vision that we have discussed—the Fackenheim view that Jews have been morally anointed as exceptional and must be honored, and heeded, as such. However understandable this kind of lens might still be after the Jewish history of persecution, the lens is distorted and shows a too-common tendency to view the world's human interactions as always involving Jews, Judaism, and Zionism. This is a worldview that is more than commonly inclined to demand a kind of special love of Jews and of Israel, and more than commonly inclined to see hostile intent in even mildly critical commentary about Israel. This sensitivity is evident not only in religious and theological commentary such as Levine's, but also in some of the most mundane secular discourse: in the heated accusations in 2021, for instance, that the decision of Ben & Jerry's Ice Cream to stop sales in the occupied territories was "antisemitic" and constituted "terrorism," or in comedian Sarah Silverman's much-publicized dismay at the fact that non-Jewish actors are sometimes cast as Jewish characters in films and television.

Levine carries her sweeping indictment of Christianity into her examination of liberation theology in general and of Palestinian liberation theology in particular. She asserts, without providing much evidence beyond a few problematic quotes, that "the language of liberation all too often veers off into anti-Jewish rants." This all amounts, she believes, to "appalling" and "dreadful" history, and conveys an impression of Judaism as "obscene."[12] In a serious misrepresentation of liberation theology as it emerged throughout Latin America and especially as it is professed in Palestine, she observes that, when liberation theologians turn to the Jesus of the gospels as liberator, they do not identify the oppressor as "Roman imperialism or colonialism," but rather "find Judaism and Jews to epitomize systemic evil."[13]

This is patently false. Jews hardly figure at all in liberation theology. As we have seen, when liberation theologies hold up Jesus' teachings and actions as models for spiritual and physical liberation from oppression, they do clearly identify the Roman occupiers under whom Jesus lived and was crucified as the oppressors, not Jews. Moreover, the modern oppressors held up by these several liberation theologies as analogous to the oppressor of Jesus' time are today's dictatorial, colonial and post-colonial governments and the Christian churches that collude with these governments. No one holds today's Jews—or indeed today's Romans or Italians—responsible for having persecuted Jesus. The fact that Israel happens to be one of the modern oppressive systems targeted by liberation theology has nothing to do with its Jewishness: liberation is sought because Israel is oppressive, not because it is Jewish; Palestinians also sought liberation from British rule during the British Mandate era between the World Wars, although Great Britain was obviously not Jewish.

Levine uses the same dubious logic and almost the same dramatic condemnatory adjectives when she turns directly to discussing Palestinian liberation theology and Naim Ateek himself—and again appears not to have a clear knowledge of what the Palestinian theology is about. Her principal contention is that, when "forms of Palestinian liberation

12. Levine, *Misunderstood Jew*, 9. The two quotes Levine provides from liberation theologians—which she labels "anti-Jewish obscenities," "evil," "pernicious," and poisonous—appear on 169: from Gustavo Gutiérrez, writing that the "infidelities of the Jewish people made the Old Covenant invalid"; and from Leonardo Boff, writing, "In the world as Jesus found it, human beings were (. . .) under the yoke of absolutization of religion, of tradition, and of the law. Religion was no longer the way in which human beings expressed their own openness to God. It had crystallized and stagnated in a world of its own, a world of rites and sacrifice. Pharisees had a morbid conception of their God." (Ellipsis in Levine's quote from Boff.) Although dismissive of Jewish teaching and practice in Jesus' day, these quotes, particularly the skimpy quote from Gutiérrez, do not seem to rise to the level of rants, or poison, or others of Levine's characterizations, and do not, as she charges, portray Judaism as "obscene."

13. Levine, *Misunderstood Jew*, 168.

theology appropriate Jesus for political ends," a stereotypical anti-Jewish message is conveyed to churches and the world—largely, she seems to be implying, simply because of the Palestinians' identity as Palestinians. Any teaching, Levine says, "that separates Jesus and his first followers from Jewish identity, associates these proto-Christians with the Palestinian population, and reserves the label 'Jew' for those who crucified Jesus and persecuted the church is not only historically untenable but theologically abhorrent."[14]

The references to "appropriating Jesus" and "separating Jesus and his followers from Jewish identity" indicate, whether Levine intends this or not, that she is unaware that Palestinian liberation theology is a theology formulated in modern times by Palestinian Christians—and in fact that there have been indigenous Christians in Palestine from the days of Jesus' earliest followers. Palestinians today, and those who in Jesus' time identified themselves as followers of Jesus (as "people of the way") are not merely "associated" with the Palestinian population. They *are* the Palestinian population today, and they *were* the Palestinian population then. As we have seen, Palestinians today of all faiths are largely descended from exactly the first-century population of Palestine of whom Levine speaks, which was made up primarily although not exclusively of Jews. If Jesus belongs to the Jews—"one of ours," by Levine's lights—it is equally and, one might say, even more true that, for Palestinians today, he is "one of ours too." Palestinians do not need to "appropriate" him.

Many Jews in this first-century population obviously followed Jesus' disciples and ultimately adopted Christianity because of Jesus; many did not. Many of this population were Gentiles living among the Jews and also adopted this new faith; many did not. Six centuries later, some of the early Christians, and perhaps some contemporaneous Jews, converted to Islam; many Muslims moved to Palestine; some Muslims probably converted back to Christianity when the Crusaders invaded, or intermingled with these Europeans and produced more changes in the ethnic composition of Palestine's multi-faith population. Undoubtedly, most of those Jews who lived in Palestine through the millennia and identified as "Palestinian Jews" until Israel's establishment were also descended from Jews of the first century. The admixture of ethnicities and religions in Palestine over a period of two thousand years—considering the several periods of exile and the history of living in diaspora that Jews

14. Levine, *Misunderstood Jew*, 183.

endured, considering also the periods of massive migration in and out that occurred in Palestine, and the fact that this land has always been at the crossroads of trade and commercial routes—renders it a fantastic leap of reasoning to imply that Palestinians ever deliberately dissociated themselves from ancient Jews.

It is also fantasy, frankly, that Palestinians devote much thought to who, other than the Roman occupiers who now symbolize their modern oppressors, was responsible for crucifying Jesus. It bears repeating that modern Israel as an oppressor is on Palestinian liberation theology's radar today not because Israel is a Jewish state, nor for any reason having to do with Jews, but simply because Israel has been the instrument of Palestinian oppression. Once again, Jews and Judaism are not the center of this liberation theology story.

When she turns her assault to Naim Ateek personally, Levine presents nothing about him or his writing that could legitimately be called, as she does, "theologically abhorrent." It appears that she never read his 1989 book *Justice and Only Justice*, published almost two decades before she wrote; she cites only quotes from Ateek's speeches that she has found in articles about him written by others (those others being in disagreement with him). On the basis of these few quotes, she finds Ateek's rhetoric "overblown" and "slippery" and also, just for good measure, "pernicious." She opposes everything she has discovered Ateek saying, but offers no cogent counterarguments. Her particular condemnations are directed at Ateek's (accurate) depiction of Jesus as "a Palestinian [living] under occupation"; his metaphorical characterization of Israel's oppressive system as a "crucifixion system"; his (correct) statement that "Palestinians have been condemned as a nation by Israel, and sentenced to destruction"; his (accurate) observation that, like Palestinians today, Jesus faced charges of being a "terrorist, evildoer, or rebel and a subversive person"; and his (honest) assertion that Israel is an exclusivist state.[15]

Levine concludes her assault on Ateek and on Palestinian liberation theology as she began, by reiterating the political and theological nonsequitur that drives her thesis: the straw man that "any prejudicial commentary that divorces Jesus from Judaism and then uses the story of Jesus to condemn all Jews is not a 'Christian' message. It is, rather, a recycled anti-Judaism that depicts Israel as a country of Christ killers."[16] Levine

15. Levine, *Misunderstood Jew*, 183–85.
16. Levine, *Misunderstood Jew*, 185.

either cannot tell the difference between antisemitic criticism of Jews as Jews and Ateek's criticism of Zionism as a political governing system, or actually sees no difference herself between Judaism and Zionism. In either case, she appears to be so absorbed in her own thought processes about Jewishness that she does not devote any thought to what Ateek has actually written and preached—failing to notice, or deliberately ignoring, that Ateek never condemns Jews individually or collectively, never blames Jews or Israel for crucifying Jesus, always directs his criticism at Israel-the-state or Zionism-the-political-movement for the human rights violations Israel is inflicting on modern-day Palestinians. Regarding Levine's specific objections above, Ateek does not "divorce Jesus from Judaism"; his reference to Jesus as a Palestinian living under occupation is a reference to Jesus' residence in Palestine under Roman occupation, not to his religion. Nor is Ateek's use of the crucifixion as a metaphor for the suffering of oppressed Palestinians today an effort to revive or hark back to the horrific charges of deicide that characterized the vicious antisemitism of the Middle Ages. As we saw in German theologian Jürgen Moltmann's use of the same metaphor, the mystical understanding that, because God knows suffering on the cross, God understands and stands with suffering humanity, is a profoundly liberating insight.

As Jewish liberation theologian Mark Braverman has noted, Levine is "tarring a theological formulation arising from a contemporary context with the brush of historic church anti-Semitism" and, in so doing, is essentially attempting to silence the Palestinian voice. Liberation theology is a form of nonviolent resistance against an oppressor, and in Palestinian theology, the oppressor is Israeli Zionism, not Jews or Judaism; Palestinian theologians cannot be held hostage to whatever unpleasant associations the reminder of medieval antisemitism may raise for Jews, or to whatever discomfort Israel and Zionists may feel at being labeled the oppressor. Braverman believes that Jews are ultimately responsible themselves for this uncomfortable association: "We—the Jewish people—set this up," he declares. "We did so by declaring a Jewish state established on the ruins of Palestinian towns and villages."[17]

Ultimately it would appear, in Levine's singular focus on Jews and Judaism—the people and the faith that define her own being and spirituality—she is unable to appreciate that other oppressed peoples are also focused chiefly on their particular experience of suffering, and on the

17. Braverman, "Moment of Grace," 68. Emphasis in original.

spirituality and the faith that define them, rather than on what may or may not have occurred millennia ago. Worship is intimate and personal. It is about one's relationship or a community's relationship with God, far more than it is about the intricacies of centuries-old theological issues. When a liberation theologian enumerates the abuses of oppressors—as indeed Ateek does about Israel in writing and from the pulpit, and as all liberation theologians do in their own contexts—the focus is far more on resistance to those abuses, and on the search for personal and community spiritual comfort and healing, than it is on the religious origins of the oppressor or even necessarily on the religious origins of Jesus and his early followers.

Levine's commentary does not by any means, of course, cover the extent of learned Jewish commentary on Christianity or on Palestinians. But it is offered as a small sampling of Jewish thought—almost a lone example in fact of any Jewish thought devoted in depth to Palestinian Christians and their theology. More thoughtful commentary, as well as more political action in solidarity with Palestinians, is emerging from the Jewish community, as we have seen. But the general paucity of commentary on Palestinians is itself a striking indication of the self-absorption of so much of Jewish thinking in the aftermath of the Holocaust and of what so many have seen as the Jewish redemption achieved in statehood. It is actually quite remarkable that it was the late 1980s, forty-plus years after the Holocaust and Israel's establishment, before any Jewish theologian began to break the silence about what Israel had been doing for decades to erase Palestine—forty years before a serious Jewish commentator began to listen to Palestinians and show interest in them *as Palestinians*, rather than merely as what Edward Said called "errata" and "dislocations" in the Israeli Jewish narrative.

Marc Ellis was that serious, radical young Jewish thinker deeply concerned about the ethics of what he termed Jewish "empowerment" in a sovereign state, at a time during the first intifada when Palestinians were rising up in opposition to Israel's oppression. Ellis focused primarily on the moral condition of the Jewish people and what Jewish empowerment meant for the future of the Jewish prophetic tradition, but that inextricably entailed a concern as well about the suffering Palestinians were experiencing at the hands of Jews. Ellis's first book on the moral implications of Jewish empowerment arising out of the Holocaust, *Toward a Jewish Theology of Liberation*, was a plea to Jews to liberate themselves from empowerment. The book was initially published in 1987, before the intifada began late that year, and was then reissued in 1989. In the later edition, Ellis used the intifada to plead that Jews everywhere begin to recognize that "the future of what it means to be Jewish" lay "in the faces of the Palestinians"—that "at the center of the struggle to be faithful as a Jew today is the suffering and liberation of the Palestinian people." He saw Israel's brutal treatment of Palestinians during the intifada as having stripped empowered Jews of the innocence—the aura of weakness and helplessness—that the Holocaust had given them, and he viewed the fundamental integration of Jewish and Palestinian political, cultural, and religious life as "integral to the Jewish future."[18] Ellis published a second, much expanded treatment of his thesis about Jewish ethics, *Beyond Innocence and Redemption*, only a year later, and in that time he connected with Naim Ateek and the Palestinian and other theologians helping Ateek formulate Palestinian liberation theology and establish Sabeel.

Ellis's awakening to Palestinian suffering at the hands of an empowered Jewish state was revolutionary among Jewish thinkers at the time. This was something clearly evidenced by the hostility he faced from Jewish commentators and, in retrospect, by the almost two decades that passed before there emerged any significant support for his critique of Israel and of Jewish ethics. Even though his concern was focused at this early stage far more on the state of Jewish ethics than on Palestinian suffering and he remained supportive of Zionism and of Israel's legitimacy as a state, the mere fact that he criticized Israel and showed any awareness of the Palestinian plight still led to accusations that he was betraying the Jewish people, something he actually foresaw with some anxiety.[19]

It is important to look briefly at the state of discourse thirty years ago when Ellis wrote: at the strongly pro-Israeli discourse, in Israel and around the world, that had been shaped around the romantic narrative of Israel's founding, built on stories of Israeli military prowess and wondrous civic progress juxtaposed with the tragic realities of Jewish suffering in the Holocaust. As Edward Said made clear, there was no realization, nor even any conception, in public discourse that this progress had come at the cost of another people's dispossession. Entire generations grew up

18. Ellis, *Toward a Jewish Theology*, 128, 136.
19. Ellis, *Beyond Innocence and Redemption*, xiii.

around the world knowing nothing of the Palestinians, of their history in the land, of their humanity. This was the state of knowledge when the first intifada erupted and Marc Ellis began to pay heed to the plight of Palestinians who had paid the price for Israel's establishment. Ellis was far ahead of his time in being able to perceive the painful Palestinian narrative of loss.

Here, for instance, is one story, of a multitude being told today, of an Israeli born in the 1970s who, like all Israeli children and most diaspora Jews born in the first decades after Israel's founding, learned the myths surrounding that founding but heard the unvarnished history only as an adult. "Throughout my childhood in Israel," Jonathan Ofir writes,

> there was a word that had a distinctly frightening aura: "terrorists"—"*mehablim*" in Hebrew (literally meaning "sabotagers"). I knew they were invariably Arab, long before I understood that Palestinians even existed, and I somehow knew they were out to get us, but that courageous soldiers would protect us. In my young mind, all of the enemies were all one thing. They were Arabs, surrounding us and even in our midst, and we were Jews trying to fight for our survival in this jungle (. . .). They, the Arabs, were always somewhere out there in the dark jungle. Thank God we had those soldiers, always at the ready to shoot a Mehabel—an Arab terrorist. I didn't learn the stories of our massacres of [Palestinian] civilians in school. Not the Kafr Qasim massacre (on the eve of the 1956 war), nor the Qibya massacre of 1953, nor the various massacres of the 1948 Nakba (. . .). So in some general way, the wars for me, as a child, were always wars against terror. We were being terrorized and had to fight back.[20]

Rabbi Brant Rosen, a Chicago-area rabbi now known for his activism on behalf of and solidarity with Palestinians, tells a similar story of having grown up in the United States identifying deeply with Israel and its perceived overriding need for safety and security. Rosen was born a decade earlier than Ofir and says that for most of his life he identified intimately with Israel, having visited more times than he can count and lived there for two years while studying. He writes that throughout the decades of the late twentieth century, during which he was ordained, his Jewish identity was "profoundly informed by the classic Zionist narrative: the story of a small underdog nation forging a national and cultural

20. Ofir, "I Understand the Terrorists."

rebirth out of the ashes of its near-destruction." A self-described "liberal Zionist," Rosen experienced occasional periods of doubt about Zionism through these years because of Israel's harsh treatment of the Palestinians, including injustices committed because of "the ethnic nationalism at the heart of Zionism." But he was able to suppress the doubts for a long time. Despite having some awareness of the Palestinian plight, Rosen says the "redemptive nature" of that classic Zionist narrative occasionally "assumed a quasi-sacred status" for him. Moreover, once he was ordained, any impulse to stand openly in solidarity with Palestinians or to criticize Israel would have been a career risk for a congregational rabbi, something seen as "tantamount to communal heresy." So he submerged his doubts about Zionism, along with his empathy for Palestinians, in "a carefully cultivated avoidance of the Israel/Palestine issue." This lasted through one aggressive Israeli round of settlement-building or war after another, until finally Israel's unprovoked assault on Gaza beginning in the last days of 2008 brought him to the realization that he had no more excuses for Israeli brutality and had to acknowledge that this "was not about security at all—*this is about bringing the Palestinian people to their knees.*"[21] This was twenty years after Marc Ellis had first raised critical questions about Zionism.

Mark Braverman, a psychologist turned theologian whom we will meet in depth later, tells a story of his own slow awakening. Born in the United States still another decade earlier than Rosen and Ofir, in fact just a month before Israel's establishment in 1948, Braverman grew up with more or less the same sensibility; as he puts it, "Zionism was mother's milk to me—a Zionism framed in religion." This was fairly ordinary for a practicing Jew born in the United States in the postwar years, he believes: all were raised "in a religion that was a mixture of political Zionism and Rabbinic Judaism. In this quasi-messianic stew, love of the State of Israel was completely intertwined with faithfulness to the commandments." During his school years, "the mythologically tinged history of the Zionist settlement and the history of the State of Israel [were] as much a part of the curriculum of my Jewish day school education as was study of Jewish ritual and theology. In our prayers, we beseeched God three times a day to protect and bless the State of Israel (. . .). I was taught that a miracle,

---

21. Rosen, *Wrestling in the Daylight*, 17–20. Emphasis in original.

born of heroism and bravery, had blessed my generation. The State of Israel was not merely a historical event, *it was redemption*."[22]

As with so many others, Braverman vaguely felt seeds of doubt arising about Zionism and its exclusivist policies, but he ignored them. When as a teenager he first visited relatives living in Israel and later during a year spent living on a kibbutz, like so many others, he buried those seeds under his busy life, his "ecstatic" love for Israel, and the embedded narrative he clung to: "the occupation, although lamentably abusive of human rights, was the price of security," he told himself. It was forty years later, during a visit in 2006 that took him to the West Bank, where he saw Israel's massive encroachment on Palestinian land and the strangulation this was causing Palestinians, that Braverman says the narrative he had held onto for so long crumbled and his "relationship with Israel changed forever." Suddenly, during a prayer service commemorating the destruction of the Temple in Jerusalem, a day of mourning and pain for Jewish suffering, he felt the *Palestinians'* suffering instead.[23]

Even these stories of waking from a dream of Jewish redemption to the harsh realities of Israeli colonialism and oppression are still unusual in the general public discourse about Israel and the Palestinians, as well as in most Jewish religious/theological discourse. It must be assumed that Amy-Jill Levine's thinking about Israel and Palestine was formed in this same dream world and still underpins her theology; although her *Misunderstood Jew* was written almost two decades ago, she still mentions it among her other published works whenever a new book of hers is published.

When he wrote *Beyond Innocence* in 1990, Ellis addressed what he viewed as an urgent need "for Jews to come to grips with the history we are creating in Israel." He recognized as few others did that, whatever Israel's efforts to ignore the Palestinians and deny their presence, this "created history" so profoundly affected Palestinians that there could be no honest or moral coming-to-grips for Jews without working with Palestinians in their liberation struggle. There could be no true Jewish liberation if there were not also a political and a theological liberation for Palestinians. For Ellis, the task of theology is to raise and nurture a people's or a faith community's questions about their present condition, the course they are on as a community, how this course affects others, and where their future

22. Braverman, *Fatal Embrace*, 28. Emphasis in original.
23. Braverman, *Fatal Embrace*, 28–32.

lies. And he questioned whether the post-Holocaust theology then being widely advanced by the Jewish thinkers who glorified Israel was even addressing the questions raised by the reality of the Palestinian intifada.[24]

Not one major Jewish theologian, he noted bluntly—including theologians who "functioned brilliantly when confronting the oppression of Jews in Christian Europe"—had spoken out about the realities of oppression wrought by Jewish state power, something painfully obvious to Ellis that he thought should be evident also to a great many Jews. He catalogued and analyzed the uncomfortable realities that seemed so clear to him: what Jews had done to Palestinians since Israel's establishment in 1948 was wrong; in conquering and displacing Palestinians, Jews were doing what had been done to them for millennia; Jews had thus "become almost everything we loathe about our oppressors"; only by confronting Israeli state power could Jews move beyond being either victim or oppressor; such forward movement by Jews was possible only through solidarity with those whom Jews have oppressed.[25]

Ellis framed his own liberation theology as a response to the Holocaust theology of eminent Jewish intellectuals and theologians like Emil Fackenheim and Elie Wiesel, among others. Formulated not immediately after the Holocaust but years later in the triumphant aftermath of Israel's military successes in the 1967 war, Holocaust theology held up an image of the Jewish people that was becoming, as Ellis put it, normative in Jewish discourse and policies: an image of a suffering people that gave them an aura of innocence and at the same time was accompanied by empowerment. The combination of perceived innocence and actual empowerment in this Holocaust theology frame lent Jews impunity from moral judgment because they had suffered so greatly. By extension, this combination enfolded Israel itself in that impunity because Israel was the defender of the Jewish people. Because the state of Israel empowered the Jews, the Holocaust theologians taught, the state's establishment redeemed them from suffering, forestalled further catastrophe, and almost certainly secured the Jewish future.[26]

The essence of Holocaust theology as Ellis described it was that a "helpless people abandoned by the world" had ensured its own continuity and was consolidating its survival against a new enemy, Arabs. This time,

24. Ellis, *Beyond Innocence and Redemption*, xiv–xv.

25. Ellis, *Beyond Innocence and Redemption*, xiv–xv.

26. Ellis, *Beyond Innocence and Redemption*, 2–6.

instead of Nazis, it was Arabs and especially Palestinians who constituted the enemy. They were seen as the new persecutor of Jews, the new Nazis, whom Jews now had license, and the power, to combat. The task of Holocaust theologians was to defend and normalize whatever policies the state put forth. Their reasoning, as described by Ellis, was as follows: because the Holocaust had raised ultimately unanswerable questions about how Jews could relate to God and whether Jews could believe in a God who allowed the Holocaust's devastation, Holocaust theology elevated survival of the Jewish people as a more immediate commandment than belief in God. Because empowerment was critical to survival, empowerment took on religious significance; therefore, rather than act as moral arbiter of Israel's actions in relation to God's commands, Holocaust theology eschewed moral prescription and followed whatever the state prescribed. This theology was belligerent—uncompromising and almost vindictive. Nowhere in Holocaust theology, Ellis pointed out, was there ever "an attempt at a critical history of Zionism or of Israeli state policy."[27] Secular state policy became theology.

The theology encouraged "self-absorption, almost to the exclusion of others," Ellis believed, and all non-Jews were judged according to their support or lack of support for Israel. "Palestinians hardly exist[ed] at all," in this universe; "if they [did] exist, it [was] as a mass of people threatening the survival of the Jewish people."[28] Describing another Holocaust theologian, the renowned Elie Wiesel, Ellis observed that Wiesel also always centered *the Jew* unapologetically in his numerous writings, even before he became well-known. Palestinians seemed not to exist for him. When Israel defeated several Arab armies in 1967 and captured vast expanses of Arab territory, including the remainder of Palestine, Wiesel hailed the conquest as a miraculous, almost mystical happening. Ellis quotes him as calling Israel's victory a "great mystery in which we [the Jews] are encloaked, as if by the command of the Almighty." Wiesel saw Israel's very existence as a moral victory, and Israel's military success as thus also moral. "My pride," he declared in a later lecture, "is that Israel has remained human because it has remained so deeply Jewish."[29]

Similarly, when Wiesel won the Nobel Peace Prize in 1986, he declared that he had long before sworn "never to be silent whenever and

27. Ellis, *Beyond Innocence and Redemption*, 2–6.
28. Ellis, *Beyond Innocence and Redemption*, 30.
29. Ellis, *Beyond Innocence and Redemption*, 7, 11, 195n10.

wherever human beings endure suffering and humiliation. Silence encourages the tormentor, never the tormented." But he always remained studiously silent about Israel's treatment of Palestinians. National borders and "sensitivities" become irrelevant, he said, when "human lives are endangered, when human dignity is in jeopardy (. . .) wherever men or women are persecuted because of their race, religion, or political views."[30] But in his moral declarations, this preeminent Holocaust theologian remained notably silent about the suffering and oppression Israel inflicted on Palestinians, never exhibiting concern for the "tormented" and never admonishing Israel as the "tormentor." He remained silent when it was Israel's "national borders and sensitivities" that enveloped the oppression of the Palestinians.

Ellis's analysis of theologian Emil Fackenheim, whom we encountered earlier in his affirmation of Jewish exceptionalism, provides a further insight into the character of Holocaust theology. Fackenheim addressed the fundamental contradiction of Jews as religious versus Jews as secular. "Even the most Orthodox Jew of today," Ellis quotes him as writing, "is a secularist insofar as, and to the extent that, he participates in the political and social processes of society. And even the most secularist Jew is religious insofar as, and to the extent that, he must fall back on the religious past in his struggle for a Jewish future." Evoking the traditional 613 commandments or *mitzvot* governing Jewish life, Fackenheim posited a 614th commandment, by which he commanded Jewish survival. "If the 614th commandment is binding on the authentic Jew," he explained,

> then we are, first, commanded to survive as Jews, lest the Jewish people perish. We are commanded, second, to remember in our very guts and bones, the martyrs of the Holocaust, lest their memory perish. We are forbidden, thirdly, to deny or despair of God, however much we may have to contend with him or with belief in him, lest Judaism perish. We are forbidden, finally, to despair of the world as the place which is to become the kingdom of God, lest we help make it a meaningless place in which God is dead or irrelevant and everything is permitted. To abandon any of those imperatives, in response to Hitler's victory at Auschwitz, would be to hand him yet other, posthumous victories.[31]

As it happened, Fackenheim published this "commandment" only a few months before Israel's success in the 1967 war, which seemed to come

30. Wiesel, "Nobel Prize Acceptance Speech."
31. Ellis, *Beyond Innocence and Redemption*, 11–14.

both as a fulfillment of his command to survive and as an answer to the Jews' religious-secular contradiction. For Fackenheim, Ellis explained, the Holocaust and Israel's existence were now irrevocably tied together "in the survival and creative future of the Jewish people."[32]

It is not difficult to feel the true anguish that gave rise to the Holocaust theology that Fackenheim, Wiesel, and other Jewish thinkers developed—the personal suffering so many had endured, the pain felt for the whole Jewish people, the intense fear of more catastrophes to come, the indescribable feelings of hope and triumph that came with Israel's creation and the 1967 victory. But it is also not difficult to see the darkness of supremacy and exclusivity arising in this theology, based as it is in pride, in a moral vantage point that is inward-looking and dismissive of any "other"—a sense that no other people has suffered as the Jews have and thus no other is as worthy. Both Wiesel and Fackenheim, as Ellis showed, tended to become indignant and confrontational toward anyone who held differing views. Neither, obviously, tolerated or even fathomed Palestinian viewpoints. Fackenheim, writing in 1977 in response to what he called "post-Holocaust anti-Jewishness," observed that Palestinian hostility to Jewish "invaders" (a word he put in quotation marks himself) was initially understandable. But then—because he was unable to see Palestinians in their own right, with their own lives, their own humanity, their own history, independent of their relationship to Jews—he wondered whether, "had these invaders not been Jews, their [i.e., Palestinian] hostility—to say nothing of [that of] the Arab world—would have remained implacable. Indeed, except in the context of Muslim and post-Muslim Arab anti-Jewish attitudes, Arab policies toward Israel would appear to be unintelligible."[33]

This statement is so brimming over with erroneous assumptions and misunderstanding of the situation in Palestine-Israel—prevalent when it was written almost fifty years ago, and still prevalent today—that it is difficult to know where to begin a parsing. What did Fackenheim mean by the odd term "post-Muslim" and did he actually understand so little about this major monotheistic religion that he believed Islam was somehow fading away? Did he truly think Islam was so inherently anti-Jewish that this was the only reason for Arab anger toward Israel? Could he not credit a Palestinian sense of nationalism or "peoplehood"

32. Ellis, *Beyond Innocence and Redemption*, 15.
33. Ellis, *Beyond Innocence and Redemption*, 195n21.

as the prime reason for opposing the Zionist conquest of Palestine? Did he know so little about the Palestinians that he believed all Palestinians were Muslim? Did he truly not understand that the reason Palestinians opposed the "invaders" had nothing to do with their own or the Zionists' religion, but arose because they were precisely invaders? Was he so utterly self-absorbed and so much enamored of Jewishness and the Jewish people that he could not understand why non-Jews might not share his personal affection for Jews and might object to being dispossessed and expelled from homes and land?

But Fackenheim's worldview was indeed the worldview fashioned in the aftermath of the Holocaust and of Israel's creation—exactly the "empowered innocence" that Ellis described in 1990 but that had already been shaping global discourse about Israel for forty-plus years.

Ellis also wrote about a "liturgy of destruction" that Jews had articulated over the millennia, a liturgy that continued to memorialize times of destruction in Jewish history and lifted up archetypes of Jewish suffering through the ages. But by the late twentieth century, with the creation of Israel, this liturgy had come to be used "in the service of power rather than [of] a precarious survival." Moreover, by the time Ellis wrote— when Palestinians had begun an uprising to bring attention to their own powerlessness in the face of this Israeli power—the Jewish liturgy of destruction had begun to ring hollow. Ellis recognized, although not many others in the Jewish community did, that the Jewish Holocaust liturgy had begun to be emptied of meaning because it failed to "acknowledge those who have suffered (. . .) because of that liturgy—the Palestinian people." Ellis wanted Jews to begin to see themselves and their history honestly, as having themselves risen from suffering to empowerment, but he wondered how such self-awareness would be possible unless Jews began to take seriously the fact that Palestinians also had a history and were also struggling. Answering his own question, he found that, as far as the Holocaust theologians were concerned, Palestinians existed "primarily within the Jewish framework of interpretation." One Jewish theologian actually wrote, in a tone that Ellis described as typical, that the "Palestinians will have to earn their power by living peacefully and convincing Israel of their beneficence or by acquiescing to a situation in which Israel's strength guarantees that the Arabs cannot use their power to endanger Israel."[34] Palestinians were apparently worthy of mention by these Jewish

---

34. Ellis, *Beyond Innocence and Redemption*, 95–96, 102, 109–10.

theologians only when the theologians wanted to demand that they reassure Israel of their goodwill and "earn" their rights.

The first intifada and Israel's brutal, very public response clearly disturbed a great many Israelis and supporters of Israel in the United States. But, unlike virtually all others, Ellis was able to break out of that "Jewish framework of interpretation" and begin to see Palestinians in their own framework: as human beings with human dignity and human rights like any other people, reacting to legitimate grievances as any other people would, rather than as terrorists or merely an amorphous mass of dehumanized "enemies." Acting on his misgivings about Israel's conduct, Ellis read the growing number of Palestinian intellectuals—including Edward Said, Walid Khalidi, and Muhammad Hallaj—who had begun in the 1980s to write about the Palestinian situation with a newly awakened consciousness. Most importantly, he connected with Naim Ateek and discovered Palestinian liberation theology—a theology that came to Ellis as a reflection "formulated on the other side of the crucible of Jewish power" and one that could provide Jews with new insights into "the consequences of the power they wield." Working from Ateek's first book, *Justice and Only Justice*, Ellis saw Ateek's mission, developed in the wake of the first intifada, as having opened a new period in the Palestinians' "long struggle for justice and peace"—and as seeking a path on which both Palestinians and Jews could move beyond mutual opposition and destruction.[35]

Ellis wanted all Jews to join the Palestinians on this path. His awakening thirty-plus years ago brought him, as we have seen, to the point of questioning the very ways in which Jewish history was evolving in the wake of the Holocaust. As he framed it, with a wide-open and critical but still compassionate eye, Jews began to "create" a new history and a new theology for themselves when Israel was established and, without noticing or caring, they created a new history for others as well, especially the Palestinians. This was history-cum-theology, now framed as a polity that gave Jews power and impunity: from suffering came innocence, from innocence came empowerment, from empowerment came impunity. What this Holocaust theology also created, in fashioning a path from suffering to impunity, was a degree of self-absorption among Jews so complete that very few could even recognize the harm, and the suffering, it brought to others.

---

35. Ellis, *Beyond Innocence and Redemption*, 125, 127.

Ellis believed that this theological-political movement, having so awakened him, would also stand as an invitation to all Jews to change direction.[36] Although there has now, thirty years later, been a considerable awakening among many Jews and other erstwhile supporters of Israel, when Ellis first began to write he was virtually alone among Jewish scholars and theologians, as well as secular intellectuals, in perceiving and analyzing the blinkered focus of the post-Holocaust worldview. Other commentators began at the time to lament what Israel's harsh treatment of Palestinians might mean for Israel's moral condition and the "Jewish soul," but it was some time before any showed concern for what Israel's conduct meant for the Palestinians it was oppressing.

Change in the discourse continues to be glacial, but it has been perceptible in the first decades of the twenty-first century, especially among younger generations of Jews. Very few of those who still feel the sense of Jewish "empowerment" of which Ellis spoke, and fewer still of those who hold actual power in the Israeli and the American Jewish communities, have responded to the need for change that Ellis perceived decades ago. But a significant few, residing somewhat below the level of what might be termed the empowered elite of Jewish political discourse, are gaining traction.

Two well-known Jewish theological thinkers have been able to free themselves from the self-absorption that Ellis described and respond boldly to the "invitation" he saw for a change of moral direction. Although certainly not the only thinkers now speaking out against Israel's brutal apartheid policies against Palestinians, these two—Rabbi Brant Rosen and Mark Braverman, both of whom we have heard discussing their conversions from dedicated Zionists to strong opponents of Zionism—are notable for their outspoken theological condemnation of Zionist principles and objectives. Rosen founded and leads an avowedly non-Zionist congregation in Chicago. Braverman worked closely with Sabeel and now is part of the global network of Kairos organizations founded to promote liberation theology worldwide following issuance of the *Kairos Palestine* document in 2009.

Rosen founded the Tzedek Chicago congregation in 2015—a congregation designed to "create a religious space for those in the Jewish

36. Ellis, *Beyond Innocence and Redemption*, 114.

community who did not consider themselves to be Zionists."[37] Even earlier, in 2011, he co-founded the Rabbinical Council established by the secular Jewish Voice for Peace, a national grassroots organization that stands in solidarity with Palestinians, speaks out for Palestinian rights, and has explicitly expressed its opposition to Zionism.[38] Rosen speaks to a widening audience of American Jews and Palestinian supporters. He writes a blog that usually deals with issues of Zionism: its abusive, supremacist impact on Palestinians, its moral impact on Jews both in Israel and in the United States, the emerging transformation of American Jewish attitudes from full, unquestioning support for Zionism toward the vision of a return to a Judaism that thrives without Zionism.

This last is Rosen's principal mission and motivation. As part of its core values, Tzedek Chicago in fact enunciates a desire to see "a Judaism beyond nationalism"—a Judaism that rejects Jewish exclusivity in Israel, condemns the injustice done to Palestinians, and lifts up the Palestinian right to self-determination and equality. "While we appreciate the important role of the land of Israel in Jewish tradition, liturgy and identity," this statement declares,

> we do not celebrate the fusing of Judaism with political nationalism. We are anti-Zionist, openly acknowledging that the creation of an ethnic Jewish nation state in historic Palestine resulted in an injustice against the Palestinian people—an injustice that continues to this day. We reject any ideology that insists upon exclusive Jewish entitlement to the land, recognizing that it has historically been considered sacred by many faiths and home to a variety of peoples, ethnicities and cultures. In our

37. Rosen, "Judaism Beyond Zionism."

38. Jewish Voice for Peace states that it "is guided by a vision of justice, equality and freedom for all people. We unequivocally oppose Zionism because it is counter to those ideals (. . .). The Zionism that took hold [in Israel] and stands today is a settler-colonial movement, establishing an apartheid state where Jews have more rights than others. Our own history teaches us how dangerous this can be. Palestinian dispossession and occupation are by design. Zionism has meant profound trauma for generations, systematically separating Palestinians from their homes, land, and each other. Zionism, in practice, has resulted in massacres of Palestinian people, ancient villages and olive groves destroyed, families who live just a mile away from each other separated by checkpoints and walls, and children holding onto the keys of the homes from which their grandparents were forcibly exiled. Because the founding of the state of Israel was based on the idea of a 'land without people,' Palestinian existence itself is resistance. We are all the more humbled by the vibrance, resilience, and steadfastness of Palestinian life, culture, and organizing, as it is a deep refusal of a political ideology founded on erasure." See Jewish Voice for Peace, "Our Approach to Zionism."

advocacy and activism, we oppose Israel's ongoing oppression of the Palestinian people and seek a future that includes full civil and human rights for all who live in the land—Jews and non-Jews alike.[39]

Rosen is at the forefront of Tzedek Chicago's mission to lift up solidarity with the Palestinians as a "sacred imperative"—an imperative that arises directly in opposition to the ways most American synagogues have sacralized Israel's creation. This typical sacralization of Israel includes, for instance, reciting during liturgy a "Prayer for the State of Israel," which is hailed as the "first flowering of our redemption." The Israeli flag is often displayed in synagogues next to the ark containing sacred Torah scrolls, and Israel's independence day is celebrated in synagogue as a religious occasion, along with traditional religious festivals. Because Tzedek Chicago, by contrast, considers the Palestinian Nakba to be an historic injustice, it has made an effort to learn what Zionism and Israel's creation have meant for Palestinians, exploring, for instance, Palestinian resistance movements like the Boycott, Divestment, Sanctions (BDS) campaign as legitimate nonviolent calls for Palestinian liberation, as well as profound challenges "to all people of conscience." Even more importantly, Rosen and the congregation have established rituals and prayers that mark occasions of Palestinian pain. On Israel's independence day, for instance, which most synagogues mark as part of the Jewish religious calendar, Tzedek Chicago expresses Jewish solidarity with Palestinians by celebrating Nakba day and saying a "Jewish Prayer for Nakba Day" that uses traditional Jewish liturgical imagery to mark the day as one of mourning, remembrance, and repentance. This long prayer is explicit in naming aspects of the Palestinian Nakba, praying to God for mercy for the dispossessed—as well as, ultimately, for healing and wholeness for the dispossessors. It is a prayer and a theology of liberation.

Rosen also takes a broad and notably anti-Zionist position on the theology of the land. In response to a key speech and a follow-up interview in May 2022 by Anti-Defamation League CEO Jonathan Greenblatt equating anti-Zionism with antisemitism,[40] Rosen affirmed a strong be-

39. Tzedek Chicago, "At Tzedek, We Value (. . .)." Until March 31, 2022, this "core values" statement affirmed that "we are non-Zionist (. . .)" but the congregation voted on that date to affirm what had been a unanimous board decision to change the wording to "anti-Zionist." The vote followed months of membership meetings and a process of "collective discernment." See "Tzedek Chicago Adds Anti-Zionism."

40. Greenblatt, "Remarks by Jonathan Greenblatt." An interview of Greenblatt, to which Rosen directly responded, is here: Chotiner, "Is Anti-Zionism Anti-Semitism?"

lief that "the notion of creating a sovereign Jewish nation state was *never* part of the Jewish land tradition until the rise of political Zionism in 19th century Europe." Pointing to Greenblatt's stated position that the Jews' longing for Zion is a fundamental, millennia-old part of Judaic prayer and ritual and thus the reason Zionism fulfills and essentially equates with Judaism, Rosen acknowledged that Jewish longing for Zion is undeniable, but he framed it as always having been a spiritual rather than a concrete vision, an "idealized messianic vision" that Jewry has lifted up since the destruction of the Temple in 73 CE. In contrast, he said, the modern political Zionist movement is a conscious, radical break from traditional Judaism as it was practiced and believed until very recently. In fact, far from being antisemitic, the anti-Zionism being embraced today by growing numbers of young Jews is a "matter of Jewish conscience" fervently held as part of their Judaism and in recognition of the injustice that Zionism and the creation of a Jewish-majority state have brought to the Palestinians.[41]

Rosen's ability to see clearly that God does not bless power, does not favor power or the powerful, but rather stands with resistance to power, makes him a universalist and a true liberation theologian. By recognizing how destructive "Jewish empowerment" is—what a "monstrous fantasy" it has been to turn Judaism the religion into nationalism and an instrument of state power, as commentator Philip Weiss laments in the epigraph above—Rosen has opened a path toward justice and reconciliation and, ultimately, toward genuine peace. He has said in fact that justice must be achieved by ending Israel's oppression of the Palestinians before discussing the shape of a peace solution—two states or one state or something else—will even be possible.[42] In being able to step away from Holocaust theology's singular focus on Jews and Jewish pain to see the Other, recognizing that in fact no one is really an "other," Rosen has shown true solidarity, giving of himself and entering into a more universal vision of liberation.

Mark Braverman has not only been walking this same path away from the destructiveness of Jewish exceptionalism and toward meaningful solidarity with suffering Palestinians, but he has put action behind his

41. Rosen, "On Anti-Zionist Jews." Emphasis in original.
42. Rosen, "Jewish Perspective."

theology, and impetus behind his solidarity, by attempting to bring mainstream Christian churches along on the same path. Having experienced
the collapse of the Zionist narrative structure and witnessing the error of
so much of that narrative, Braverman recognizes that Israel's creation and
existence explicitly as a state for Jews came totally at the expense of the
Palestinians indigenous to the land. The fundamental Israeli-Zionist belief
in Jewish "chosenness" and Israel's policy and practice of Jewish exclusivity, he believes, constitute the root cause of the Palestine-Israel conflict.
In his awakening, Braverman came to realize—as we have also seen with
Marc Ellis and Brant Rosen and, as has occurred more recently, with a
number of other Jews of conscience—that the romanticized Zionist narrative that so captivated the world decades ago and has shaped global discourse for so long was possible only because it entirely omitted the story of
the Palestinians and the huge price they have paid for Israel's existence.[43]

Like the liberation theologian he is, Braverman recognizes that the
fundamental issue in Palestine-Israel is justice: justice in redress for "the
massive abrogation of [Palestinian] human rights that accompanied the
birth of the State of Israel and that continues to the present day." The
inescapable reality, he wrote over a decade ago and still believes, is that
there will never be an end to the conflict until there is wide public recognition—in the media, from pulpits, and in synagogues—that Israel's
"systematic project" has always been to rid the land of its indigenous
population, for the reason that they are not Jews. The evidence for this
project, he affirms, is "horrifyingly clear"—clear to anyone able to see
and recognize what is happening on the ground. This is a reality that has
motivated his own journey.[44]

Braverman has spent the last decade and more attempting to convince Christian churches of this reality, and also to promote Palestinian
liberation theology, through lectures around the world, articles and, importantly, a book describing what he characterizes as the "fatal embrace"
of Jews and Israeli Jewish supremacy by post-Holocaust Christian theologians trying to atone for centuries of Christian antisemitism. Because
of the responsibility they have felt for historical antisemitism and their
consequent belief that as Christians they have no right to criticize Israel
in any way, these Christian theologians have played a major part in shaping a global discourse that is Israel-centered and almost totally ignorant

43. Braverman, *Fatal Embrace*, 3–10.

44. Braverman, *Fatal Embrace*, 10–11.

of the Palestinians. Braverman believes the embrace between these "two powerful, deeply-seated forces" inevitably enabled the Zionists' objective of ignoring and deliberately obscuring the very existence of Palestinians and Palestinian rights. The "persistence and power" of a narrative framework like this—uniting Judeo-Christian sympathies in a long-established, never-questioned belief system that lifts up Israel as always to be supported—have been a major factor in sustaining the so-called Judeo-Christian culture of the United States, reinforcing the inviolability of Israel's position and ultimately thwarting any progress toward a peaceful resolution of the conflict.[45]

Braverman has described and analyzed the thinking of several American Christian post-Holocaust theologians whose criticism of past Christian doctrine and effort to atone for past antisemitism have produced a profound transformation in Christian theology since the Holocaust. We will discuss the specifics of this theological teaching in the next chapter, but it is important for now to note the impact this revisionist thinking has had in the mainstream of US Christianity and even beyond, in general public discourse on Israel. Revisionist Christian theologians like Paul van Buren, Franklin Littell, R. Kendall Soulen, and others have essentially taught in the decades since the Holocaust that Christianity is theologically subordinate, even subservient, to Judaism and that Christian identity is irrevocably tied to and dependent on Judaism and the Jewish people. Their writings have been taught in seminaries, influencing generations of clergy and their congregants in turn. Although no longer necessarily explicit, the sense of guilt and of the need to seek atonement that these theologians taught Christians to feel have become a part of popular culture in the United States, combining seamlessly with the already sympathetic attitudes of general public discourse toward Jews and Israel.[46]

The Christian theologians' acceptance of Judaism's primacy as part of the atonement process has played out as a perceived need to dialogue with Jewish interfaith partners, and essentially seek permission from them to narrate and ultimately to formulate their own thinking. This is a reality that has maintained Christians as the junior partners in Christian-Jewish dialogue. These attitudes, Braverman says, have so thoroughly permeated Christian thinking that the slightest criticism of Judaism or

45. Braverman, *Fatal Embrace*, 7–8.
46. Braverman, *Fatal Embrace*, 105–9.

of Israel has long been taboo for church leaders. Although this taboo is loosening in some churches, it remains the case that in interfaith discussions, it is totally acceptable, as Braverman obsrves, for Christians to criticize their own doctrines, history, and attitudes, while no such criticism of Judaism or of the behavior of Jews or their institutions is permissible. "Christian sins are fair game," but any critique of "things Jewish is simply out of bounds."[47] What Braverman calls a "brittle détente" rather than a mutual and mutually respectful sharing is what Marc Ellis has labeled the "ecumenical deal," the mutual understanding in interfaith dialogue that criticism flows only toward Christians and never raises the subject of Israel's treatment of Palestinians.[48]

Indeed, Braverman points out that, while the profound question about the Holocaust that has tormented so many Jewish theologians was *how could God do this to us?*, Christian Holocaust theologians turned the question away from God and toward themselves by asking *how could we have done this to God's people?* In their intense and, one might say, immoderate effort to atone, these theologians threw out fundamental Christian beliefs along with their renunciation of centuries of Christian anti-Jewish theology and have fashioned an altogether new theology. As Braverman observes, anti-Jewish theology was "replaced by a theology and hermeneutic that restored the Jewish people's standing as God's chosen and conferred theological status on the modern State of Israel as the fulfillment of biblical promises."[49]

Note Braverman's use of the word "replaced." The irony here is rich: part of the belief system of many of the Christian Holocaust theologians, as well as of today's zealous Christian Zionists, is that Christianity's greatest sin has been supersessionism, the teaching that Christianity and the gospels constitute a completely new and separate covenant with God, superseding or *replacing* God's original covenant with the Jews.[50] As framed by the most zealously pro-Israeli Christians, the accusation of

47. Braverman, *Fatal Embrace*, 105–9, 125.

48. Braverman, *Fatal Embrace*, 188, and Ellis, *Future of the Prophetic*, 44.

49. Braverman, "Theology in the Shadow," 151–52.

50. It should be noted that neither the notion of "replacing" or superseding God's original covenant with the Jews nor the term "replacement theology," meaning supersessionism, has anything to do with the so-called "replacement theory" that has recently been put forth by radical White supremacists and racists. This is the idea that so-called political liberals who encourage immigration and any accommodation to non-White populations are doing so in order to "replace" the White population with Black people and others of color.

supersessionism holds that Christianity abandoned Judaism and established itself millennia ago as a replacement for Judaism and God's covenant with Abraham and the Jews. This rejection of Jews and Judaism, the accusation goes, ultimately encouraged virulent Christian antisemitism, which in turn eventually led to the Holocaust. Braverman, however, points out that the rigid, black-and-white theology of the post-Holocaust Christian theologians who embrace Judaism so strongly and reaffirm God's promise of the land to the Jews in fact positions them as "reverse supersessionists."[51] These theologians have replaced one orthodox theological totality with another.

Citing one of the several Christians he has studied, Braverman quotes Kendall Soulen, now a professor at Emory University's Candler School of Theology. Soulen asserts that one of Christianity's principal theological requirements today is repudiating supersessionism and affirming "God's fidelity to God's covenant with Israel," thus upholding what Soulen calls "God's irrevocable election of the people Israel." Braverman argues that this thinking, intended as a rejection of antisemitic Christian triumphalism, actually lifts up Jewish triumphalism. Soulen's repeated references to Jewish specialness, to God's particular love for Israel, and to God's election of Israel for a special role in history in fact raise up Israeli superiority politically as well as theologically and replace Christian supersessionism with Jewish exceptionalism.[52]

By affirming Jewish specialness, Braverman believes, Soulen is actually preserving Christian exceptionalism. One can detect a hint of self-importance in these Christian expressions of atonement, a kind of righteousness that lifts repentant Christians up as special and good. The words that Braverman frames as the Christian theologians' theoretical question about Christian guilt—*how could we have done this to God's people?*—have the ring of breast-beating that verges on the self-congratulatory. The question reflects the same sort of self-absorption that we have seen in some Jewish theologians. In uncovering the Christian exceptionalism conveyed in Christian post-Holocaust theology, Braverman demonstrates not only that these Christians ignore and even attempt to overturn the most fundamental teachings and spiritual orientation of Jesus Christ, but also that, in their attempted solicitousness toward Judaism, they completely ignore the existence of the Palestinians, precisely

51. Braverman, *Fatal Embrace*, 113.
52. Braverman, *Fatal Embrace*, 110–13.

the human beings who have been disadvantaged by their unilateral rein-
statement of the Abrahamic covenant.[53]

Braverman's own clear-eyed view is that the original covenant between God and the Jews was "tribal and exceptionalist in nature." Jesus'
prophetic voice, he says, was raised "in fierce opposition" to this tribal
framework of the first-century Jewish establishment and its theology.
Even if one does not fully accept Braverman's suggestion that Jesus' universalism and the challenge he posed to Judaism rendered the eventual
separation between Judaism and Jesus' new faith inescapable[54]—although
there is, in fact, little cogent reason to reject the suggestion, or to regard
difference and separation as necessarily supersessionist—the reasonable
solution to the issue of two faith traditions going in different directions is
not the total reversal of that change and return to the original covenant
advocated by the Christian Holocaust theologians. Rather, as Braverman
suggests, what is need is a critical theological examination of the original
covenant and the reasons for reshaping it. Jesus brought something new;
he came to "recast" but not reject the narrative of the Hebrew scriptures,
Braverman says, and to transform the nature of God's relationship with
humanity from the tribal to the universal. He was working toward "a
radical shift to a *universal* covenant, one that would be available to all of
humankind." It is critical to recognize that Christianity thus "arose out
of Judaism in a transformative, revolutionary process." Overturning this
transformation and reincorporating the exclusivist Abrahamic covenant
into Christianity absolutely undermines Jesus' revolution.[55]

This glaring negation of the essence of Jesus' mission and message
to humanity not only has huge theological implications, but has had an
enormous impact on the Palestinians who are the forgotten victims of
repentant Christianity's embrace of Israel and its exclusivist policies and
actions—policies and actions that have from the beginning been specifically anti-Palestinian. Braverman frames Christianity's *fatal embrace* of
Jewish exceptionalism in blunt analogy: "if Christian triumphalism as
expressed in supersessionism led to the ovens of Auschwitz, then Jewish triumphalism as expressed in political Zionism has led to the ethnic
cleansing of Palestine."[56] What emerges most notably from Braverman's

53. Braverman, "Theology in the Shadow," 151–52.

54. Braverman, *Fatal Embrace*, 118.

55. Braverman, *Fatal Embrace*, 114–16, 119–20. Emphasis in original.

56. Braverman, *Fatal Embrace*, 114.

analysis of these Christian Holocaust theologians is their total absence of any sense of the need for justice for—or, in most cases, even any recognition of—the Palestinians who have always been a part of the land that God supposedly granted only to Jews. If the theologians recognize Palestinians at all, it is most often only, à la Emil Fackenheim, as somehow foreign and implacably hostile. Most often, these Christians make no mention of Palestinians at all. Their assumption that God's covenant with the Jews naturally includes a total Jewish right to possess the land negates any rights that Palestinians, as non-Jews, might enjoy.

Jesus' challenge was to the power and exceptionalism of temporal rule and of empire. Institutional Christianity did indeed later corrupt Jesus' universalist challenge and assume a triumphal character by allying with empire from the fourth century onward. But, as Braverman believes, Christianity's imperative now is to move back toward universalism rather than further enable the corruption of Judaism by returning to the tribal exceptionalism of two thousand years ago. Christianity's task now is to move away from exceptionalism in any form: from Jewish tribalism, the Israeli atrocities this tribalism gives rise to, and any Christian accommodation of Israel's triumphant dominance. And, finally, to simply say "Sorry" and "let Jesus be Jesus."[57]

In a rare acknowledgement by a Jewish theologian and intellectual, Braverman believes that Jews must turn away from their self-absorption— "our fixation," as he calls it—on the evils done over the centuries to Jews, toward a recognition "that our story today is what we are now doing to others." The era now is a post-Nakba rather than a post-Holocaust time, he affirms, and Christians too must recognize that there is a "dark side" to supporting the Jewish/Israeli position.[58] He appeals to Christians not to enable what he views as the Jews' self-destructive tendency over the ages to "legitimize and intensify our separation from humankind."[59]

57. Braverman, *Fatal Embrace*, 118–20.

58. Braverman, "Theology in the Shadow," 164–65.

59. Braverman, *Fatal Embrace*, 237.

6

Christian Guilt, Christian Zionism

Palestine's Christian Antagonists

There has been no misfortune worse for us than that we are ineluctably
viewed as the enemies of the Jews. No moral and political fate worse
(. . .). The Holocaust has victimized us too, but without the terrifying
grandeur and sacrilegious horror of what it did to the Jews. Seen from
the perspective of the Holocaust, we are (. . .) inconsequential.

—EDWARD W. SAID[1]

We ask our sister Churches not to offer a theological cover-up for the
injustice we suffer, for the sin of occupation imposed upon us. Our
question to our brothers and sisters in the Churches today is: Are
you able to help us get our freedom back, for this is the only way you
can help the two peoples attain justice, peace, security and love?

—*KAIROS PALESTINE*[2]

IT IS PROBABLY NOT an exaggeration to say that Western Christianity
itself—many theologians and critical segments of the institutional
church—has been a major nemesis of Palestinian Christians in the

1. Said, *After the Last Sky*, 134.
2. *Kairos Palestine*, para. 6.1.

modern era. As we saw briefly in the last chapter and will discuss in greater detail here, a few key theologians, wishing to clear Christianity's conscience and expiate guilt for centuries of antisemitism, turned Christian theology on its head in the aftermath of the Holocaust. By essentially reassigning Christianity's theological sinecure, rendering God's primary love and God's promise of the land of Palestine exclusively to the Jewish people, these theologians effectively subordinated their own Christian faith to a narrow political interpretation of Judaism and unquestioningly blessed and embraced Israel's creation as a specifically Jewish state in a land populated overwhelmingly by non-Jews. Christianity's long, reprehensible history of teaching anti-Jewish doctrine was totally replaced, as theologian Mark Braverman has stated categorically, "by a theology and hermeneutic that restored the Jewish people's standing as God's chosen and conferred theological status on the modern State of Israel as the fulfillment of biblical promises."[3]

This embrace was so whole-hearted, the effort to reconcile with Judaism so complete, that the fate of Israel's victims, the Palestinians, was utterly ignored, even while great numbers were being physically expelled from their own homeland and the entire Palestinian polity was politically and theologically upset and eclipsed. Because the Palestinians' existence stood in the way of Zionism's drive to establish a Jewish sanctuary in Palestine—and to do so by ridding the land of non-Jews—and because institutional Christianity wholly supported every Israeli action, Palestinians were condemned to political oblivion.

This pro-Israeli and baldly anti-Palestinian thinking has thoroughly permeated Christian attitudes throughout the West for the last seventy-five years and more, and in combination with the powerful and sustained impetus of the pro-Israel lobby's political efforts, has been responsible for molding a global narrative about Israel that has essentially, at least until very recently, excluded the Palestinians. The major import of the discourse is that, in the global political conversation and mindset, Palestinians have no place in Palestine and no inherent human or political rights there. In addition, the embrace of Israel and Zionism by mainstream Christian post-Holocaust theologians, along with the growth of the Israeli narrative as an innate element of US political discourse, inevitably reinvigorated the older, more fundamentalist theology of Christian Zionism.

3. Braverman, "Theology in the Shadow," 151.

Growing out of a biblical literalism focused on preparing for the Second Coming of Jesus Christ, Christian Zionism is the belief that the establishment of the Israeli state and the "return" and "ingathering" of Jews to the Holy Land are biblically mandated steps necessary before Jesus' reappearance on earth can occur. Christian Zionism's beliefs, shared principally among several evangelical traditions, arise from a literal interpretation of the Hebrew Scripture that in fact distorts both God's promises in these texts and Jesus' gospel message of justice and love. Ironically, and despite its stated vision of seeking the return of Jesus, Christian Zionist beliefs focus so intently on the Hebrew texts and the supposedly unalterable promise to Abraham that Jesus is actually eclipsed in this "Christian" theology. As Palestinian Lutheran pastor the Rev. Munther Isaac has lamented, "Christian Zionism places Israel at the center of the biblical narrative—not Jesus. The Hebrew Scripture prophecies are mainly about Israel, we are told, not Jesus. The offspring of Abraham is ethnic Israel, we are told, not Jesus and those who are in him."[4]

Although, as we will see, Christian Zionism is a uniquely Christian, basically rightwing, and ultimately antisemitic theology that differs markedly in theological terms from the political Zionism that animates the Jewish Israeli state, its vociferous support for Israel's existence is so similar on the surface to mainstream Christianity's support that it has become difficult to distinguish one Christian strain from the other. Mainstream Christianity's stance effectively morphs into Christian Zionism's far more strident, more literalist theology. The perception that Palestinians have no rights in Palestine is shared to a greater or lesser extent by both strains of Christianity. As a result, Christian thinking for the most part avoids the Palestinian issue altogether, generally failing to recognize Israel's oppressive policies and rejecting criticism of those policies. Palestinians are denied legitimacy in their own land, and any reasonable explanation for their resistance to Israeli domination is ignored.

For Palestinians, the impact of this thinking has been cataclysmic. The shattering reality of the Holocaust and the Holocaust theologies that arose from it have indeed, as Edward Said lamented, rendered Palestinians and their lives inconsequential in the geopolitical scheme and in public opinion the world over. Palestinians have been regarded, if they are not forgotten altogether, as two-dimensional characters, enemies and haters of the Jews, props playing opposite Israel and indeed on stage

4. Isaac, *Other Side*, 95.

only in relation to Israel. Few are even aware that there are Christians among indigenous Palestinians, and have been for millennia. Rarely if ever viewed even before the Holocaust as a people in their own right, Palestinians have been further consigned because of the Holocaust to a kind of existential limbo—as a people, as a nation and, most critically, as a legitimate claimant to their own homeland. With their fate already effectively sealed by Israel's total disruption of their society in 1948, the addition of Christianity's theological seal of approval on Israel's appropriation of the land seriously undermined any possibility of political or psychological redress.

Although this grim situation has been changing in recent years as more and more social justice elements in mainstream Christian denominations have awakened to the realities of Israel's oppressive system and have begun to stand openly in solidarity with Palestinians, change at the level of institutional church hierarchies has been extremely slow at best. The road to a true embrace of Palestinians by Western Christianity remains steep and winding and encumbered with numerous obstacles. The plea addressed by *Kairos Palestine* more than a dozen years ago to the Palestinian Christians' "sister Churches"—a plea "not to offer a theological cover-up for the injustice we suffer, for the sin of the occupation imposed upon us"[5]—is still largely disregarded.

Strong impressions created in the years following the Holocaust and Israel's establishment helped construct a dominant mindset about Palestine and Israel—a mindset significantly impervious to new thinking—that lingers today among many Christians, clergy and laity, who absolutely will not criticize Israel. One of the most notable expressions of this rigid adherence to one unchanging perspective was James Carroll's bestselling, award-winning 2001 book *Constantine's Sword: The Church and the Jews.* A prolific writer, former Roman Catholic priest, and avowed Catholic dissident, Carroll framed this long, nearly encyclopedic history of Christian persecution of Jews as part of his own personal theological struggles. But he principally intended this epic popular history (and the publisher emphasized this theme in multiple cover blurbs) as a book with a broad popular reach, a dramatic account of what is termed the church's "battle against Judaism." The book is labeled, in sweeping terms, a "dark history

5. *Kairos* Palestine, para. 6.1.

[of] the central tragedy of Western civilization, its fault lines reaching deep into our culture (. . .) [an] affecting reckoning with difficult truths that will touch every reader."[6]

Throughout this seven-hundred-page paean to Judaism and criticism of Christianity, Carroll barely mentions the Palestinians. In the book's index, there is only one mention of the words Palestine or Palestinian. Although there are in fact a few additional mentions of Palestinians that the index failed to pick up, this scant reference is a measure of the minimal consideration Carroll gave to the people whom Israel displaced and dispossessed.[7] There was no mention whatsoever of the hundreds of thousands ethnically cleansed, no apparent awareness of the history of Palestine before 1948, no recognition that there are Christians among the Palestinian population, only glancing references, as in the index, to the Jews' "conflict" and other problems with Palestinians—and no sense that Palestinians are real people with legitimate interests and grievances, nor any recognition that there might be other claimants to what Carroll assumed is a God-given Jewish land. Speaking of the continued importance to Judaism of the ancient Jewish Temple and its remaining remnant, the Western Wall, he wrote in a remarkable analytical leap that the "Temple *and, by extension, the land* are tied to the unbreakable covenant God has made with the Jewish people." One cannot, he maintained, understand Judaism or even modern Israeli politics "until the significance of that tie is grasped."[8]

Judaism, and what he defined as Israel's moral rights as the Jewish state, loomed so large in Carroll's account that he appeared to have no ability even to conceive of any other moral agenda. He clearly regarded the Palestinians as having none. Like so many Israeli advocates today, Carroll "weaponized" anti-Zionism and criticism of the Israeli state as antisemitism—that is, conflated political criticism of a state's policies with hatred of Jews as Jews. Carroll did not distinguish between Israel and Jews as a people or evidently understand that the Palestinians' struggle is against Israel because of its state actions, rather than against Jews. Commenting on the 1972 murder of eleven Israeli Olympic athletes in Munich by

6. Carroll, *Constantine's Sword*. Quotes are from the cover of the paperback edition.

7. The one mention of Palestinians in the index is strangely constructed, as if to avoid a direct reference. The citation—"Palestinians, Jews' conflict with"—addresses the Jewish perspective on Palestinians, dealing with them not in their own right but merely as obstacles to Jewish life.

8. Carroll, *Constantine's Sword*, 108. Emphasis added.

Palestinian terrorists from the group Black September, he called this "an exclusive targeting of Jews *as Jews*," an event that he said "spoke to [him] of the anti-Jewish genocide."[9] In fact, although this act of terrorism was horrific and inexcusable, the Palestinian terrorists targeted these athletes because they were Israelis representing Israel, not primarily because they were Jews. The terrorists did not attack any other Jews at that Olympics. Carroll's failure to understand why Palestinians opposed Israel is typical of most misguided commentators, then and now.

Whether or not Carroll's book is historically on point, and no matter whether it might be slightly overdrawn to say, as a publisher's cover blurb claimed, that the Holocaust and Christian persecution of Jews have constituted the "central tragedy" of Western civilization, the book was nonetheless widely hailed and welcomed as a major proclamation of love from Christians to Jews, and it has probably emotionally touched millions of readers around the Western world, if not precisely every reader, as the publisher hoped. But here is the issue: this book, arousing deep empathy for Jews and strong support for the Jewish state growing out of Carroll's profound and often agonized personal theological struggle, almost totally ignores the Palestinians, as if they are and have always been inconsequential. The book was published more than fifty years after Israel ethnically cleansed a majority of the indigenous Palestinian population and was continuing to oppress this people and deprive them of freedom and self-determination. This fact demonstrates that, even in the face of decades of oppressive Israeli policies and actions against Palestinians, convictions formed out of psychological guilt and religious piety die very hard. *Constantine's Sword* is a moral tract about Christianity's oppression of Jews, but its morality is selective, extending only to Jews and, moreover, seeming to free Jews themselves of any moral constraints.

Early in the book, Carroll framed his intent in writing it as an imagined, deeply powerful question from Jews to Christians: "Where in your theology of redemption is there any room for the bottomless evil that the death camp had to have been for those who died here?" He went on to say that every question he would ask in the book "will be a way of asking, How did this happen?"[10] This of course is a profound and profoundly appropriate question, one that virtually every Jewish theologian and intellectual, and many Christians, had asked before Carroll. But for

9. Carroll, *Constantine's Sword*, 49. Emphasis in original.
10. Carroll, *Constantine's Sword*, 61.

Palestinians and for all who support them, whether Christian, Muslim, Jew, or none of these, the next question, equally profound and following naturally from Carroll's, should be the same: "How did this—meaning in this case the attempted ethnocide, even perhaps genocide, of the Palestinians by the Jewish nation—happen?" It is perhaps natural that Jewish post-Holocaust theologians would not think to ask this second question. But one would expect Christian post-Holocaust theologians, supposedly more steeped in Jesus' teaching of universalism and love of neighbor, to think beyond themselves and their own framework and be aware of suffering everywhere—in this case specifically, to think of the question of how Palestinians became the victims of Jews. Carroll's thinking apparently did not take him this far. Nor does the thinking of most Christian theologians, as we will see.

If Western Christianity had a guilty history for centuries of persecuting Jews, for which the institutional church and theologians have been atoning for decades, Christianity is now in more recent times living out a further sad history, of which it seems oddly unaware: a history of ignoring the moral and theological calls of the oppressed for justice. While this has been the fate of many liberation theologies, as we have seen, the church tendency to ignore the cries of the oppressed is nowhere more striking than in Palestine.

The eminent biblical scholar Walter Brueggemann, one of the few modern Christian theologians to speak out in support of justice for Palestinians, writing the foreword of an essay collection about Zionism and the pursuit of justice in Palestine, has observed that Christians nowadays "are held in hock by accusations of anti-Semitism if they criticize Israel, or by a fear of such accusations that might come." Citing the post-Holocaust theologies of several prominent theologians who embraced the creation of Israel at a time of crisis for Jews but have since then avoided close examination or critique of Israel's treatment of Palestinians, Brueggemann urges Christian leaders to move away from earlier romanticized images of Israel and look honestly at today's realities on the ground—which he says include Israel's enormous economic and military power and "a seemingly unrestrained practice of abuse, exploitation, and ruthless assaults on the vulnerable."[11]

11. Brueggemann, "Foreword," xiv–xv.

In the volume Brueggemann was introducing, one of the book's editors and a longtime advocate of Palestinian rights and scholar of rightwing Christian Zionism, the Rev. Donald Wagner, has traced the growth of support for Zionism among mainstream Christian theologians from its beginnings in the political-theological opposition to Nazism in the 1930s, before the Holocaust began. Renowned German theologian and philosopher Paul Tillich left Germany for the United States in the early 1930s after being harassed by pro-Nazi university officials and immediately began campaigning against Nazi ideology, particularly its anti-Jewish policies, on theological grounds. Tillich joined forces in those early years with Reinhold Niebuhr, who would soon himself rise to prominence and influence as a public intellectual and theologian. The two men began working to urge Christian churches to support Judaism and join in opposing Nazism's distorted expression of nationalism and its persecution of Jews.[12]

When Zionist leaders met in the United States in 1942 and formally expressed support for creation of a Jewish state, Tillich and Niebuhr both supported this vision and strove to push Christian leaders to back Zionist aims. The pro-Zionist attitudes of these two theological giants did differ slightly. Tillich viewed creation of a Jewish state as a political necessity in the face of Nazism but not as something divinely inspired. Niebuhr, on the other hand, was an uncritical promoter of Zionism on all counts and worked closely with the pro-Zionist lobby in the 1940s. He viewed US support for Jewish statehood as a political as well as a moral necessity, and in fact lobbied in support of a Jewish state over a single democratic or a binational state in which all citizens, Palestinians as well as Jews, would be equal. In the general post-Holocaust push to relieve Jewish suffering, however, political differences such as those between Tillich and Niebuhr were lost, and neither theologian appeared even to notice that there might be a downside to Jewish nationalism. Their early and vociferous support, however qualified, ultimately resonated as full and unquestioned endorsement of Israel, influencing later theological thinking about Israel and effectively shutting out serious thinking about the Palestinians.[13] Niebuhr later went so far in the aftermath of the Holocaust as to pronounce cavalierly on the disposability of Palestinians, urging that the

---

12. Wagner, "Mainline Protestant Churches," 146–53.
13. Wagner, "Mainline Protestant Churches," 146–53.

needs of stateless Jews be given precedence over the rights of Palestinians, who he said could move to other Arab territories.[14]

Wagner goes on to discuss later mainstream Christian theologians who in their writing and advocacy have supported the Zionist agenda, along the way influencing generations of the American public and, importantly, of the political leaders and policymakers who have fashioned an official policy stance that consistently favors Israel and denies equal rights to Palestinians.[15] Another essay in this volume, by Catholic theologians Rosemary and Herman Ruether on the history of Christian attitudes toward Jews and Zionism, points to broad support among Christians in the United States, well beyond the evangelical sects that have long supported Zionism, for the notion of Jewish "restoration" to the land of ancient Israel. This support has extended even late into the twentieth century and beyond: a poll published in 1987 indicated that, while only one-third of Catholics believed that Israel's creation constituted the fulfillment of a biblical prophecy that "Jews would be restored to their land," considerably more than half of Protestants—57 percent—held this belief.[16]

As we have briefly discussed, the penitential Christian response to the Holocaust occasioned the rise of a revisionist theological movement in US Christianity, focusing heavily on repairing relations with Jews and Judaism, that had a profoundly transformative impact on Christian, particularly Protestant, attitudes and beliefs. Paul van Buren, an Episcopal priest and theologian, wrote voluminously during the 1980s about Christianity's long dismal relationship with Judaism and is widely regarded as the principal theological re-educator of the church. In the belief that Christianity could rid itself of antisemitism and achieve true reconciliation with Judaism only through a radical redirection and redefinition, van Buren sought to forge Jewish and Christian traditions into "the embrace of a single, continuous tradition" and a "new revelation" that would honor both faiths. His vision of this single embrace, however, was effectively to subsume Christianity into Judaism: Christianity would have to "refer to Judaism in order to make sense of itself," he declared, and reversing Christian anti-Judaism meant acknowledging the "eternal covenant between God and Israel."[17]

14. Wagner, "Protestantism's Liberal/Mainline Embrace," 6.

15. Wagner, "Mainline Protestant Churches," 157.

16. Ruether and Ruether, "Vatican, Zionism, and the Israeli-Palestinian Conflict," 120.

17. Braverman, *Fatal Embrace*, 106–9.

Van Buren espoused and promoted a narrow Zionist definition of Judaism, ignoring texts in the Hebrew Scriptures that speak to inclusivity rather than to the tribal Judaism that he was promoting. Although Jesus' very life and teachings in the gospels directly challenge van Buren's theology, he insisted that Christians must accept God's covenant with the Jews as eternal, as exclusive to the Jewish people, and as the foundation for Christian revelation. Because Christianity "spiritualized" God's promise of the land, van Buren believed that Christians, whom he defined as "gentiles who worship the God of the Jews," might be allowed to join with Jews spiritually in Jerusalem but that Jews hold the deed to actual land ownership, something evidenced and affirmed by the "return" of Jews to that land via the creation of Israel.[18]

Kendall Soulen, the Emory University theologian briefly discussed in the last chapter, is a leading disciple of van Buren, whom he regards as "a pioneer among theologians" striving to repair and renew Jewish-Christian relations. Soulen identifies himself in his faculty profile as devoting most of his scholarship to demonstrating that "Christian faith becomes more authentically Christian as it overcomes its stubborn legacy of anti-Judaism." Although it is not immediately clear what he means by becoming "more authentically Christian," he is a strong advocate of rejecting so-called supersessionism, meaning that he rejects, and believes Christianity must also repudiate, any notion that the New Testament and the Christian belief system have replaced or superseded the Hebrew Scriptures. In his view, outlined in several books and articles over the last almost three decades—and also the view of van Buren and other like-minded theologians—supersessionism has been the root cause of Christian antisemitism, and overcoming this legacy is the church's most important theological task. For these theologians, undoing supersessionism means restoring the Jewish covenant to primacy.[19]

Supersessionism is a particular bugbear for those post-Holocaust Christian theologians and especially for Christian Zionists who accord primacy to Jewish over Christian tradition and to the Abrahamic covenant over any notion that Jesus and the New Testament texts fulfill and complete the covenant but are not meant to replace it. In fact, the accusation of supersessionism arises from a false premise, a baseless fear, and the use of this accusation, however sincere, borders on being coercive and

18. Braverman, *Fatal Embrace*, 106–9, and personal email communication from Donald Wagner, July 6, 2022.

19. Braverman, *Fatal Embrace*, 106.

bullying. In this modern era and especially in the aftermath of the Holocaust and Christian atonement for past antisemitism, supersessionism
is a manufactured charge and should be a non-issue. As noted religious
scholar Diana Butler Bass has declared, "Jesus does not replace. Jesus rei-
magines and expands, inviting an alternative and often innovative reading of Jewish tradition." Citing the Sermon on the Mount in Matthew's
Gospel, Bass points out that Jesus made it clear that he loved the Jewish
tradition and law ("Do not think that I have come to abolish the law or
the prophets; I have come not to abolish but to fulfill. For truly I tell you,
until heaven and earth pass away, not one letter, not one stroke of a letter,
will pass from the law until all is accomplished" [Matt 5:17–18, NRSV]).
Jesus restated and interpreted the Torah and the law in his own words, a
practice common among Jewish teachers, then and now.[20] Interpretation
is not rejection or replacement.

Biblical scholar Colin Chapman has traced the growth of the modern Christian belief in the "restoration" of Israel and the concomitant fear
that mainstream Christian theology has replaced or superseded Judaism
and the Abrahamic covenant—beliefs most commonly found among
Christian Zionists—and he concludes that the fear is not legitimate.
The New Testament itself clearly insists that everything in the Hebrew
Scriptures "points forward to Jesus the Messiah," he says; the church is
a *continuation* of, not a replacement for, Israel, and far from replacing
Jews or taking over their identity or their privileges, Gentile believers
were incorporated into Judaism. Although many Christian Zionists
regard the integration of Gentiles into Israel as illegitimate, Chapman
maintains that this is illegitimate only if "Jesus has no right to claim to be
the fulfillment of all the hopes of Israel." In fact—and this is the essence of
true Christianity—Jesus "has the right to throw open membership of the
chosen people to every human being of every race. Those who accept his
invitation are not 'replacing' anyone or 'taking anyone's place.'"[21]

The fundamentalist movement commonly referred to as Christian Zionism—as distinct from the more moderate Zionism of the mainline Protestant and Roman Catholic churches—is an amorphous movement with
vaguely defined boundaries but a well-defined doctrine and mission. It is

20. Bass, *Freeing Jesus*, 39–41.

21. Chapman, *Christian Zionism*, 86–88.

less a distinct Christian denomination—there is no "Church of Christian Zionism"—than a theologically based, singularly focused political campaign founded on a particular biblical interpretation. The term Christian Zionist goes well beyond simply signifying any Christian who happens to support Israel, but rather defines a specific political objective of supporting Israel unquestioningly for precise religious and theological reasons. The numerous churches that espouse this pro-Israeli theology are often not connected to a discrete denomination but, in political terms, are pointedly pro-Israeli, frequently even displaying the Israeli flag and/or the Star of David outside the church or inside at the altar. As distinguished from political Zionism—the late nineteenth-century Jewish movement that ultimately led to the founding of the Israeli Jewish state, and forms the ideological foundation of that state—Christian Zionism is a theology formulated and expounded by Christians. It focuses single-mindedly on preparing for the Second Coming of Jesus and, to facilitate this event, on ensuring that the whole land of Palestine-Israel is peopled entirely by Jews and emptied of Palestinians and other non-Jews. Christian Zionists believe that the establishment of the Israeli state in the entire land, and the "ingathering" and "return" of Jews to this land, were mandated by God and must be accomplished completely before Jesus can come again. Christian Zionism sees the establishment of the state of Israel in 1948 and the expansion of Israel's borders in 1967 as the stimuli that initiate the so-called End Times process.

Found primarily among evangelicals—although not including all evangelicals—Christian Zionists are biblical literalists who believe that, as written millennia ago in Genesis, God promised to make Abraham "into a great nation" and to bless those who bless him and curse whoever curses him.[22] In today's Christian Zionist theological interpretation, this means that God blesses whoever unconditionally supports the state of Israel and condemns all who criticize Israel and its policy. More liberal biblical scholars, including two experts on Christian Zionism, both British Anglican priests—Colin Chapman and Stephen Sizer—reject the validity of connecting God's blessing on Abraham four thousand years ago to the modern state of Israel. Sizer, who has written voluminously on this movement, believes this ancient promise carries no requirement for

22. See Gen 12:2–3, NRSV: "I will make of you a great nation, and I will bless you, and make your name great, so that you will be a blessing. I will bless those who bless you, and the one who curses you I will curse; and in you all the families of the earth shall be blessed."

"entire nations 'blessing' the Hebrew nation, still less the contemporary and secular State of Israel."[23]

Besides corrupting God's message in the Hebrew texts and undermining Jesus' gospel message of justice and love, Christian Zionism's uncompromising doctrine negates the very existence of the Palestinians, even Palestinian Christians, despite their indigeneity. In the Christian Zionist worldview, the biblical promise to Abraham is eternal and today mandates total support for Jewish Israel's colonization of all parts of Palestine, as well as support for its displacement and dispossession of Palestinians and the rejection of all Palestinian political demands. Christian Zionists reject as sinful any move toward a Palestinian-Israeli peace agreement that would require Israel to cede control of land to the Palestinians.

Christian Zionism has a history extending back at least to the early to mid-nineteenth century, a time when British exploration societies, Victorian-era adventure travel, and American and British religious travelers, pilgrims, and missionaries sparked a massive wave of interest in travel to the Holy Land. Most of these travelers, and the hugely popular travel literature they produced, portrayed Palestine as a land either empty of Palestinian Arabs or barren and ugly because of them—and a land romantically reminiscent of biblical times simply waiting for the return of Jews and Judaism, and ultimately of Jesus Christ. In the United States, Mark Twain, although certainly no theologian or religious scholar, was one of the leading writers who helped create a popular culture and psychological atmosphere eager to absorb the teaching and preaching of Christian religious leaders who began to formulate a theology about the Holy Land.[24]

Gary Burge, noted New Testament scholar, author, and expert on Christian Zionism, has summarized how rapidly Christian Zionist belief grew in this receptive atmosphere: the "unity of political destiny and religious fulfillment was given its theological form" in the mid-nineteenth century, he writes,

> in the hands of an Irish pastor, J[ohn] N[elson] Darby. As Herzl was the father of Jewish Zionism, one could argue that Darby was the father of Christian Zionism, laying out many of its principal theological foundations. During his 60-year ministry, Darby (. . .) called for a return to a literal biblical faith. But it was

23. See Sizer, "What is the Relationship?"

24. Christison, *Perceptions of Palestine*, 16–25, and Burge, "Theological and Biblical Assumptions," 45–46.

> Darby's eschatology (. . .) that taught a literal fulfillment of proph-
> esies [sic] in the near-present age. He used the biblical books of
> Daniel, Ezekiel, Zechariah and Revelation to weave a consistent
> picture of the Last Days: the church is raptured, the anti-Christ
> arises, Armageddon erupts, and Christ returns to establish his
> thousand-year reign on earth. But above all, Darby believed, the
> revival of Israel would be the catalyst of the End Times.[25]

As Burge notes, Darby's eschatology soon came to be widely called
by the term he coined: Dispensationalism, referring to the belief that God
divided biblical history into dispensations, or temporal periods, to which
God dispensed administrative principles or covenants, each adminis-
tered by humanity in accord with God's plan. The final dispensation was
to be Jesus' return to earth. Darby's theology attracted several prominent
contemporary followers among evangelicals in the United States, including most notably Chicago evangelist William Blackstone, who lobbied for
establishment of a Jewish state as early as the 1890s, and Cyrus Scofield,
whose 1909 Scofield Reference Bible popularized dispensationalism. This
bible has sold millions of copies and, in the words of one commentator,
"has made uncompromising Zionists out of tens of millions of Americans." The text of the Scofield Reference Bible is the King James Version
of the Bible, but it is Scofield's annotations that have given it such prominence. Highlighting the Genesis 12 text on blessings and curses, Scofield
wrote that these verses have been "wonderfully fulfilled in the history
of the dispersion." Indeed, he affirmed, "It has invariably fared ill with
the people who have persecuted the Jew—well with those who have protected him. The future will still more remarkably prove this principle."[26]

Until the 1960s, strict adherence to Darby's dispensationalist theology was what Burge calls "the litmus test of fundamentalist orthodoxy."
But Israel's creation, along with its 1967 expansion and capture of all of
Jerusalem and the remainder of Palestine, appeared to fundamentalist
evangelicals to be bringing the future forward more rapidly, and strict dispensationalism gave way to what is now usually called pre-millennialism.
Whatever its name and whatever the changes in some particulars of the

25. Burge, "Theological and Biblical Assumptions," 46. There is an extensive literature on the rise and growth of Christian Zionism in Britain and the United States,
including volumes authored by Burge. See Burge, *Jesus and the Land*; Burge, *Whose
Land?*; Sizer, *Zionism*; Sizer, *Zion's Christian Soldiers?*; and Wagner, *Anxious for
Armageddon*.

26. Cathail, "Scofield Bible," 45–46.

theology, belief in Darby's original eschatology remains strong, as does belief in the inerrancy of Scofield's biblical interpretation and predictions. The broad outlines of pre-millennialism today are essentially the same as Darby's eschatology, only now on an accelerated time schedule: Israel's "return" to the Holy Land has added urgency to the perceived advent of the End Times. The next steps are envisioned, according to Darby's sequence, as the church's rapture, followed by a period of tribulation that brings the final battle of Armageddon, leading ultimately to Jesus' return to pass judgment and establish his kingdom on earth.[27] Israel's existence in the whole land is now inevitably viewed by Christian Zionists as the essential step that will finally bring Jesus back.

Christian Zionism experienced a notable popular, and political, resurgence in the 1980s, helped by warm support from President Ronald Reagan. Despite ups and downs, the evangelical resurgence has continued into the twenty-first century. By Reagan's era, the noted evangelist Billy Graham had long been a firm supporter of Israel. Others of the movement's early proponents in this period are also well-known: Hal Lindsey, author of *The Late Great Planet Earth* and numerous other books; Tim LaHaye, author of the *Left Behind* series; and several prominent evangelists, such as Jerry Falwell, Pat Robertson, Tony Perkins, Ralph Reed, and Gary Bauer. Most of these preachers, who espoused notably conservative political positions along with their support for Israel—and several of whom tried running for political office—have for years been broadcasting their message primarily via radio and television programs that reach millions. In addition, the Lindsey and LaHaye books were, and remain, hugely influential, selling in the tens of millions of copies; according to Burge, their books "popularized and solidified the foundation of many laypersons' eschatology" and established a belief system that would endure well into the future.[28] The books widely popularized the idea, still preached by many evangelical leaders, of the so-called Rapture: the expectation that, when Jesus returns to earth, believers will be taken bodily up to heaven.

A somewhat later generation of evangelists, televangelists, and writers is ensuring that this belief system does indeed endure. John Hagee, for instance, who leads the 20,000-plus-member Cornerstone Church in San Antonio, Texas, broadcasts his Christian Zionist message on a

---

27. Burge, "Theological and Biblical Assumptions," 46–48, and Wagner, "From Blackstone to Bush," 32–34.

28. Burge, "Theological and Biblical Assumptions," 49.

dedicated television station and leads a major nationwide organization called Christians United for Israel (CUFI) that claims eight to ten million followers beyond the Cornerstone Church. Another Christian Zionist preacher, Robert Jeffress, pastor of a Dallas, Texas, megachurch, hosts daily radio and television programs broadcast nationally and internationally, is a regular Fox News Contributor, and appears frequently on mainstream television news programs. His First Baptist Church claims a membership of fifteen thousand, and his broadcast audiences run into the millions.

Mike Evans has been preaching and writing for decades about his view that the United States must ally itself with Israel and support God's covenant with the Jewish people as irrevocable and eternal. Evans founded the Jerusalem Prayer Team, an activist organization with a Facebook following in the tens of millions, whose mission is to build a worldwide network of "Friends of Zion" prepared "to guard, defend, and protect the Jewish people and to pray for the peace of Jerusalem." The Prayer Team website publishes news of Israel and of Jews around the world, raises funds "to meet humanitarian needs of the Jewish people in Israel," and following Russia's attack on Ukraine in 2022 began distributing food and other relief to Jewish Ukrainians. In 2015, Evans established the Friends of Zion Museum in Jerusalem, a state-of-the-art museum enshrining the non-Jewish contribution to Zionism and to the establishment of Israel.[29]

It is difficult to pin down exact membership numbers for the broad Christian Zionist movement. Various assessments from the 1980s put the number of evangelicals in the United States at anywhere between a low of twenty-five million and a high of one hundred million, the latter number claimed by the likes of Pat Robertson and Jerry Falwell. More recent estimates seem most often to settle on about eighty million, nearly one-quarter of the entire United States population. Not all evangelicals by any means espouse Christian Zionism, and increasing numbers of evangelicals are reportedly disturbed by the politicization of the movement, but the number of pro-Israeli evangelicals who can be called Christian Zionists is nonetheless quite high. A 2017 poll conducted by an evangelical polling firm indicated that fully three-quarters of older White evangelicals had a positive view of Israel.[30] The strength of Christian Zionist beliefs is further confirmed by a 2022 Pew Research Center poll that

29. See Jerusalem Prayer Team website.
30. Skibell, "Questioning the Covenant."

put the proportion of evangelicals who believe God gave the land to the Jewish people at 70 percent. Ironically, a Pew poll from two years earlier indicated that only 30 percent of Jews in the United States held this belief and, among the US population as a whole, the figure stands at a similar 30 percent.[31]

There are numerous indications, including from these polls, of diminishing support for Israel among younger evangelicals. Like their peers in the Jewish community, many of these younger people are pulling back from full, unquestioning support for Israel as they discover the facts of the situation on the ground in Palestine. Nonetheless, whatever the numbers and whatever the changes in support, the Christian Zionist movement remains strong and zealous. One expert noted in the 1980s— and this remains true, especially after the era of Donald Trump, as we will see—that the movement was "not composed of 'crazies' so much as mainstream, middle to upper middle-class Americans" who gave literally millions of dollars every week to the preachers and televangelists who promise them rapture, heavenly salvation, and Jesus' return to earth if they support Israel's absorption of the land.[32] This so-called "theology" illustrates a clear idolatry of the land.

The extent of Christian Zionist support for Israel's right wing and its increasingly blatant anti-Palestinian policies and actions is massive. Many Christian evangelicals, along with numbers of rightwing American Jews, donate lavishly to an Israeli group working to reestablish the ancient Jewish temple destroyed two millennia ago by Rome, expecting to replace the present Muslim Dome of the Rock and al-Aqsa Mosques that have been located atop the Temple Mount in the heart of Jerusalem for over a thousand years. The many millions of dollars raised by televangelists are also directed to multiple other projects in the Israeli-occupied West Bank and East Jerusalem—land evangelicals freely call, in concert with Israel's terminology, "Judea and Samaria" and "Greater Israel." Groups of evangelicals on pilgrimage to Israel-Palestine, altogether numbering in the tens of thousands, are taken to visit and often work at archeological digs specifically designed to "prove" a millennia-long Jewish history on this land—sites that credentialed biblical scholars say are not authentic. A group called Passages, jointly founded and funded by conservative Jews and Christians in the United States, takes thousands of students from

31. Samuels, "Pew Survey Reveals Huge Gap."
32. Quoted in Sizer, "Historical Roots," 21.

Christian colleges during school breaks on trips designed to connect the biblical history they study in school with today's Israeli state. According to one assessment, Passages "glorifies Israel as a modern state that manifests providential continuity with a biblical past."[33] In the process it deliberately ignores the history of Palestinians in the land, as well as Israel's oppression of Palestinians.

Christian Zionist churches and groups, which operate individually as well as in larger cooperative networks, spend millions of dollars received in donations to help illegal Israeli settlements in the West Bank and East Jerusalem and also to send volunteers to work on agricultural and construction projects in the settlements. One such organization among many, called Hayovel, founded years ago by a married Christian Zionist couple from Missouri, has sent three thousand volunteers to help in wineries established in Israeli West Bank settlements, primarily picking grapes. The organization's goal, according to its literature, is to be a "positive voice from Judea and Samaria into the nations [i.e., to the non-Jewish world]—a voice declaring the amazing, restorative things that we were seeing with our own eyes and touching with our own hands."[34]

In a massive effort intended, according to Hayovel's founder, to "see the land come alive [as] the prophets spoke about," the organization began a project in 2022 designed eventually to plant hundreds of thousands of trees throughout the central West Bank, which Hayovel refers to as "part of Israel's biblical heartland." Beginning in an area near the Palestinian city of Nablus and adjacent to the Israeli settlement of Har Bracha, Hayovel has kicked off the project with a fundraising effort to cover the cost of planting three thousand trees by the end of the year. The plan thereafter is to plant twenty thousand trees every year. Although the land confiscated for the initial planting is privately owned by Palestinian farmers from the village of Burin, who have been prevented for years by Israeli settlers and the Israeli military from reaching their land, the Hayovel leader says he believes these Palestinians have no jurisdiction over the land. Hayovel enjoys US tax exempt status on the basis that its mission is to "serve and support agricultural communities in Israel."[35]

33. Among numerous sources for these activities, see Roth-Rowland, "On the Temple Mount"; Kirk, "Christian Zionist Archaeology"; Fache and Parent, "Digging in the Holy Land"; and Ahmad, "Tourism."

34. Maltz, "Despite COVID-19 Travel Ban."

35. Maltz, "'Biblical Mandate.'"

Lara Friedman, president of the Foundation for Middle East Peace in Washington, DC, and a former US Foreign Service officer who served for several years in Israel, has characterized Christian Zionism and the reach of its activities as an "industry in evangelical America," all supported by huge grassroots donations. In addition to the activities named above, the movement's numerous activist organizations also lobby politicians directly, for instance by taking congresspeople on tours to Israel and, when they return, pressing them to introduce legislation supporting Israeli settlements and other activities in the occupied territories. Friedman labels the overweening Christian Zionist support and affection for Israel as a kind of philosemitism, a disturbing fetishization of Israeli Jews that is deeply embedded in the psyche and the religious fiber of Christian conservatism. She equates the Christian right's passionate embrace of Jews to conservatism's vehement, deep-seated opposition to abortion, other women's rights, and LGBTQ rights.[36]

The Christian Zionist movement received a critical boost during the presidency of Donald Trump between 2017 and 2021. Trump's pro-Israeli and notably anti-Palestinian viewpoint, and the policy changes he pursued in carrying that viewpoint to fruition, constituted a ringing endorsement of the fundamental beliefs and aspirations for Israel that Christian Zionists had been advocating for decades. Trump's unconventional personal style of policymaking benefited these evangelists in several ways: they enjoyed easy access to the White House for prayer meetings because they were his so-called pastoral advisers; they had frequent contact with Trump's closest Jewish advisers, son-in-law Jared Kushner and personal friend appointed ambassador to Israel David Friedman; and they were able to count as several of their own at least three key Trump administration officials: Vice President Mike Pence, Secretary of State Mike Pompeo, and UN Ambassador Nikki Haley, all strong Christian Zionists themselves.

The serendipitous combination of fervent Christian Zionist religious leaders, avowed Christian Zionists in the cabinet, strong Zionists among family and friends who played key policymaking roles, and a personal friendship with Israel's then-Prime Minister Benjamin Netanyahu, together produced unprecedented policy changes toward Israel and cemented the United States' relationship with Israel more firmly than

36. Presbyterian Church Webinar, "Israel/Palestine."

any previous president had done. These policy changes have not been reversed by the administration of his successor, President Joe Biden, and it is entirely possible that Trump himself might be reelected in 2024 or that one or another of his strongly Christian Zionist lieutenants will seek election and win.

What can be called the Trump "phenomenon"—the remarkable level of support he enjoyed, and continues to enjoy, from a broad array of Christian evangelicals, including but not limited to Christian Zionists— has been described by Sarah Posner, an expert on the broad Christian conservative movement, as driven by "a politicized theology" that believes the US government is endangered by and must be protected from "the demonic influences of liberalism and secularism."[37] Although Posner's assessment was written shortly before Trump's electoral defeat in 2020 and the heavily "Christian nationalist" assault on the US Capitol on January 6, 2021, she seems to have captured well the paroxysm of religious zeal that ultimately fueled that attack and indeed that fuels the zeal of fervent Christian Zionists, although on a less intense and less militant level.

There appears to be little direct connection, or at least few strong ties, between the Christian nationalists who were involved in or continue to support the Capitol attack and Christian Zionists, whose principal interest is more in supporting Israel than in directly controlling the US government. Posner wrote of these two strains of evangelical Christianity almost interchangeably, and they do share a religious ardor of greater or lesser intensity: both preach a highly politicized theology, and they share deeply held viewpoints on a range of issues, including abortion, gay rights, racism, immigration, even antisemitism. But since the Capitol attack, Christian Zionists have appeared to keep their distance from, and expressed occasional distaste for, the more militant Christian nationalism that has risen to prominence in recent years.

Although clearly not religious himself, Trump was able to put himself forth as someone who did not simply share the Christian right's pet aversions to issues like abortion and gay rights, but who was also deeply displeased by liberal America's increased awakening to the rights of marginalized groups like African Americans and other racial minorities, women, immigrants, refugees, and gays. To the point of our interest here, he was seen as someone who shared Christian Zionism's deep love for Israel and theological convictions about its importance. In their fervor,

37. Posner, *Unholy*, 10–11.

Christian conservatives have been able to excuse Trump's personal behavior because they see him as the kind of strong leader who does not
sway with shifting political winds and does not bow to the left: "a savior
from the excesses of liberalism," in Posner's assessment, and someone
who, moreover, had raised the sagging fortunes of the evangelicals' con-
stituency by energizing them and sending them to the polls. Evangelicals
voted for Trump in large numbers. Although, according to polls cited by
Posner, the Christian evangelical population dropped from 23 percent of
American adults in 2006 to only 17 percent a decade later, on election day
in 2016 they made up fully 26 percent of voters.[38]

If it seems strange to hear Trump hailed as a savior or regarded
as someone admired by religious personalities, Posner points out that
Trump's politics and political style were defined by the very kind of
televangelism and showmanship that mark the ministries of Christian
evangelicals and that his Christian voter base finds so appealing. Because
he came to prominence through a career in reality television, where he
studied Christian television and befriended many of its celebrities, Christian conservatives came to see him as anointed by God to protect Christians, save America, and save Israel. They seemed to view him as a kind
of prophet simply because he espoused their views and prayed with them.
According to Posner, for White evangelicals, defending Trump became
indistinguishable from defending White Christian America. Trump was
a warrior in a battle they believe is raging between good and evil. Robert
Jeffress, for instance, gave politicized sermons during which he invoked
Trump as a warrior on the side of right (in the sense both of moral right
and of the political right). In one 2019 sermon, Jeffress said the Democratic Party was "a godless party" and liberal Christians worshiped an
"imaginary God (. . .) who loves abortion and hates Israel." The true God
of the Bible, he asserted, "is one who hates abortion and loves Israel!"[39]

Trump was clearly the warrior defending that "true God," as well as
those evangelical Christians and, of course, Israel. Christian conservative
leaders prayed earnestly over Trump and began openly declaring him
"God's chosen one," sent to "rule and judge over us (. . .) in our government." Even Trump's personal flaws were seen as part of a divine plan:
"God uses imperfect people through history," said former Texas governor Rick Perry. "King David wasn't perfect. Saul wasn't perfect. Solomon

38. Posner, *Unholy*, 10–11.

39. Posner, *Unholy*, 13–15, 39, 254, 260.

wasn't perfect."[40] In the view of the several Christian Zionists who were part of Trump's evangelical prayer group, even if Trump himself was not one of God's chosen, God was nonetheless involved in Trump's decision-making on Israel. When Secretary of State Mike Pompeo announced in late 2019 that at his direction, the United States would no longer regard Israeli settlements in the occupied West Bank as illegal, Christian Zionist leaders hailed the decision as God's answer to their prayers—prayers they had indeed been offering fervently. Invoking the Genesis 12 passage and claiming that God's issuance of blessings and curses applies to modern Israel, not merely to biblical Abraham, Mike Evans proclaimed the move "a tremendous answer to prayer from evangelicals." Evans viewed the Pompeo decision as "recognizing the Bible as legal."[41]

The particular triumph of Christian Zionism during the Trump years was that Trump was in fact induced to "legalize" a Zionist version of the Bible, ignoring and manipulating both international law and biblical morality and turning the biblically based illusions of the most hardcore Zionists into official US policy. Thanks to an extraordinary—and, from the participants' viewpoint, quite fortuitous—combination of Christian Zionist, American Jewish Zionist, and rightwing Israeli Zionist influences, and impelled by Trump's own free-wheeling personal style, a non-diplomatic team utterly lacking in any policymaking experience turned itself into a working alliance that crafted a peace plan and a body of official policy positions that promoted Israel's demands and totally ignored Palestinian interests.

That peace plan, the so-called "Deal of the Century" put forth in January 2020, followed after, as a kind of *coup de grâce*, a series of concrete policy decisions unprecedented in the history of the United States-Israeli relationship. In 2017, Trump declared all of Jerusalem to be the capital of Israel, something the United States had refused to do since Israel's 1948 establishment; in 2018 actually moved the US embassy from Tel Aviv, where it had been located since 1948, to Jerusalem, which the United States and international law had never recognized as belonging to Israel; closed the US consulate in East Jerusalem, which had served Palestinian consular needs for decades; closed the official Washington, DC, office of the Palestine Liberation Organization, which had diplomatically represented the Palestine Authority since the Oslo Accords of the 1990s;

40. Scott, "Fix."

41. Jenkins, "Trump Advisor."

recognized the occupied Syrian Golan Heights, seized militarily by Israel in 1967, as Israeli territory; eliminated the United States' contribution, averaging $350 million annually, to the United Nations Relief and Works Agency (UNRWA), the international organization established in 1949 to provide social welfare assistance to Palestinian refugees; and eliminated another $200 million in annual US aid to various projects in Palestine.

Not only were Trump's policy changes unprecedented in the seven decades of US Middle East policymaking, but almost all were illegal under international law. Although every US president had winked at Israel's 1948 capture of West Jerusalem (which was part of an area designated by the 1947 UN Partition Plan to be an "international zone" belonging to neither Jews nor Arabs), the United States had never formally recognized Israeli sovereignty in Jerusalem and had kept the US embassy in Tel Aviv. Neither had the United States recognized the legitimacy of Israel's further capture in 1967 of East Jerusalem and other Palestinian territories. Every one of Trump's moves—further embellished by Mike Pompeo's personal recognition in 2019, while serving as Secretary of State, of Israeli settlements in occupied Palestinian territory as legal—thus constituted a significant US policy change.

The so-called Abraham Accords of 2020, another Trump initiative, which normalized diplomatic relations between Israel and several Arab states, were not illegal, but the agreement was a broad multipurpose geopolitical accord engineered to enhance Israel's status in the Middle East, to forge a regional alliance against Iran and, not incidentally, to marginalize the Palestinians. The Accords are a cynical alliance among regimes that are undemocratic or nearly so—essentially ties between Arab authoritarianism and Zionist settler-colonialism. They amount effectively to a violation of trust by Arab states that have previously championed Palestinian interests. Palestinians themselves had no role in negotiating the agreement; their interests were deliberately ignored, and the Accords are unpopular among the masses of ordinary Arab citizens, who generally support the Palestinians.[42]

Whatever their legality, every one of Trump's policy moves was a gift on a silver platter to Israel, came as a "godsend" to Christian Zionists who had been lobbying unsuccessfully for policies such as these for decades, and constituted yet another catastrophe—another step in the ongoing Nakba—for Palestinians. Trump is the notable exception to the reality

42. Klippenstein and Grim, "Biden Administration."

that foreign policy rarely changes significantly from administration to administration, and the Biden administration has done virtually nothing to dismantle any of Trump's policy innovations on Palestine and Israel. These Trump policies continue to undergird Biden administration policy despite Trump's electoral defeat in 2020, the change from a Republican to a Democratic administration, and President Biden's supposedly more liberal perspective.

Although Biden is not a Christian Zionist in theological terms, not an evangelical who believes in the End Times or other Christian Zionist orthodoxy, he is and has always been strongly Zionist and an unquestioning supporter of Israel. Since coming to office, he has been distinctly reluctant to confront Israel on any issue and, during a visit to Israel in July 2022, made a point of endorsing the entirety of Israel's policy agenda. Biden did restore the aid monies to UNRWA and to Palestinian hospitals that Trump had cut, but other Trump policy changes remain in place, and in fact Biden fully endorsed Israel's anti-Palestinian agenda by making it clear that there will be no US pressure to halt the expansion of Israeli settlements or stop Israel's continuing action to dispossess, displace, and oppress Palestinians. Even Israeli commentators took note of Biden's surrender to Israel's agenda. One noted that Biden's visit gave "new meaning to the terms doing the minimum and lip service," even as "Palestinians [were] bleeding on the ground."[43]

Ardent Israeli supporter that he is, Biden has also made an effort to strengthen the Abraham Accords, for the specific reason that they normalize Israel's relationship with its Arab neighbors and further its integration into the greater Middle East. Biden and his foreign policy experts view the Accords as a stabilizing factor that guarantees against the eruption of violence in the region. In addition, despite promises to renew the Iran nuclear agreement—negotiated by President Barak Obama in 2015 and from which Trump unilaterally withdrew in 2018—Biden has dragged his feet because Israel has been strenuously opposed to the agreement since its signing. Christian evangelical leaders also strongly support the Abraham Accords and oppose renewal of the nuclear agreement with Iran.

This Biden administration inertia on Palestine issues sets the scene in a critical way for the possible reentry of a strong Christian Zionist administration in a few years if Trump is reelected in 2024 or another

43. Levy, "Biden Signs."

rightwing candidate like Mike Pence or Mike Pompeo wins election. Pence and Pompeo, both strong Christian Zionists as we have seen, have made it known that they intend to run for president and actually began competing in 2022 for political support among their rightwing friends and allies in Israel. During a visit in early 2022, Pence courted the right wing, meeting with both Benjamin Netanyahu and then-Prime Minister Naftali Bennett, and dining with the widow of casino magnate and political kingmaker Sheldon Adelson, who before his death in 2021 contributed lavishly to American Christian Zionist causes, to rightwing US presidential candidates, and to an array of Israeli causes. Pence, who is fond of quoting the Genesis passage about blessings and curses, promising that "we stand with Israel because we cherish that ancient promise that those who bless her will be blessed," also met and sang the praises of an Israeli politician who soon afterward became notorious for his flaming rightwing, anti-Palestinian views. Itamar Ben-Gvir, widely regarded as the ideological successor of the late American-Israeli terrorist Meir Kahane, won election to the Knesset in late 2022, assumed a key security-related cabinet position, and has been pressing punitive anti-Palestinian legislation that also undermines Israel's judiciary. Pence promised Ben-Gvir to "stand with you."[44]

Pompeo seems less fervently religious than Pence in his public statements, although he has been quoted as insisting that "God sent Trump to save the Jews" and that "the Lord is at work" with Israel.[45] But whatever the depth of his religious feeling, he is no less right-leaning in his politics. Visiting an Israeli winery in the West Bank settlement of Psagot in late 2021, Pompeo campaigned hard for his view, first enunciated two years earlier when he was secretary of state, that "Israel is not an occupier in Judea and Samaria [the West Bank]." He called this declaration perhaps his most important statement as a US official. Going further as a private citizen, even dubbing his position the "Pompeo Doctrine," he declared, "This is the rightful homeland for the people of Israel here in Judea and Samaria." To cheers from a West Bank settler who said Pompeo was "doing what God wanted you to do," he reiterated his position that the West Bank is not an occupied territory and Israel is not an apartheid state.[46] At a Zionist Organization of America (ZOA) gala in early 2022, Pompeo

44. Sommer, "Israel's Far Right."

45. Quoted in Isaac, *Other Side*, 51.

46. Lazaroff, "Pompeo: Israel Is Not an Apartheid State."

declared, in a striking distortion of the role of the United States' principal foreign policy official, that there "is no more important task of the secretary of state than standing for Israel." The extreme rightwing ZOA later issued a news release calling Pompeo's speech the most pro-Israeli speech ever delivered by a public official.[47]

What emerges most notably from studying the teachings of Christian post-Holocaust and Christian Zionist theologians and politicians is the near total absence from their thinking of any sense of the need for justice for the Palestinians, and indeed any recognition even that Palestinians exist and have always lived in the land these people claim God granted exclusively to Jews. If these theologians recognize Palestinians at all, it is most often only as somehow foreign.

In terms of the beliefs passed down and absorbed by Western Christian church people—seminarians, clergy, lay leaders, and ordinary faith practitioners—there is little real difference between the radical fundamentalism of a Christian Zionist like John Hagee and the more mainstream theology of a Reinhold Niebuhr, who saw both a moral and a practical imperative in supporting Israel's creation and, as a "realist," considered it a morally acceptable pragmatic solution to displace Palestinians in order to make room for establishment of a Jewish state. The impact of these differing theologies is the same. Although the basic politics of conservative Christians and those in mainstream denominations differ significantly, the theologies they profess concerning Israel are all Zionist, whether they believe in the Rapture and the End Times and the return of Jesus, or take the Abrahamic covenant more seriously than the gospels, or simply regard the Jewish ethos as morally superior to the Palestinian. No matter where they reside theologically, they all ignore the legitimacy of the Palestinians. They teach in unmistakable terms the supremacy of the Jewish, and only the Jewish, people in the land of Palestine—even though this land has been continuously inhabited since Jesus' day by Palestinians—including Palestinian Jews who remained Jews, Palestinian Jews who followed Jesus and became Christian, Palestinian Gentiles who may or may not have followed Jesus, may or may not later have adopted Islam, but who remained in the land. These are the indigenous people

47. Arria, "Pompeo at ZOA Gala."

of Palestine, who over the centuries have become the Palestinian Jews, Christians, and Muslims of this land.

It is thus critical to reiterate that Western Christianity in its post-Holocaust embrace of Israel and ignorance of Palestinians, and especially in its Christian Zionist manifestations, has emerged prominently as a force that is deeply antagonistic toward the Palestinians.

The *Kairos Palestine* document, noting that "certain theologians in the West try to attach a biblical and theological legitimacy to the infringement of our rights," declares forthrightly that clinging to the exclusivity of the Abrahamic covenant is "a menace to our very existence" and that the fundamentalist Christian interpretation of the gospel "has become 'a harbinger of death' for us."[48] A decade later, as we saw in Chapter 3, the *Kairos* theologians issued two further, more desperate alarms over being abandoned by mainstream Christian churches. "The global Church is failing us," they cried. Another anguished appeal said that the "very being of the church (. . .) and the credibility of the Gospel [are] at stake."[49]

These Palestinian theologians declared—as a theological statement made in the context of a confession of faith—that any "support for the oppression of the Palestinian people, whether passive or active, through silence, word or deed, is a sin." This, and similar statements in *Kairos Palestine* itself, are the kind of statement that should commit Christian churches to oppose the sinful ideology or theology as a matter of faithfulness to the gospel.[50] The response from Western Christian churches to these Palestinian appeals has for the most part been silence, with the exception, as we have seen, of only a few mainstream churches. Even these have come only very slowly.

We have heard much about the theology of Naim Ateek. In a 2014 essay in a book about the ways Zionism has affected the struggle for justice in Palestine, Ateek wrote that "Zionism *is* the problem." It is a doctrine, he writes, that provides Israel with "a firm—even dogmatic—religio-national identity justified by an appeal to God's will, to historical memory, and to mythical racial ancestry (. . .). It is a theologically infused ideology of Jewish identity" whose "dark side" has resulted in a century of Palestinian suffering and dispossession.[51] The mainstream Christian church

48. *Kairos Palestine*, para. 2.3.3.

49. See *Kairos Palestine*, "*Kairos Palestine* 10th Anniversary Conference Statement," and *Kairos Palestine* & Global Kairos for Justice, "Cry for Hope."

50. Ateek, "Concluding Theological Postscript," 219.

51. Ateek, "Concluding Theological Postscript," 217. Emphasis in original.

has been largely oblivious to that dark side—to Zionism's insistence on Jewish supremacy and Jewish exclusivity in the land—and to Christian Zionism's support for it. A well-informed church person noted some years ago that "silence in the mainstream church" on the truth of this critical situation "has allowed Palestine to be defined by Zionists."[52]

While it has been absolutely necessary and appropriate for Western Christianity to repudiate its own centuries of antisemitism and Christian triumphalism, the turn toward accomplishing this by advocating the theological reemergence and re-ascendancy of Jewish exclusivity and triumphalism, as discussed in the last chapter, is an utterly inappropriate and destructive assault on Christian theology. Not only does this reaffirmation of the Abrahamic covenant as an exclusive promise from God negate any rights that Palestinians, because they are non-Jews, might enjoy in their own homeland, but it also, as theologian Mark Braverman has rightly pointed out, effectively negates the revolutionary nature of Jesus' message: Jesus came both to challenge tribalism and actually to "challenge the power of empire—the triumphalism of temporal rule"—and in fact to introduce instead "the triumph of the spirit."[53]

Jesus, the original liberation theologian, preached a liberating message of universalism and love for all people, as all equally children of God. This is a message that Western Christianity has never fully taken on board, although it is now at last beginning to heed the message on behalf of the oppressed, including even of Palestinians, in small, incremental ways.

52. Essa, "'Tip of the Spear.'"
53. Braverman, *Fatal Embrace*, 116, 131.

Conclusion

Hope in the Absence of All Hope[1]

I saw a peasant woman crouching down [in the field], in her lap a child, its eyes wide in terror (. . .). "Didn't we warn you," [the Israeli governor] yelled, "that anyone returning there will be killed? (. . .). Go back anywhere you like to the east. And if I ever see you again on this road I'll show you no mercy." The woman stood up and, gripping her child by the hand, set off toward the east, not once looking back. Her child walked beside her, and he too never looked back. At this point I observed the first example of that amazing phenomenon that was to occur again and again (. . .). For the further the woman and child went from where we were (. . .) the taller they grew. By the time they merged with their own shadows in the sinking sun they had become bigger than the plain of Acre itself. The governor still stood there awaiting their final disappearance (. . .). Finally he asked in amazement, "Will they never disappear?"

—EMILE HABIBY[2]

1. *Kairos Palestine* begins with these lines: "We, a group of Christian Palestinians (. . .) cry out from within the suffering in our country, under the Israeli occupation, with a cry of hope in the absence of all hope, a cry full of prayer and faith in a God ever vigilant, in God's divine providence for all the inhabitants of this land."

2. Habiby, *The Secret Life of Saeed The Pessoptimist*, 15–16. Habiby (1922–96) was a Christian Palestinian writer from Haifa who remained in Israel after 1948. He was a leader of the Palestine Communist Party before Israel's establishment and later co-founded the Israeli Communist Party, serving several terms in the Israeli Knesset. One of several novels about the Palestinian condition, *The Pessoptimist*, written in 1974, is a tragi-comic tale of Palestinian hardships under Israeli rule, laced throughout with satire and a dose of the absurd.

EMILE HABIBY, A PALESTINIAN Christian and professed communist who most likely never thought much about God or theology, would probably not be surprised that, half a century after he wrote the prophetic lines above, Palestinians have indeed "become bigger than the plain of Acre itself." Habiby knew Palestinians well enough that he would have been fairly certain that by the 2020s, Palestinians would still be there as a force in Palestine. But Israel, represented by the governor in that story and the Zionist expansionism he symbolizes, most certainly is surprised and chagrined that any Palestinians remain on that plain of Acre or anywhere else in the land Israel has been striving to make wholly its own.

"Will they never disappear?" the Israelis are still wondering.

Yet Palestinians are there still, growing in population despite having been ethnically cleansed and driven out in massive numbers; still bonded to each other by "hearts of living stone" and to the land by love, despite Israel's concerted efforts to take the land and transform it into a Jewish place; still steadfast and determined never to surrender. Steadfastness and numbers do not mean Palestinians have the upper hand in this long-running struggle; Israel clearly has all the military might, as well as all the international and particularly US political support and the huge advantage that comes with simply being a sovereign state in a world of nation states. But Israel is losing the contest to make this land over and rid it of its indigenous people, of that never-disappearing woman and her son in Habiby's story, and their progeny.

The decades since Habiby wrote and especially more recently, since the time of awakening when the first intifada, a grassroots uprising, and a grassroots theology of liberation arose together to struggle for Palestinian freedom, have brought immense tragedy for Palestinians, collectively and in innumerable individual instances. There have been times of despair, but also times of hope. Israel has gained immeasurably in physical strength as Palestinians have gained in numbers and in moral strength. The tragic, utterly mismatched struggle continues. But Palestinians persist. Through all of this, it is clear that, however uneven the struggle, Palestinians have achieved a real measure of victory simply through the enduring fact of their resistance. Resistance is its own inspiration: the mere act of resistance, even in the absence of any clear reason for hope, nurtures and builds hope, nurtures more resistance. Resistance is built on hope, and generates continuing hope in turn.

The oppression visited on the Palestinian people over the last century remains a haunting problem. Haunting because it is so morally reprehensible on its face; Palestinians have long been and are still being squeezed and cleansed, only because they are not of the "right" ethnicity and religion, not ethnically Jewish, not of the Jewish faith. Haunting also because the perpetrator of this oppression is the Jewish state of Israel, built by a people who themselves suffered horribly through centuries of oppression and into the genocide of the Holocaust. Haunting because the oppression of Palestinians is enabled and paid for in full by the United States. Haunting because Israel's domination is motivated by an exclusivist theology that depicts God, the God of all, as a God of injustice, an evil God who would murder and dispossess and steal from one part of humanity solely for the benefit of another.

In his first book on liberation theology thirty years ago, Naim Ateek said that, in the face of Israel's Jewish triumphalism, Palestinian Christians were questioning the very nature and character of God. "Is God partial only to the Jews? Is this a God of justice and peace? (. . .). The focus of these questions is the very person of God. God's character is at stake. God's integrity has been questioned."[3] These are the questions, the doubt, out of which Palestinian liberation theology grew, a theology that reassures that God is not a God of injustice or partiality, but one who loves all God's children equally, whether Jew or Palestinian, Euro-American colonialist or Native American, White or Black or any other color, of any faith, gender, ethnicity, level of wealth or poverty.

It is from these questions and the theology arising from them that the hope comes that sustains Palestinians, Muslims as well as Christians, and that reaches out to Jews as well. The essence of liberation theology, as Ateek wrote years after first formulating these questions, is to lift up a strong prophetic voice affirming in faith and hope that "the one God in whom we all believe is the God of justice, peace, love, mercy, and compassion, and there is no God besides this God (. . .). God cannot be pleased when injustice is done against others."[4]

A God of justice is a God of hope. The South African *Kairos* theologians affirmed that their prophetic, liberating theology was one of hope, that "God is at work in our world turning hopeless and evil situations to good," that because God is with everyone, injustice and oppression cannot last forever.[5] The Palestinian *Kairos* theologians are equally positive:

3. Ateek, *Justice and Only Justice*, 78.
4. Ateek, "Liberation Theology as a Test," 51.
5. *Kairos Document.*

in the land of Jesus' resurrection, Palestinians cannot but live in hope that the evil facing them will be overcome. Like Jesus' resurrection from the dead, the impossible is possible.

Hope is a paradox, always in tension with impossibility. *Kairos Palestine* speaks paradoxically of "hope in the absence of all hope." But the mere issuance of that document at a time of hopelessness was an act of hope over despair. Sabeel and Naim Ateek speak often of how faith and hope transform the seemingly impossible into the possible. Theology alone can never expect to confront political, or certainly military, power as great as that of Israel and the United States. But liberation theology looks beyond concrete temporal power. A people inspired by the rightness, and indeed sacredness, of their demand for *justice* have within themselves a spiritual power that can be conquered only by their own despair. Liberation theology is a paradox of many dimensions. A paradox of hope in the midst of despair. A paradox of grace in the midst of darkness: *Kairos* is "the moment of God's grace," even as both Palestinians and Israelis experience "the darkest moments lived by individuals."[6] A paradox of patience in the face of urgent need; of powerlessness against insuperable physical and political power; of faith and love in the face of misery and oppression. The prophetic voice of Palestinian liberation theology rises up from the place where hope confronts impossibility.

But hope rejects impossibility. "In the Palestinian context," says Father Fadi Diab, a Palestinian Episcopal priest in Ramallah, "hope is a sustenance of life and mission"; it is a sign of "God's liberating presence among the suffering." The subjugated and oppressed are able to endure precisely because they have hope in a just and loving God who hears their cry and is always present with them. Father Diab is the rector of St. Andrew's Episcopal Church in Ramallah, was a signatory of *Kairos Palestine*, and for years has been a beacon of hope for Palestinian Christians. Hope is present in the daily lives of Palestinians, he says, and "in the daily struggles for liberation": in the determination of the six Palestinian prisoners who in 2021 managed to do the impossible by escaping briefly from a high-security Israeli prison; in the many prisoners who go on hunger strike to protest unjust incarceration; in every Palestinian who has opted to remain in Palestine despite the oppression; in every one of

6. This image is from Sabbah, "Preface," *Kairos for Global Justice.*

the innumerable pieces of street resistance art that defiantly adorn walls all over Palestine.[7]

"Every decision to stay, learn, live, find joy, join in community, and *be*—these are all embodiments of resistance and the fight for liberation and justice." Echoing the Palestinians' feeling of close connection with Jesus' death and resurrection—a connection, as we have seen, that even Muslims often feel—Diab asserts that a major aspect of Palestinian hope is the knowledge that "crucifixion and death don't have the last word. The empty tomb in Jerusalem continues to witness to the fact that the last word is God's."[8]

The sacredness of Christian hope lies in the enfolding comfort of God's embrace that it evokes. Catholic spiritual leader Father Richard Rohr has said that "mystical hope offers us an experience of trust that God's presence, love, and mercy [are] all around us, regardless of circumstances or future outcome." Theologian and mystic Cynthia Bourgeault expands at length on this notion of God's presence as the source of hope. It dwells deep within us, as a kind of fullness that she calls "the Mercy." This ineffable mercy is "the length and breadth and height and depth of what we know of God," and it is "unconditional—always there, underlying everything. It is literally the force that holds everything in existence." Hope is this gift of mercy; it is "divine love itself," as this love "floods forth into our being as strength and joy."[9]

Hope, Bourgeault concludes "fills us with the strength to stay present" no matter what confronts us[10]—the strength, as Fadi Diab says, to decide in favor of remaining and simply *being*, of surviving and staying in the struggle for liberation and justice. Hope is not only a theological matter. A young climate activist, lamenting the rise of depression among American youth over the planet's endangered future, recently declared that "hope is a right we must protect." Highlighting the endurance of Native Americans as an example of how the oppressed live in hope, she quoted indigenous scholar Robin Wall Kimmerer, whose best-selling book *Braiding Sweetgrass* is a story of Native wisdom and hope: "Despite

7. Diab, "Hope Not Despair."
8. Diab, "Hope Not Despair." Emphasis added.
9. Bourgeault, *Mystical Hope*, 20, 25, 34
10. Bourgeault, *Mystical Hope*, 87.

exile, despite a siege four hundred years long, there is something, some heart of living stone, that will not surrender."[11]

The preeminent Palestinian poet Mahmoud Darwish wrote often of endurance—of *being* and of the Palestinians' survival in hope. Palestinians did not come to Palestine from anywhere else, he once wrote. "We came from pomegranates, from the glue of memory, from the fragments of an idea."

11. Florsheim, "Don't Tell Me to Despair."

Bibliography

Abdulhadi, Rabab Ibrahim, and Jade Musa. "A Virtual Reunion 10 Years Later: Indigenous and Women of Color Feminists Reflect on Historic Delegation to Palestine." *Mondoweiss*, July 15, 2021. https://mondoweiss.net/2021/07/a-virtual-reunion-10-years-later-indigenous-and-women-of-color-feminists-reflect-on-historic-delegation-to-palestine/.

Abraham, Yuval, and Basil al-Adraa. "Scenes from a Jewish Pogrom." *+972 Magazine*, September 29, 2021. https://www.972mag.com/settler-violence-sukkot-pogrom/.

Abuata, Tarek. "Stand in Conviction." *Friends of Sabeel North America*, April 21, 2019. https://www.fosna.org/standinconviction. https://www.fosna.org/standinconviction.

Abunimah, Ali. *The Battle for Justice in Palestine*. Chicago: Haymarket, 2014.

———. *One Country: A Bold Proposal to End the Israeli-Palestinian Impasse*. New York: Metropolitan, 2006.

Abu Sway, Mustafa. "Concerns of Palestinian Muslims." *Cornerstone* 77 (2018) 8.

———. "Jerusalem: The City of Peace for All—Challenges and Opportunities," July 17, 2021. https://www.facebook.com/1621299340/videos/136601481934611/.

Adewunmi, Bim. "Kimberlé Crenshaw on Intersectionality: 'I Wanted to Come Up with an Everyday Metaphor that Anyone Could Use.'" *The New Statesman*, April 2, 2014. https://www.newstatesman.com/politics/welfare/2014/14/kimberl-crenshaw-intersectionality-i-wanted-come-everyday-metaphor-anyone-could-use.

Ahmad, Halah. "Tourism in Service of Occupation and Annexation." *al-Shabaka*, October 2020. https://al-shabaka.org/wp-content/uploads/2020/10/Ahmad_PolicyBrief_Eng_Oct2020.pdf.

Alatar, Mohammed. *The People's Patriarch*. Sabeel Jerusalem, February 6, 2021. https://www.youtube.com/watch?v=64_ihtzLbFE.

Amnesty International. *Israel's Apartheid Against Palestinians: Cruel System of Domination and Crime Against Humanity*. London: Amnesty International, February 1, 2022. https://www.amnesty.org/en/documents/mde15/5141/2022/en/.

Angel, Arielle. "Responsa: On Loving Jews." *Jewish Currents* (Fall 2021) 14–21.

———. "The Use and Abuse of 'Jewish Peoplehood.'" *On the Nose Jewish Currents Podcast*, October 8, 2021. https://jewishcurrents.org/the-use-and-abuse-of-jewish-peoplehood.

Arria, Michael. "Pompeo at ZOA Gala: 'Israel Is Not an Occupier.'" *Mondoweiss*, January 5, 2022. https://mondoweiss.net/2022/01/p0Smpeo-at-zoa-gala-israel-is-not-an-occupier/.

Arrison, Edwin, with Farid Esack. "Palestine Israel: A Christian Perspective with Reverend Edwin Arrison." *#Africa4Palestine #NC4P*, September 18, 2020. https://www.youtube.com/watch?v=v736b3I-sn4.

Arrison, Rev. Edwin. Zoom interview (May 19, 2021).

Ateek, Naim Stifan. "Bible Study on Mark 5:21–43." *A Sabeel Initiative, Kumi Now: An Inclusive Call for Nonviolent Action to Achieve a Just Peace*, 19–23. Jerusalem: Sabeel Ecumenical Liberation Theology Center, 2018.

———. "Biblical Perspectives on the Land." In *Faith and the Intifada: Palestinian Christian Voices*, edited by Naim S. Ateek et al., 115. Maryknoll, NY: Orbis, 1992.

———. "A Concluding Theological Postscript." In *Zionism and the Quest for Justice in the Holy Land*, edited by Donald E. Wagner and Walter T. Davis, 219. Eugene, OR: Pickwick, 2014.

———. "Invitation to Kumi Now." In *A Sabeel Initiative, Kumi Now: An Inclusive Call for Nonviolent Action to Achieve a Just Peace*, 12–13. Jerusalem: Sabeel Ecumenical Liberation Theology Center, 2018.

———. "The Israeli Occupation and Theological Thinking." *Cornerstone* 56 (2010) 1–4.

———. *Justice, and Only Justice: A Palestinian Theology of Liberation*. Maryknoll, NY: Orbis, 1989.

———. "Naim Ateek Responds to Episcopal Divestment Vote." FOSNA email newsletter (July 13, 2015).

———. "Liberation Theology as a Test for Authentic Religion." In Sabeel Documents No. 4, 36–52. Jerusalem: Sabeel Ecumenical Liberation Theology Center, 2020.

———. *A Palestinian Christian Cry for Reconciliation*. Maryknoll, NY: Orbis, 2008.

———. *A Palestinian Theology of Liberation: The Bible, Justice, and the Palestinian-Israeli Conflict*. Maryknoll, NY: Orbis, 2017.

———. "Sermon: Today the Scripture is Fulfilled." 2–3. *Cornerstone*, no. 68 (Winter/Spring 2014).

Awad, Rev. Alex. "Colliding Forces During the Christmas Season: A Sermon About the Situation in Palestine." 24–25. *Washington Report on Middle East Affairs* (January/February 2022).

Barber, Rev. Dr. William J., II. "Moral Movements Are Never Just About One Issue." Email from Repairers of the Breach, info@breachrepairers.org, March 14, 2022.

Baroud, Ramzy. *The Last Earth: A Palestinian Story*. London: Pluto, 2018.

———. ed. *Searching Jenin: Eyewitness Accounts of the Israeli Invasion, 2002*. Seattle: Cune, 2003.

———. *The Second Palestinian Intifada: A Chronicle of a People's Struggle*. London: Pluto, 2006.

"The Basic Law: Israel—The Nation-State of the Jewish People," November 2018. https://www.adalah.org/uploads/uploads/Final_2_pager_on_the_JNSL_27.11.2018%20.pdf.

Bass, Diana Butler. *Freeing Jesus: Rediscovering Jesus as Friend, Teacher, Savior, Lord, Way, and Presence*. New York: Harper One, 2021.

Battle, Michael. *Desmond Tutu: A Spiritual Biography of South Africa's Confessor*. Louisville: Westminster John Knox, 2021.

B.C. "What Happened to Liberation Theology?" *The Economist*, November 5, 2018. https://www.economist.com/the-economist-explains/2018/11/05/what-happened-to-liberation-theology.

Blumenthal, Max. *Goliath: Life and Loathing in Greater Israel*. New York: Nation, 2013.

Bourgeault, Cynthia. *Mystical Hope: Trusting in the Mercy of God*. Lanham: Cowley Publications, 2001.

Braverman, Mark. *Fatal Embrace: Christians, Jews, and the Search for Peace in the Holy Land*. Austin: Synergy, 2010.

———. "The Moment of Grace and Opportunity: The Global *Kairos* Movement For Justice in the Holy Land." *Theologies and Cultures* 11 (2014) 42–83.

———. "Theology in the Shadow of the Holocaust: Revisiting Bonhoeffer and the Jews." *Theology Today* 79 (2022) 146–65.

Brueggemann, Walter. *Chosen? Reading the Bible Amid the Israeli-Palestinian Conflict*. Louisville: Westminster John Knox, 2015.

———. "Foreword." In *Zionism and the Quest for Justice in the Holy Land*, edited by Donald E. Wagner and Walter T. Davis, xiv–xv. Eugene, OR: Pickwick, 2014.

———. "Permission to Narrate." *Church Anew*, February 16, 2021. https://churchanew.org/brueggemann/permission-to-narrate.

B'Tselem. *A Regime of Jewish Supremacy from the Jordan River to the Mediterranean Sea: This is Apartheid*. Jerusalem: B'Tselem. January 2021. https://www.btselem.org/sites/default/files/publications/202101_this_is_apartheid_eng.pdf.

———. "2021 Was the Deadliest Year Since 2014, Israel Killed 319 Palestinians in OPT, 5-Year Record in House Demolitions: 895 Palestinians Lost Their Homes." *B'Tselem Press Release*, January 4, 2022. https://www.btselem.org/press_releases/20220104_in_deadliest_year_since_2014_Israel_killed_319_palestinians_in_opt.

———. Website. https://www.btselem.org/about_btselem.

Burge, Gary M. *Jesus and the Land: The New Testament Challenge to Holy Land Theology*. Ada: Baker Academic, 2012.

———. "Theological and Biblical Assumptions of Christian Zionism." In *Challenging Christian Zionism: Theology, Politics and the Israel-Palestine Conflict*, edited by Naim Ateek et al., 45–46. London: Melisende, 2005.

———. *Whose Land? Whose Promise?: What Christians Are Not Being Told about Israel and the Palestinians*. Cleveland: Pilgrim, 2013.

Burnley, Lawrence Burnley. "The Movement for Black Lives Has Always Been Spiritual." *YES! Magazine*, June 19, 2020. https://www.yesmagazine.org/opinion/2020/06/19/black-lives-movement-spiritual.

Cannon, Mae Elise, and Andrea Smith, eds. *Evangelical Theologies of Liberation and Justice*. Downers Grove, IL: InterVarsity, 2019.

Carroll, James. *Constantine's Sword: The Church and the Jews: A History*. New York: A Mariner Book, Houghton Mifflin, 2002.

Cathail, Maidhc Ó. "The Scofield Bible—The Book That Made Zionists of America's Evangelical Christians." *Washington Report on Middle East Affairs* (October 2015) 4546.

Chacour, Elias, with David Hazard. *Blood Brothers*. Grand Rapids: Chosen, 1984.

———, with Mary E. Jensen. *We Belong to the Land: The Story of a Palestinian Israeli Who Lives for Peace and Reconciliation*. New York: HarperSanFrancisco, 1990.

Chapman, Colin. *Christian Zionism and the Restoration of Israel: How Should We Interpret the Scriptures?* Eugene, OR: Cascade, 2021.

Chotiner, Isaac. "Is Anti-Zionism Anti-Semitism?" *The New Yorker*, May 11, 2022. https://www.newyorker.com/news/q-and-a/is-anti-zionism-anti-semitism.

Christian Church (Disciples of Christ). *Compelled to Witness*: "A Christian Church (Disciples of Christ) Pastoral Letter Affirming Justice, Rights, and Accountability in Promoting Peace in Israel/Palestine," February 23, 2022. https://www.globalministries.org/compelled-to-witness/.

Christison, Kathleen. *Perceptions of Palestine: Their Influence on U.S. Middle East Policy*. Berkeley: University of California, 2001.

————. *The Wound of Dispossession: Telling the Palestinian Story*. Santa Fe: Sunlit Hills/ Ocean Tree, 2001.

Christison, Kathleen, and Bill Christison. *Palestine in Pieces: Graphic Perspectives on the Israeli Occupation*. London: Pluto, 2009.

Cook, Jonathan. *Blood and Religion: The Unmasking of the Jewish and Democratic State*. London: Pluto, 2006.

————. *Disappearing Palestine: Israel's Experiments in Human Despair*. London: Zed, 2008.

————. "Palestinian Christians." *The Link* 53 (2020).

Cone, James H. *A Black Theology of Liberation*. Rev. ed., 40th anniversary ed. Maryknoll, NY: Orbis, 2010.

————. *Black Theology and Black Power*, 20th anniversary ed. Maryknoll, NY: Orbis, 1997.

————. *The Cross and the Lynching Tree*. Maryknoll, NY: Orbis, 2013.

Davidson, Lawrence. *Foreign Policy Inc.: Privatizing America's National Interest*. Lexington: The University Press of Kentucky, 2009.

Davies, Janet. "Longtime Friends of Sabeel." *Cornerstone* 66 (2013) 6.

de Gruchy, John W. *Reconciliation: Restoring Justice*. Minneapolis: Fortress, 2002.

————. "Foreword." In *The Kairos Document: Challenge to the Church: A Theological Comment on the Policical Crisis in South Africa*, 7–9. Grand Rapids: Eerdmans, 1986.

Diab, Fadi. "Hope Not Despair." December 2021. *The Anglican Peacemaker*, 8. https://www.anglicanpeacemaker.org.uk/wp-content/uploads/2021/12/ANG-28719-Anglican-Peacemaker-Issue-21_3.pdf.

Duaybis, Cedar. "Becoming Whole: The Challenge of the Palestinian Christian Woman." In *Faith and the Intifada: Palestinian Christian Voices*, edited by Naim S. Ateek et al., 120–21. Maryknoll, NY: Orbis, 1992.

————. "Theologies of Palestine." *Cornerstone* 81 (2019–20) 19.

————. "The Three-Fold Nakba." *Cornerstone* 66 (2013) 8–9.

Dugard, John. *Confronting Apartheid: A Personal History of South Africa, Namibia and Palestine*. Auckland Park, South Africa: Jacana Media, 2018.

East, Brad. "Jewish Jesus, Black Christ." *Christian Century* (February 9, 2022) 20–25.

El-Ad, Hagai. "The Bloody Legacy of 'Shared Values.'" *+972 Magazine*, July 13 2022. https://www.972mag.com/biden-israel-values-palestinians/.

————. "We are Israel's Largest Human Rights Group—and We Are Calling This Apartheid." *The Guardian*, January 12, 2021. https://www.theguardian.com/commentisfree/2021/jan/12/israel-largest-human-rights-group-apartheid.

Ellis, Marc H. *Beyond Innocence and Redemption: Confronting The Holocaust And Israeli Power: Creating a Moral Future for the Jewish People*. New York: Harper & Row, 1990.

———. *Finding Our Voice: Embodying the Prophetic and Other Misadventures*. Eugene, OR: Cascade, 2018.

———. *Future of the Prophetic: Israel's Ancient Wisdom Re-Presented*. Minneapolis: Fortress, 2014.

———. "Judaism." In *The Hope of Liberation in World Religions*, edited by Miguel A. De La Torre, 65–89. Waco: Baylor University Press, 2008.

———. *Toward a Jewish Theology of Liberation: The Challenge of the 21st Century*. 3rd expanded ed. Waco: Baylor University Press, 2004.

Erakat, Noura. *Justice for Some: Law and the Question of Palestine*. Stanford: Stanford University Press, 2019.

Essa, Azad. "'Tip of the Spear': The US Christian Movement Praying for Trump and Israel." *Middle East Eye*, Mach 24, 2019. https://www.middleeasteye.net/news/tip-spear-us-christian-movement-praying-trump-and-israel.

Fache, Wilson, and Salomé Parent. "Digging in the Holy Land: Evangelicals Are Excavating Occupied Soil to Help Their Cause, and Israel's." *The National*, July 29, 2019. https://www.thenational.ae/world/mena/digging-in-the-holy-land-evangelicals-are-excavating-occupied-soil-to-help-their-cause-and-israel-s-1.892323/.

Flapan, Simcha. *The Birth of Israel: Myths and Realities*. New York: Pantheon, 1987.

FOSNA. "Liberation Theology: The Theology of Sabeel—What We Believe." https://www.fosna.org/content/liberation-theology.

FOSNA webinar. "Tied in a Single Garment of Destiny: Black Christian Reflections on Palestine," May 22, 2020. https://www.youtube.com/watch?v=OT35i2-OAPo&feature=youtu.be.

FOSNA website. https://www.fosna.org/.

Florsheim, Morgan. "Don't Tell Me to Despair about the Climate: Hope Is a Right We Must Protect." *YES! Magazine*. June 15, 2021. https://www.yesmagazine.org/opinion/2021/06/15/climate-despair-hope.

Freire, Paulo. "Foreword to the 1986 Edition." In *A Black Theology of Liberation*, by James H. Cone. Rev. ed., 40th anniversary ed. Maryknoll, NY: Orbis, 2010.

———. *Pedagogy of the Oppressed*. Translated by Myra Bergman Ramos. 50th anniversary ed. New York: Bloomsbury Academic, 2018.

Gordon, Neve. *Israel's Occupation*. Berkeley: University of California Press, 2008.

Greenblatt, Jonathan. "Remarks by Jonathan Greenblatt to the ADL Virtual National Leadership Summit," May 1, 2022. https://www.adl.org/news/remarks-by-jonathan-greenblatt-to-the-adl-virtual-national-leadership-summit.

Gutiérrez, Gustavo. *A Theology of Liberation: History, Politics, and Salvation*. Translated and edited by Sister Caridad Indo and John Eagleson. Rev. ed., 15th anniversary ed. Maryknoll, NY: Orbis, 1988.

Habiby, Emile. *The Secret Life of Saeed the Pessoptimist*. Translated by Salma Khadra Jayyusi and Trevor LeGassick. London: Zed, 1985.

Halper, Jeff. *Decolonizing Israel, Liberating Palestine: Zionism, Settler Colonialism, and the Case for One Democratic State*. London: Pluto, 2021.

———. *An Israeli in Palestine: Resisting Dispossession, Redeeming Israel*. London: Pluto, 2008.

———. "A Prophetic Judaism of Human Rights: Rene Cassin and Resistance to the Israeli Occupation." In *Peace, Justice, and Jews: Reclaiming Our Tradition*, edited by Murray Polner and Stefen Merken, 277. New York: Bunim and Bannigan, 2007.

Hanna, Archbishop Atallah. "An Easter Reflection from the Holy City of Jerusalem." *Mondoweiss,* April 4, 2021. https://mondoweiss.net/2021/04/an-easter-reflection-from-the-holy-city-of-jerusalem/.

Haramy, Omar. Prayer at Sabeel Holy Saturday Service, April 3, 2021. https://www.youtube.com/watch?v=jNZ5g-O5ep0

Hedges, Chris. "The Heresy of White Christianity." *Truthdig.com,* December 10, 2018. https://www.truthdig.com/articles/the-heresy-of-white-christianity/.

———. "Dr. Cornel West on the Decay of the American Empire." *ScheerPost.com,* April 18, 2022. https://scheerpost.com/2022/04/18/the-chris-hedges-report-dr-cornel-west-on-the-decay-of-the-american-empire/.

Heim, David. "Bill McKibben: The End of Being Human." *Christian Century* (July 3, 2019), 3033.

Hewitt, Garth. *Palestine is Calling:* "No. 2, Cry for Hope," and "No. 3, Standing Against Apartheid."

Hill, Mark Lamont, and Marshall Plitnick. *Except for Palestine: The Limits of Progressive Politics.* New York: The New Press, 2021.

Holmes, Barbara A. *Joy Unspeakable: Contemplative Practices of the Black Church.* 2nd ed. Minneapolis: Fortress, 2017.

———. *Race and the Cosmos,* 45, quoted in "Richard Rohr's Daily Meditation: A Foundational Sense of Awe." meditations@cac.org, January 6, 2021.

hooks, bell. *Teaching to Transgress: Education as the Practice of Freedom.* Oxfordshire: Routledge, 1994.

Human Rights Watch. *A Threshold Crossed: Israeli Authorities and the Crimes of Apartheid and Persecution.* New York: Human Rights Watch, April 27, 2021. https://www.hrw.org/report/2021/04/27/threshold-crossed-israeli-authorities-and-crimes-apartheid-and-persecution.

"An Interview in Mr. Balfour's Apartment, 23 Rue Nitot, Paris, on June 24th, 1919, At 4;45 P.M." In *From Haven to Conquest: Readings in Zionism and the Palestine Problem until 1948,* edited by Walid Khalidi, 198. Washington: Institute for Palestine Studies, 1987.

Isaac, Munther. *The Other Side of the Wall: A Palestinian Christian Narrative of Lament and Hope.* Downers Grove: InterVarsity, 2020.

Jenkins, Jack. "Trump Advisor Calls Pompeo's West Bank Decision an Answered Prayer." *Religion News Service,* November 18, 2019. https://religionnews.com/2019/11/18/trump-advisor-calls-pompeos-west-bank-decision-an-answered-prayer/.

Jerusalem Post Staff. "Desmond Tutu: Israel Guilty of Apartheid in Treatment of Palestinians." *Jerusalem Post,* March 10, 2014. https://www.jpost.com/diplomacy-and-politics/desmond-tutu-israel-guilty-of-apartheid-in-treatment-of-palestinians-344874.

Jerusalem Prayer Team website. https://jerusalemprayerteam.org.

Jewish Voice for Peace. "Our Approach to Zionism." Jewish Voice for Peace website. https://jewishvoiceforpeace.org/zionism.

The Kairos Document: Challenge to the Church: A Theological Comment on the Political Crisis in South Africa. Grand Rapids: Eerdmans, 1985.

Kairos for Global Justice. Jerusalem: *Kairos* Palestine, 2012. https://www.kairospalestine.ps.

Kairos Palestine. "Kairos Palestine Christmas Alert 2020," October 2020. https://www.kairospalestine.ps/images/kairos-palestine-christmas-alert-2020.pdf.

———. "*Kairos Palestine* 10th Anniversary Conference Statement & Call to the Church," November 29, 2019. https://www.kairospalestine.ps/index.php/resources/statements/kairos-palestine-10th-anniversary-conference-statement-call-to-the-church.

———. *A Moment of Truth: A Word of Faith, Hope and Love from the Heart of Palestinian Suffering.* Jerusalem: *Kairos* Palestine, 2009. https://kairospalestine.ps/sites/default/files/English.pdf.

———. Website. https://www.kairospalestine.ps.

Kairos Palestine and Global *Kairos* for Justice. "Cry for Hope: A Call to Decisive Action," July 1, 2020. https://www.cryforhope.org.

Kairos USA. "Call to Action: U.S. Response to the *Kairos* Palestine Document: A Word of Confession and Faith from Christians in the United States," 2012. https://kairosusa.org/wp-content/uploads/2013/12/Kairos-USA-Call-to-Action.pdf.

Kane, Alex. "Black-Palestine Solidarity Is Making Its Way to Capitol Hill." *+972 Magazine*, June 16, 2021. https://www.972mag.com/black-democrats-palestine-congress/.

Karcher, Carolyn L., ed. *Reclaiming Judaism from Zionism: Stories of Personal Transformation.* Northampton: Olive Branch, 2019.

Kassis, Rifat Odeh. *Kairos for Palestine.* Palestine: Badayl/Alternatives, 2011.

———. "*Kairos* Palestine: The Great March to Freedom." *This Week in Palestine* 260 (2019) 58–62.

Khalidi, Rashid. *The Hundred Years' War on Palestine: A History of Settler Colonialism and Resistance, 1917–2017.* New York: Metropolitan, 2020.

———. *Palestinian Identity: The Construction of Modern National Consciousness.* New York: Columbia University Press, 1997.

Khalidi, Walid. *Before Their Diaspora: A Photographic History of the Palestinians 1876–1948.* Washington: Institute for Palestine Studies, 1984.

Khoury, Samia Nasir. *A Memoir: Reflections from Palestine: A Journey of Hope.* Cyprus: Rimal, 2016.

———. "PLT: A Rewarding Way." *Cornerstone* 66 (2013) 6.

Kimmerer, Robin Wall. *Braiding Sweetgrass: Indigenous Wisdom, Scientific Knowledge and the Teachings of Plants.* Minneapolis: Milkweed Editions, 2013.

King, Martin Luther, Jr. "Letter from Birmingham Jail," April 16, 1963. https://www.africa.upenn.edu/Articles_Gen/Letter_Birmingham.html.

Kirk, Mimi. "Christian Zionist Archaeology: A Tool of Palestinian Subjugation." *Al-Jazeera*, February 16, 2020. https://www.aljazeera.com/opinions/2020/2/16/christian-zionist-archaeology-a-tool-of-palestinian-subjugation.

Klippenstein, Ken, and Ryan Grim. "The Biden Administration is Pursuing a Retread of Trump's False Peace Plan." *The Intercept*, May 27, 2022. https://theintercept.com/2022/05/27/biden-middle-east-abraham-accords/.

Konrad, Edo. "Washington's Three Gifts to Naftali Bennett." Email message to *+972 Magazine* subscribers (September 26, 2021).

Kovel, Joel. *Overcoming Zionism: Creating a Single Democratic State in Israel/Palestine.* London: Pluto, 2007.

Kubovich, Yaniv. "Violence Against Palestinians on the Rise Amid Israel's 'Hands-Off' Approach in West Bank." *Haaretz*, October 3, 2021. https://www.haaretz.com/israel-news/2021-10-03/ty-article/.premium/sharp-increase-in-anti-palestinian-settler-violence-amid-israels-hands-off-policy/0000017f-e1dc-d568-ad7f-f3ff7bec0000.

KumiNow website. https://www.kuminow.com.

Kurtz, Carolyn. "Introduction: Who Was Oscar Romero?" In *The Scandal of Redemption: When God Liberates the Poor, Saves Sinners, and Heals Nations,* edited by Carolyn Kurtz, 1–15. Walden: Plough, 2018.

Kuttab, Daoud. "William Barber Preaches at Easter Vigil Service Spotlighting Palestinian Christians." *Religion News Service,* April 6, 2021. https://religionnews.com/2021/04/06/william-barber-preaches-at-easter-vigil-service-acknowledging-christian-palestinians/.

Lazaroff, Tovah. "Pompeo: Israel Is Not an Apartheid State." *Jerusalem Post,* October 11, 1021) https://www.jpost.com/israel-news/pompeo-israel-is-not-an-apartheid-country-681580.

Lee, Michael E. *Revolutionary Saint: The Theological Legacy of Oscar Romero.* Maryknoll, NY: Orbis, 2018.

"The Letter of Paul to the Galatians." *The New Oxford Annotated Bible,* augmented 3rd edition, edited by Michael D. Coogan, 310. New York: Oxford University Press, 2007.

Levine, Amy-Jill. *The Misunderstood Jew: The Church and the Scandal of the Jewish Jesus.* New York: Harper One, 2006.

Levy, Gideon. "Biden Signs the Palestinians' Death Certificate." *Haaretz,* July 16, 2022. https://www.haaretz.com/opinion/2022–27-16/ty-article-opinion/.highlight/biden-signs-the-palestinians-death-certificate/00000182–7db-d7d0-a3ae-cfdbafd00000.

"Liberation Theology: The Theology of Sabeel—What We Believe." Friends of Sabeel North America. https://www.fosna.org/content/liberation-theology.

Lustick, Ian. *Arabs in the Jewish State: Israel's Control of a National Minority.* Austin: University of Texas Press, 1980.

Makdisi, Saree. *Palestine Inside Out: An Everyday Occupation.* New York: Norton, 2008.

Maltz, Judy. "'Biblical Mandate': The U.S. Evangelicals Behind the Latest West Bank Land Grab." *Haaretz,* August 22, 2022. https://www.haaretz.com/israel-news/2022–28-22/ty-article/.highlight/biblical-mandate-the-u-s-evangelicals-behind-the-latest-west-bank-land-grab/00000182-c64e-d6fa-abbe-d74f90570000.

———. "Despite COVID-19 Travel Ban, Israel Lets in 70 Evangelicals to Volunteer in Settlements." *Haaretz,* September 8, 2020. https://www.haaretz.com/israel-news/2020–29-08/ty-article/.premium/despite-covid-travel-ban-israel-lets-in-70-evangelicals-to-volunteer-in-settlements/0000017f-e7a5-d62c-a1ff-ffff6c380000.

Mandela, Nelson. "Address by President Nelson Mandela at International Day of Solidarity with Palestinian People, Pretoria." Mandela website , December 4, 1997. http://www.mandela.gov.za/mandela_speeches/1997/971204_palestinian.htm

Masalha, Nur. *Expulsion of the Palestinians: The Concept of "Transfer" in Zionist Political Thought, 1882–1948.* Washington: Institute for Palestine Studies, 1992.

———. *Palestine: A Four Thousand Year History.* London: Zed, 2020.

Masalha, Nur, and Lisa Isherwood, eds. *Theologies of Liberation in Palestine-Israel: Indigenous, Contextual, and Postcolonial Perspectives.* Postmodern Ethics Series 4. Eugene, OR: Pickwick, 2014.

Mattar, Philip, ed. *Encyclopedia of the Palestinians.* New York: Facts on File, 2000.

McCarthy, Justin. "Population." In *Encyclopedia of the Palestinians,* edited by Philip Mattar, 329. New York: Facts on File, 2000.

Mearsheimer, John J., and Stephen M. Walt. *The Israel Lobby and U.S. Foreign Policy.* New York: Farrar, Straus and Giroux, 2007.

Moltmann, Jürgen. *The Crucified God.* Rev. ed., 40ᵗʰ anniversary ed. Minneapolis: Fortress, 2015.

Morris, Benny. *The Birth of the Palestinian Refugee Problem, 1947‑1949.* Cambridge: Cambridge University Press, 1987.

———. "Exodus." In *Encyclopedia of the Palestinians,* edited by Philip Mattar. 123–25. New York: Facts on File, 2000.

"Neighbors of Trees and Stones." *This Week in Palestine* 260 (2019) 70–71.

Newell, J. Philip. *Christ of the Celts: The Healing of Creation.* San Francisco: Jossey‑Bass, 2008.

———. *The Rebirthing of God: Christianity's Struggle for New Beginning.* Woodstock: SkyLight Paths, 2014.

North, James. "'NY Times' Gives in to Widespread Criticism, and Mentions Amnesty Report on Israeli 'Apartheid' 52 Days Late." *Mondoweiss,* March 24, 2022. https:// mondoweiss.net/2022/03/ny-times-gives-in-to-widespread-criticism-and-mentions-amnesty-report-on-israeli-apartheid-52-days-late/.

Office of the High Commissioner for Human Rights. "UN Experts Alarmed by Sixth Palestinian Child Killing by Israeli Forces in 2020, Call for Accountability," December 17, 2020. https://www.ohchr.org/EN/NewsEvents/Pages/DisplayNews. aspx?NewsID=26619&LangID=E.

Ofir, Jonathan. "I Understand the Terrorists." *Mondoweiss,* November 11, 2021. https:// mondoweiss.net/2021/11/i-understand-the-terrorists/.

PalestinePortal.org. "Resolution on Israeli Apartheid Comes Before the World Council of Churches" (September 16, 2022). PalestinePortal.org email.

Pappé, Ilan. *The Ethnic Cleansing of Palestine.* Oxford: One World, 2006.

———, ed. *Israel and South Africa: The Many Faces of Apartheid.* London: Zed, 2015.

———. *Ten Myths About Israel.* London: Verso, 2017.

Posner, Sarah. *Unholy: Why White Evangelicals Worship at the Altar of Donald Trump.* New York: Random House, 2020.

Presbyterian Church (USA). 225ᵗʰ General Assembly (2022). "On Recognition That Israel's Laws, Policies, and Practices Constitute Apartheid Against the Palestinian People," July 6, 2022. https://www.pc-biz.org/#/search/3000773.

———, Office of Public Witness, World Mission, and Israel Palestine Mission Network. Webinar, "Israel/Palestine: US Complicity and Accountability," May 10, 2022. https://vimeo.com/708702294?fbclid=IwAR1bu7tsQ9 MsgLdN2aayBZTWbUoNkfFWbGhPy1GyWgZeXTKvAsQo5Qtg5kI.

Qleibo, Ali. "Blood Bonds: Palestinian Christian‑Muslim Common Heritage." *This Week in Palestine* 260 (2019) 18–24.

Qumsiyeh, Mazin B. *Popular Resistance in Palestine: A History of Hope and Empowerment.* London: Pluto, 2011.

Raheb, Mitri. *Faith in the Face of Empire: The Bible Through Palestinian Eyes.* Maryknoll, NY: Orbis, 2014.

———. *I Am a Palestinian Christian.* Translated by Ruth C. L. Gritsch. Minneapolis: Fortress, 1995.

———. "Palestinian Christians in Modern History: Between Migration and Displacement." *This Week in Palestine* 260 (2019) 10–11.

Raheb, Mitri, and Suzanne Watts Henderson. *The Cross in Contexts: Suffering and Redemption in Palestine.* Maryknoll, NY: Orbis, 2017.

Rieger, Joerg. "Protestantism." In *The Hope of Liberation in World Religions*, edited by Miguel A. De La Torre, 35–49. Waco: Baylor University Press, 2008.

Rod, Marc. "Democratic Split on Israel on Display in Competing House Speeches." *Jewish Insider*, May 14, 2021. https://jewishinsider.com/2021/05/israel-gaza-hamas-congress-speeches/.

Rohr, Rev. Richard, OFM. "Knowing from the Bottom." *Richard Rohr's Daily Meditations*, February 10, 2020. https://cac.org/category/daily-meditations.

———. "Practical Christianity." *Richard Rohr's Daily Meditations*, January 24, 2019. https://cac.org/category/daily-meditations.

Romero, Oscar A. "Quotes." *goodreads.com*. https://www.goodreads.com/quotes/6880923-a-church-that-does-not-provoke-any-crisis-preach-a.

———. *The Violence of Love*. Compiled & translated by James R. Brockman, SJ. Maryknoll, NY: Orbis, 2010.

Rosen, Rabbi Brant. "On Anti-Zionist Jews and Anti-Zionist Judaism." *Shalom Rav: A Blog by Rabbi Brant Rosen,* May 13, 2022. https://rabbibrant.com/2022/05/13/on-anti-zionist-jews-and-anti-zionist-judaism/.

———. "A Jewish Perspective on Palestine/Israel and Zionism." Chicago: Lecture, *Seeking Truth and Justice in Palestine and Israel: Part 3*, October 28, 2021. https://youtube.com/playlist?list=PLs2HR3v-BRLVmTjgnzM8G7S4lcSqx4jfh.

———. "Judaism Beyond Zionism: Toward a New Jewish Liturgy." *Shalom Rav: A Blog by Rabbi Brant Rosen*, June 3, 2021. https://rabbibrant.com/2021/06/03/judaism-beyond-zionism-toward-a-new-jewish-liturgy/.

———. *Wrestling in the Daylight: A Rabbi's Path to Palestinian Solidarity*. Charlottesville: Just World, 2012.

Roth-Rowland, Natasha. "On the Temple Mount, Jewish Fundamentalists Are Winning the Day." +972 *Magazine* Email News Digest (May 31, 2022).

Rothchild, Alice. *Condition Critical: Life and Death in Israel/Palestine*. Charlottesville: Just World, 2016.

Roy, Sara. *Failing Peace: Gaza and the Palestinian-Israeli Conflict*. London: Pluto, 2007.

———. *Unsilencing Gaza: Reflections on Resistance*. London: Pluto, 2021.

Ruether, Rosemary Radford. "Catholicism." In *The Hope of Liberation in World Religions*, edited by Miguel A. De La Torre, 13–34. Waco: Baylor University Press, 2008.

———. "Preface: The Conference and the Book." In *Faith and the Intifada: Palestinian Christian Voices*, edited by Naim S. Ateek et al., xi. Maryknoll, NY: Orbis, 1992.

Ruether, Rosemary, and Herman Ruether. "The Vatican, Zionism, and the Israeli-Palestinian Conflict." In *Zionism and the Quest for Justice in the Holy Land*, edited by Donald E. Wagner and Walter T. Davis, 120. Eugene, OR: Pickwick, 2014.

———. *The Wrath of Jonah: The Crisis of Religious Nationalism in the Israeli-Palestinian Conflict*. Minneapolis: Fortress, 2002.

Sabbah, Patriarch Michel. "The Future of Christian Palestinians." *This Week in Palestine* 260 (2019) 26.

———. "Theologies of Palestine." *Cornerstone* 81 (2019–20) 23.

Sabeel. *The Contemporary Way of the Cross: A Liturgical Journey along the Palestinian Via Dolorosa*. Jerusalem: Sabeel Ecumenical Liberation Theology Center, 2020.

Sabeel website. https://sabeel.org/.

Said, Edward W. *After the Last Sky: Palestinian Lives*. New York: Pantheon, 1986.

———. "Intifada and Independence." In *Intifada: The Palestinian Uprising Against Israeli Occupation*, edited by Zachary Lockman and Joel Beinin, 8. Boston: South End, 1989.

———. "Permission to Narrate." *London Review of Books* 6 (February 16, 1984).

Said, Najla. "Diary of a Never-Ending Crisis." *The Nation* , July 29, 2020. https://www.thenation.com/article/world/new-york-city-coronavirus/.

Samuels, Ben. "For This Congressman, Support for the Palestinians is Rooted in His Blackness." *Haaretz*, July 1, 2021. http://www.haaretz.com/us-news/.premium-for-this-congressman-support-for-the-Palestinians-is-rooted-in-his-blackness-1.9959807.

———. "Pew Survey Reveals Huge Gap Between Young, Old Americans' View on Israel-Palestine Conflict." *Haaretz*, May 26, 2022. https://www.haaretz.com/us-news/2022–25-26/ty-article/.premium/huge-gap-between-young-old-americans-view-on-israel-palestine/00000180-ffc2-defc-aff4-ffc610fd0000.

Sarsar, Saliba, ed. *What Jerusalem Means to Us: Christian Perspectives and Reflections.* Bethesda: Holy Land, 2018.

Sarsar, Saliba, and Carole Monica C. Burnett, eds. *What Jerusalem Means to Us: Muslim Perspectives and Reflections.* Bethesda: Holy Land, 2021.

Scott, Eugene. "The Fix: Why Evangelicals Like Rick Perry Believe Trump is God's Chosen One." *The Washington Post* (November 25, 2019).

Seddon, Mark. "'A Scream for Life' Gaza, the Great March of Return and Its Legacy." Interview with Ahmed Abu Artema. *Palestine Deep Dive*, April 21, 2021. https://www.youtube.com/watch?v=bym3B_UTws8.

Shavit, Ari. *My Promised Land: The Triumph and Tragedy of Israel.* New York: Random House, 2013.

Shehadeh, Raja. *Palestinian Walks: Forays into a Vanishing Landscape.* New York: Scribner, 2007.

———. *Strangers in the House: Coming of Age in Occupied Palestine.* South Royalton: Steerforth, 2002.

Shlaim, Avi. *Collusion Across the Jordan: King Abdullah, the Zionist Movement, and the Partition of Palestine.* New York: Columbia University Press, 1988.

———. *The Iron Wall: Israel and the Arab World.* New York: Norton, 2000.

Singer, Olivia. "Liberation Theology in Latin America." In *Modern Latin America.* Oxford: Oxford University Press, 2018. https://library.brown.edu/create/modernlatinamerica/chapters/chapter-15-culture-and-society/essays-on-culture-and-society/liberation-theology-in-latin-america/.

Sizer, Stephen. "The Historical Roots of Christian Zionism from Irving to Balfour: Christian Zionism in the United Kingdom (1820–918)." 21. In *Challenging Christian Zionism: Theology, Politics and the Israel-Palestine Conflict.*, edited by Naim S. Ateek et al., 21. London: Melisende, 2005.

———. "What Is the Relationship Between Israel and the Church? Seven Biblical Answers," April 7, 2019. http://www.stephensizer.com/wp-content/uploads/2019/04/7-Biblical-Answers-Israel-and-the-Church-2019.pdf.

———. *Zionism: Road Map to Armageddon.* Downers Grove: IVP Books, 2004.

———. *Zion's Christian Soldiers? The Bible, Israel and the Church.* Downers Grove: InterVarsity, 2007.

Skibell, Arianna. "Questioning the Covenant." *Jewish Currents*, June 17, 2020. https://jewishcurrents.org/questioning-the-covenant/.

Sobrino, Jon. "Introductory Essay: A Theologian's View of Oscar Romero." In *Voice of the Voiceless: The Four Pastoral Letters and Other Statements*, by Archbishop Oscar Romero, translated by Michael Walsh, 26–27. Maryknoll, NY: Orbis, 1985.

Sommer, Allison Kaplan. "Israel's Far Right, Shunned by AIPAC, Is Embraced by Mike Pence." *Haaretz*, March 10, 2022. https://www.haaretz.com/israel-news/2022-23-10/ty-article/.premium/israels-far-right-shunned-by-aipac-is-embraced-by-mike-pence/0000017f-f2c9-dc28-a17f-feff50f70000.

A Survey of Palestine: Prepared in December 1945 and January 1946 for the Information of the Anglo-American Committee of Inquiry, vol. 1, reprinted with permission from Her Majesty's Stationery Office. Washington: Institute for Palestine Studies, 1991.

Tamari, Salim, ed. *Jerusalem 1948: The Arab Neighborhoods and Their Fate in the War*. Jerusalem: Institute for Jerusalem Studies and Badil, 1999.

Tent of Nations website. http://www.tentofnations.org.

Theoharis, Jeanne. *The Rebellious Life of Mrs. Rosa Parks*. Boston: Beacon, 2013.

Thurman, Howard. *Jesus and the Disinherited*. Boston: Beacon, 1996.

Tutu, Desmond. "Apartheid in the Holy Land." *The Guardian*, April 28, 2002. https://www.theguardian.com/world/2002/apr/29/comment.

———. *Hope and Suffering: Sermons and Speeches*. Grand Rapids: Eerdmans, 1984.

———. *No Future Without Forgiveness*. New York: Image Doubleday, 1999.

Tzedek Chicago. "At Tzedek, We Value (. . .)" Tzedek Chicago. https://www.tzedekchicago.org/our-values.

———. "Tzedek Chicago Adds Anti-Zionism to Our Core Values Statement." Tzedek Chicago, March 30, 2022. https://www.tzedekchicago.org/updates/tzedek-chicago-affirms-anti-zionism-as-a-core-value.

United Nations. "Two Years On: People Injured and Traumatized During the 'Great March of Return' Are Still Struggling." *The Question of Palestine*. April 6, 2020. https://www.un.org/unispal/document/two-years-on-people-injured-and-traumatized-during-the-great-march-of-return-are-still-struggling/.

———. "The Universal Declaration of Human Rights." https://www.un.org/en/universal-declaration-human-rights/index.html.

———. "Universal Declaration of Human Rights: History of the Document." https://www.un.org/en/sections/universal-declaration/history-document/index.html.

United Nations Country Team in the Occupied Palestinian Territory. *Gaza in 2020: A Liveable* [sic] *Place?* August 2012. https://unsco.unmissions.org/sites/default/files/gaza_in_2020_a_liveable_place_english.pdf.

Vail, Tiffany. "Synod Delegates Approve Resolution Decrying Oppression of Palestinian People." *United Church of Christ News*, July 19, 2021. https://www.ucc.org/synod-delegates-approve-resolution-decrying-oppression-of-palestinian-people/.

Volf, Miroslav. "Foreword." In *The Crucified God*, by Jürgen Moltmann. Rev. ed., 40th anniversary ed. Minneapolis: Fortress, 2015.

Wagner, Donald E. *Anxious for Armageddon: A Call to Partnership for Middle Eastern and Western Christians*. Scottsdale: Herald, 1995.

———. "From Blackstone to Bush: Christian Zionism in the United States (1890–2004)." In *Challenging Christian Zionism: Theology, Politics and the Israel-Palestine Conflict*, edited by Naim Ateek et al., 32–34. London: Melisende, 2005.

———. *Glory to God in the Lowest: Journeys to an Unholy Land*. Northampton: Olive Branch, 2022.

———. "Holy Land Christians and Survival." In *Faith and the Intifada: Palestinian Christian Voices*, edited by Naim S. Ateek et al., 44. Maryknoll, NY: Orbis, 1992.

—. "The Mainline Protestant Churches and the Holy Land." In *Zionism and the Quest for Justice in the Holy Land*, edited by Donald E. Wagner and Walter T. Davis, 146–53. Eugene, OR: Pickwick, 2014.

—. "Protestantism's Liberal/Mainline Embrace of Zionism." *The Link* (April/May 2016).

WCC 11th Assembly Statement. "Seeking Justice and Peace for All in the Middle East," September 8, 2022. https://www.oikoumene.org/resources/documents/seeking-justice-and-peace-for-all-in-the-middle-east.

Weiss, Philip. "Addressing the Role of My Community, Both Angrily and Lovingly." *Mondoweiss* email message to subscribers (December 18, 2021).

Wi'am website. https://www.alaslah.org.

Wiesel, Elie. "Nobel Prize Acceptance Speech," December 10, 1986. https://www.nobelprize.org/prizes/peace/1986/wiesel/26054-elie-wiesel-acceptance-speech-1986/.

Wikipedia. "Demographic History of Jerusalem." https://en.wikipedia.org/wiki/Demographic_history_of_Jerusalem#cite_note-table3–2.

—. "Demographics of Israel." https://en.wikipedia.org/wiki/Demographics_of_Israel.

—. "Hélder Câmara." https://en.wikipedia.org/wiki/Hélder_Câmara#cite_note-Bellos-10.

—. "Óscar Romero." https://en.wikipedia.org/wiki/Óscar_Romero.

—. "Tent of Nations." https://en.wikipedia.org/wiki/Tent_of_Nations.

Wright, Jeff. "How Israeli Settlers Use Archeology to Displace Palestinians from Their Land." *Mondoweiss*, September 4, 2022. https://mondoweiss.net/2022/09/how-israeli-settlers-use-archeology-to-displace-palestinians-from-their-land/.

—. "The Presbyterian Church (USA) Adds Its Voice to a Growing Choir Naming Israeli Apartheid." *Mondoweiss*, July 11, 2022. https://mondoweiss.net/2022/07/the-presbyterian-church-usa-adds-its-voice-to-a-growing-choir-naming-israeli-apartheid/.

—. "World Council of Churches General Assembly Puts Israeli Apartheid on the Global Church's Table." *Mondoweiss*, September 10, 2022. https://mondoweiss.net/2022/09/world-council-of-churches-general-assembly-puts-israeli-apartheid-on-the-global-churchs-table/.

Zoughbi, Zoughbi, and Tarek Zoughbi. "From the Chaos of Fear, Panic and Anger Towards Community Building." *Cornerstone* 82 (2020) 8–12.